Group Life and Health Insurance

PART A

Contributors

The following contributing authors, members of the Group Insurance Curriculum Subcommittee of HIAA's Insurance Education Committee, are specialists in particular areas of insurance. Their companies represent a cross-section of the life and health insurance industry. The valuable service of both authors and companies is gratefully acknowledged.

AUTHORS

Lee H. Hall
Massachusetts Mutual Life Insurance Company

Vida M. Henry
John Hancock Mutual Life Insurance Company

Donald W. Kress
Provident Life & Accident Insurance Company

James McCullough
Provident Mutual Life Insurance Company of Philadelphia (formerly)

Priscilla Miller
The Principal Financial Group

William Mullaney
Metropolitan Life Insurance Company

Ernest Nine/Larry E. Breitenbach
Lincoln National Life Insurance Company

Bernard E. Peskowitz
New York Life Insurance Company

Martin Rosenbaum
The Great-West Life Assurance Company

James P. Ross
General American Life Insurance Company

Warren A. (Fred) Shugars
Aetna Life & Casualty

EDITOR

Sherry E. Schlossnagle
Health Insurance Association of America

PRODUCTION

The authors acknowledge their gratitude to HIAA Education staff for the editing and production of this text.

Group Life and Health Insurance

PART A

Fifth Edition

HEALTH INSURANCE ASSOCIATION OF AMERICA
Washington, D.C.

The Health Insurance Association of America
Washington, DC 20036-3998

Published 1978. Fifth Edition 1994
Printed in the United States of America

ISBN 1-879143-18-6

Contents

Foreword

The HIAA Insurance Education Program aims to be the leader in providing the highest quality educational material and service in Group Life and Health insurance, Individual Health insurance, and other related health care fields.

To accomplish this mission, the Program seeks to fulfill the following goals:

1. Develop member company personnel for improved quality and efficiency of services to the public;

2. Provide a career development vehicle for member companies and other health care industry personnel; and

3. Further general understanding of the role and contribution of the health insurance industry in the financing and administration of health care services.

The Insurance Education Program provides the following services:

1. A comprehensive course of study in both Individual Health and Group Life and Health insurance;

2. Certification by examination of educational achievement for all courses;

3. A program to recognize accomplishment in the industry and academic communities through course evaluation and certification, which enables participants to obtain academic or continuing education credits; and

4. Development of educational, instructional, training, and informational materials related to the health insurance and health care industries.

Preface

This textbook and the accompanying study manual offer the benefit of knowledge and insight of people highly proficient in the health insurance business. The authors, people active in the business of life and health insurance, are qualified by education, training and experience to share with you in-depth perceptions of their special areas of work.

The course, divided into parts A, B and C, provides students with a comprehensive knowledge of the technical as well as the socio-economic aspects of the group life and health insurance business. Parts A and B present subject matter according to function and in the approximate sequence in which many insurers conduct their business. Part C builds on these basics and offers information on the specialty areas and changing concepts within the business. Completion of the full course sequence is encouraged.

Textbooks often develop and use certain premises to simplify presentation and understanding. Within the group life/health insurance industry are many insurers, doing business with policyholders of diverse size and type. In these textbooks the term "small" will identify groups under 100 lives; "medium" means 100 to 1,000 lives; "large" means over 1,000 lives. "Centralized" indicates home office administration; "decentralized," a regional or branch system of management.

In addition, the insurance business operates in an ever-changing regulatory climate, affected by both federal and state authorities. This fact, particularly for current legislation, must be kept in mind during the study of HIAA's group curricula.

The contents of this book are educational, not a statement of policy. The views expressed or suggested in HIAA textbooks are those of the contributing authors or editors and do not necessarily represent the opinion of this Association or its member companies.

1

THE CONCEPT AND HISTORY OF GROUP INSURANCE

INTRODUCTION

As early as 1000 B.C., the group insurance concept existed in the laws of the sea: "If goods are thrown overboard in order to lighten the ship, what is sacrificed for the common benefit should be made good by a common contribution." This law embodies the principle underlying not only group insurance but all insurance—a common contribution for the common good. In fact, all insurance may be considered group insurance, since an individual can be insured only by being part of a group on which the law of averages may operate.

People use various methods to manage risk—the possibility of loss that occurs in the course of everyday living. Risk management techniques include:

- elimination of the risk by avoiding its cause,
- reduction of risk by engaging in activities to prevent loss or minimize loss if it should occur,
- assumption of risk, and
- transfer of all or part of the risk to another, such as an insurance company, in return for payment of a premium.

By using the last technique, the financial consequences of a similar risk are shared by a large number of individuals. This is a fundamental characteristic of insurance. Group insurance, an American innovation of the twentieth century, differs from other forms of insurance only in details, not in basic concepts. By modifying and reshaping insurance mathematical practices that have existed for centuries, the group insurer uses mass marketing, servicing, and purchasing power of employers to provide low-cost insurance protection for employees.

In summary, group insurance can be described as an economical way of providing insurance protection against financial losses (such as those caused by death, disability, medical care expenses or retirement) of a group of individuals who are associated with the policyholder by some relationship other than insurance. Typically, the benefits, rights, and obligations of the insured group members are stated in a master policy issued by the insurer to a single entity, the policyholder.

In its broadest concept, group insurance includes a considerable list of insurance coverages: life insurance, health insurance, annuities, and property and casualty insurance. This text limits itself to detailed study of the various forms of group life and health insurance.

REASONS FOR EMPLOYEE BENEFITS

A primary purpose of employee benefits is to improve the morale and productivity of employees by relieving them of concern over the financial consequences of death, disability, medical care costs, unemployment, or retirement. Benefit plans provided through insurance for employer-employee groups are the best way to accomplish this. Group insurance plans, now often referred to as employee benefits, offer certain advantages to both employers and employees.

For an employer, group insurance fulfills four main purposes:

- The employer purchases insurance at a lower cost;
- When an accident or sickness causes a financial crisis, the benefits under a group insurance plan provide the employer with the means of aiding employees in a predetermined and businesslike manner;
- A plan of insurance is almost a necessity to compete in the labor market. It serves to make the employer's company known as a good place to work, aids in attracting and retaining employees, and can improve employee morale and productivity; and
- Under federal tax laws and regulations, the employer's contributions usually are deductible as a business expense.

Employees also receive advantages:

- The benefits under a group insurance plan may represent the difference between the adequacy of individual and family resources and the need to turn to various community programs for financial assistance;

- Group insurance can provide the greatest amount of protection for the lowest cost;

- Chronic health problems or a hazardous occupation may make buying individual life and health insurance more difficult than buying group insurance. Most group insurance is available without individual health questionnaires that provide evidence of insurability;

- If employees are contributing toward the cost, premiums are automatically withheld from earnings, thus reducing the hazard of lapsed coverages;

- Conversion privileges enable a terminated employee to convert the group insurance to an individual policy without having to produce satisfactory evidence of insurability; and

- The employer's contributions usually are not reportable as taxable income to the insured employee. In general, therefore, group insurance provides employees a greater after-tax value than a wage or salary increase.

CHARACTERISTICS OF GROUP INSURANCE

Group insurance differs in many ways from insurance sold under individual policies. Basic characteristics and concepts of group insurance mentioned below will be discussed in detail in later chapters.

THE CONTRACT

A single policy called a master contract is issued to the group policyholder to cover a group of individuals who have a defined relationship (other than insurance) to the policyholder, such as:

- employee-employer,
- member-union, and
- debtor-creditor.

The contract provides various types of insurance coverage for the individuals in a group. The individuals themselves, however, are not parties to the contract and do not receive a policy. Instead, group members receive individual certificates of insurance as evidence of their coverage under the master contract.

LIMITED USE OF EVIDENCE OF INSURABILITY

The group selection process differs significantly from insuring individuals. Individual selection requires health questionnaires, medical examinations, and inspection reports to establish insurability. Based on information, an insurer may accept, decline, or offer modified coverage to an applicant. Group insurance seldom requires evidence that individuals are insurable if they enroll when they become eligible for coverage. Under the group method of insuring, the spread of risk (number of individuals insured) and personal characteristics of the individuals (age, sex, income) should produce an acceptable ratio of claim experience to premium income.

Also, certain underwriting requirements assure an adequate spread of risk and guard against adverse selection or poorer risks dominating the insured groups. If the plan of insurance requires that the employees pay part of the premium, insurers commonly require a minimum enrollment (usually 75 percent) by persons eligible for coverage. Another requirement is that employees be actively at work on the day they become insured, and that those for whom the actively-at-work test is inappropriate (usually dependents) not be hospital-confined on that day.

REDUCED PREMIUM COSTS

The cost of group insurance usually is lower than the cost of individual insurance. Prospecting, selling, underwriting (evaluating risk and determining rates and coverage), enrolling, installing, administering, and servicing a group insurance plan take a smaller percentage of the insurance premium than is required in individual insurance. Underwriting a group of people, for example, is considerably less expensive than underwriting a comparable number of persons individually.

The administration of group insurance also is more economical than individual insurance because the insurer deals with a single entity, the group policyholder. For single-employer groups, payroll deductions provide a simple, low-cost way to collect required premium contributions from the insured members of the group.

GROUP SIZE

A fundamental concept in group insurance pertains to the minimum number of individuals needed to constitute a group. State insurance laws or insurance company practices resolve this issue. Some states set no minimum number of lives for group life and health insurance; an insurer's own underwriting practices set the requirements. In other states, the minimum number of lives required may be two, five, or ten.

TYPES OF ELIGIBLE GROUPS

State insurance laws and insurer underwriting practices also are the two major forces determining the types of groups eligible for group insurance. In practice, underwriting practices of insurers vary. Within the existing legal and underwriting framework, however, types of eligible groups may be generally classified as follows:

1. *Single Employers.* Corporations, partnerships, and sole proprietorships.

2. *Labor Unions.* Individual members insured through a local or national union.

3. *Multiple Employers.*

   - *Negotiated Trusteeships:* These groups are formed as an outgrowth of collective bargaining.

   - *Voluntary Trade Associations:* A trade association comprises employers in the same industry. The Health Insurance Association of America (HIAA), for example, has as its members insurance companies in the United States and Canada that sell health insurance products.

- *Multiple-Employer Trusts (METs):* A multiple-employer trust is a legal entity sponsored by two or more employers in the same industry, by an insurer, or by an administrator. The trust brings together a number of small employers for the purpose of insurance.

- *Professional Associations:* These groups are membership organizations of persons in the same profession—doctors, lawyers, teachers, for example—and sometimes their employees.

- *Creditor Groups:* This insurance, issued to creditors (banks, finance companies, vendors) and debtors, covers consumer debts such as time-payment purchases, charge accounts, personal loans, and mortgages.

In addition to these classifications, state insurance laws may permit other groups to have group insurance. These groups might include franchised dealers, clubs and fraternal organizations, veterans' organizations, and religious groups.

FINANCING A GROUP PLAN

Usually, employers finance a group insurance plan totally (a noncontributory plan) or partially (a contributory plan). Occasionally, where not prohibited by law or insurer underwriting practices, employees pay the entire cost of a group plan.

There are advantages to both the noncontributory and contributory plans. Traditionally, some groups, for example those that use collective bargaining, have been noncontributory. For tax reasons an employer may offer certain employee benefits instead of salary increases. A $25 benefits increase is worth more to the employer than a taxable $25 salary increase. The acceleration of health benefit plan costs to employers has led to more sharing of premium costs by employees.

ADVANTAGES OF THE NONCONTRIBUTORY PLAN

- *Employer Tax Deduction:* Employer premiums usually are deductible as an ordinary business expense for federal income tax purposes.

- *Coverage for All Employees:* Employees who have served a probationary period and are actively at work are automatically insured, assuring total participation and minimizing adverse selection. This approach avoids problems for the employer that might occur under a contributory plan when eligible employees do not elect to take the insurance or drop out of a plan without their dependents' knowledge.

- *Economy of Installation and Administration:* Since all employees are covered, the insurer and the employer avoid the expense of soliciting plan membership among individual employees, soliciting new employees, and getting waiver forms from nonsubscribing employees.

■ *Simplicity of Administration:* The insurance records of individual employees under a noncontributory plan are somewhat simpler. Since no payroll deduction procedures are necessary, the employer has fewer accounting operations.

■ *Control of the Plan:* A noncontributory plan gives the employer more control over changes in coverage and benefits.

ADVANTAGES OF THE CONTRIBUTORY PLAN

■ *Possible Larger Benefits:* The group plan may be more liberal if the employees contribute part of the premium. Because of their contributions, additional types of insurance coverages or higher amounts of existing coverages may be available.

■ *Greater Employee Interest and Appreciation:* Experience shows that employees generally have more interest in group insurance plans to which they are making some direct contribution. Also, because of greater employee awareness of the plan, they probably are more appreciative of its value.

■ *More Employee Control:* The contributory plan gives employees a greater voice in the benefits provided. The employer is more likely to respect the opinions of the employees when they are sharing the cost.

HISTORY OF THE GROUP INSURANCE CONCEPT

The concept of sharing the personal economic risks associated with injuries and illnesses on a mutual aid (insurance) principle was not new in the twentieth-century United States. Earlier examples include the artisans of Imperial Rome, the craft guilds in medieval England, and the mutual aid systems developed in Great Britain in the nineteenth century that came to be known as Friendly Societies and Saturday Funds.

As industrialization spread throughout much of Europe, systems of mutual aid or insurance also developed in Germany, Denmark, Sweden, Norway, Switzerland, and the Netherlands. These systems were mainly sick clubs, mutual benefit funds, cooperatives, or societies developed by local unions of craftspeople or other workers, by individual employers for the benefit of their employees, by physicians or medical societies, by religious groups, and by private individuals or insurance companies. A typical nineteenth-century mutual aid society collected small contributions from its members, promising to pay a cash benefit when a member became disabled by accident or sickness. The mutual aid society, in effect, was organized principally to provide a kind of group health insurance that we now call short-term disability income insurance.

Voluntary mutual protection associations developed in the United States in the second half of the 1800s. One of the earliest of these, La Societe Francaise de Bienfaisance Mutuelle, was organized in San Francisco in 1851. This society is noteworthy for having established a hospital in 1852 to provide care for its members. Fraternal benefit societies and other ritualistic social organizations also were important early providers of health insurance.

Starting in 1875 in the United States, a number of mutual benefit associations called establishment funds were formed by and for employees of a single employer, and a few of these funds were financed partially by employers. The benefits provided by these funds usually included small payments for death and disability. By the last half of the nineteenth century, the mutual aid movement was judged inadequate in many quarters because of its purely voluntary character, poor participation by eligible workers, and the low level of contributions, which frequently meant that the fund was insufficient to provide adequate benefits.

With the advent of the twentieth century and the enactment of workers' compensation laws (federal government in 1908; state of Wisconsin in 1911), United States employers and insurers alike became interested in the possibility of providing benefits for illnesses and nonwork injuries under group insurance contracts, since workers' compensation legislation did not cover such losses.

The origin of group health insurance by insurance companies is related closely to an "establishment fund" created for the employees of Montgomery Ward & Co., Inc. Following a study of its employee association plan, which provided a small death benefit and disability income benefits of $5 to $10 a week, Montgomery Ward decided in 1910 to investigate the feasibility of replacing the association plan with an insured plan. The decision was motivated by low membership in the association (scarcely more than 15 percent), frequency of special assessments, and inadequate benefits.

After protracted and complex negotiations with a number of insurers, the Montgomery Ward disability income coverage was placed with the London Guarantee and Accident Company of New York in 1911. The contract for this coverage provided, after a three-day waiting period, benefits for disabled employees under age 70 equal to one-half of an employee's weekly wage, subject to a minimum benefit of $5 a week and a maximum benefit of $28.25 a week. There was no time limitation on the indemnity; payments continued until the employee was able to return to work. This plan generally is regarded as the first group health insurance policy.

GROUP HEALTH INSURANCE

The group health insurance industry had its inception in the twentieth century. The concept was well-received; product development and numbers of insured increased rapidly.

ACCIDENTAL DEATH AND DISMEMBERMENT INSURANCE

From 1911 to 1917, the only available form of group health insurance was short-term disability income insurance for temporary disability resulting from a nonoccupational accident or sickness. During this period it became apparent to insurers that they might offer an important service to employees by providing benefits for accidental death or permanent disability as a result of the accidental loss of sight or limbs. Since non-occupational accidental losses did not fall under workers' compensation laws, individual life and health insurance policies offered this type of indemnity. By 1917, group accidental death and dismemberment insurance was offered as a supplemental group coverage.

DISABILITY INSURANCE

Short-term disability income insurance did not change substantially in the first 40 years or so following the negotiation of the Montgomery Ward contract. Insurance covered only temporary disabilities, and rarely did the plans have a duration of benefits that exceeded one year. Most plans provided coverage for 13 or 26 weeks.

Beginning in 1942, four states (Rhode Island, 1942; California, 1946; New Jersey, 1948; New York, 1949) gave impetus to the growth of disability income coverage by adopting plans that made temporary disability benefits compulsory. Hawaii and Puerto Rico also adopted compulsory disability plans in 1969. Interest in such plans by other states has since decreased; the spread of voluntary plans has removed most of the motivation for states to enact compulsory disability benefit programs.

In the 1940s, a few insurance companies began experimenting with an extension of short-term disability income insurance that resulted in what is known today as long-term disability income insurance. The early long-term plans, which provided coverage for up to five years, were devised primarily for the protection of certain classes of higher-salaried employees, such as those in management and supervisory groups. Today, plans covering all active full-time employees and providing coverage up to normal retirement age for disabilities resulting from accidents or sickness are common.

BASIC MEDICAL CARE EXPENSE BENEFITS

The U.S. Socialist Party had included proposals to provide compulsory hospital-surgical medical expense benefits in its programs for many years. Not until 1911, when Great Britain passed a National Health Insurance Act, did the concept of providing medical care expense benefits generate significant interest in the United States. Various ideas involving compulsory plans were explored during the early 1900s, but even Samuel Gompers, then president of the American Federation of Labor, rejected compulsory health insurance as being too paternalistic. In the early 1920s, individual hospitals in Rockford, Illinois; Grinnell, Iowa; New Bedford, Massachusetts; and Brattleboro, Vermont offered hospital expense benefits on an individual prepaid basis.

The principle of group prepayment for hospital expenses (premiums paid in advance for specific services covered in full) originated at Baylor University Hospital in Dallas, Texas. In 1929, some 1,500 schoolteachers, members of a mutual benefit society, were covered for 21 days of semi-private room and board and necessary hospital services and supplies during any one year. At the beginning of the Depression, hospitals, faced with declining revenues, welcomed the Baylor group concept. The Depression also focused public interest to a greater degree than ever on the problem of meeting the cost of medical care.

The Baylor Plan is considered the forerunner of what later became known as the Blue Cross plans. Other hospital prepayment programs were developed in New Jersey, Minnesota, and North Carolina in 1931. The first citywide plan was offered by hospitals in Sacramento, California in 1932, followed by Washington, D.C. in 1934 and New York City in 1935. By 1935, the shift from hospital expense benefit programs of individual hospitals to communitywide programs became general.

HOSPITAL, DOCTOR, AND MEDICAL EXPENSE BENEFITS

Meanwhile, in 1934, the General Tire & Rubber Company asked The Equitable Life Assurance Society of the United States to add hospital expense benefits to its existing group insurance program. About the same time, Occidental Life of California added hospital expense benefits to an existing short-term disability income insurance policy for a large chain of grocery stores.

The development of group hospital expense benefits was a significant step in helping employees meet the cost of medical care. The next step was coverage for surgeons' fees and physicians' charges for in-hospital, home, and office visits. In 1938, private insurers introduced group surgical expense benefits, followed by group medical expense benefits (Physicians' Visits Expense Benefits) in 1943. In 1939, the first Blue Shield Surgical-Medical Plan (California Physicians' Service) developed a statewide, prepaid, medical-society-sponsored plan.

MAJOR MEDICAL EXPENSE BENEFITS

Basic medical expense coverages developed during the 1930s and 1940s, although beneficial for most illnesses and accidents, were inadequate for prolonged confinements and expensive procedures. To provide insurance against such catastrophic medical events, the Liberty Mutual Insurance Company introduced major medical in 1949 to supplement basic medical care expense benefits. This dramatic new approach to medical care expenses resulted in a 90 percent enrollment of the members of the Elfun Society (a voluntary association of approximately 4,000 General Electric management employees) when the first group major medical expense benefits plan was written on February 2, 1949.

Originally, insurers wrote major medical expense benefits policies as a supplement to their own basic medical care coverages or to coverages provided by Blue Cross/Blue Shield. Today, major medical insurance encompasses virtually all types of medical care expenses, both in and out of a hospital. It either supplements a basic medical care plan or integrates basic and supplemental medical care expense benefits into a single comprehensive insurance plan.

DENTAL EXPENSE INSURANCE

As early as 1945, the American Dental Association (ADA) adopted recommendations for experimental prepayment dental plans on a nonprofit basis. In so doing, the ADA was aware that individuals who visit their dentists regularly can budget the cost of dental needs to some extent. The ADA recognized also that only scant factual information was available on whether dental plans could be financially sound.

In the years that followed, several illuminating studies of the need for, and the incidence and costs of, dental care were made. Experimental dental prepayment programs, initiated cautiously in the 1950s, provided dental care benefits to select groups. In August 1959 the first comprehensive group dental expense insurance plan, covering all types of services, was written by the Continental Casualty Company.

OTHER HEALTH BENEFITS

American enterprise has developed other group health insurance benefits, in addition to those previously discussed—credit health insurance in 1950, vision care expense benefits in 1957, extended care facility expense benefits (skilled nursing facilities) in 1959, prescription drug expense benefits in 1964, and hospice care expense benefits in the 1980s. Home health care and long-term care are recent benefit additions.

CURRENT STATUS

The development of new coverages over the years is merely one measure of the expansion of the industry. At the end of 1987, more than 181 million Americans were protected by one or more forms of private health insurance, according to the U.S. Census Bureau. In 1940, it was estimated that about 12 million persons had coverage; in 1960, about 122 million. The number of insureds has grown steadily during the past half century. Even among persons age 65 and older, despite Medicare benefits, over 21 million older Americans hold policies that supplement benefits available through Medicare.

Health insurance benefits today are provided in several ways. More than 1000 private insurance companies in the United States write individual and group health policies covering over 85 million persons of all ages for hospital care. In the continental United States, the joint Blue Cross/Blue Shield plans and single Blue Cross or Blue Shield plans cover about 70 million persons for hospital care. Private insurers (commercial and Blues) account for over one-quarter of all HMO enrollees.

Health care coverage also is provided through health maintenance organizations (HMOs) for nearly 30 million persons. A growing number of insurance plans are self-insured—those where an employer or union assumes all or part of the responsibility for paying claims. An additional expanding area for the private health insurance business is providing administrative services only (ASO) to self-insured plans. Under such arrangements, a fee is paid by the self-funding group to process claims and provide other administrative services.

Health care benefits are available also through various government programs. These include: Medicare for persons over age 65, Medicaid for a portion of the indigent population as well as certain categories of the medically needy, and various other programs described later in the text. However, despite the development of government health insurance benefit programs, recent years have witnessed a dramatic growth in the number of uninsureds. In 1991, there were an estimated 37 million persons who were uninsured. Of the nonelderly who are uninsured, 56 percent are working, 17 percent are nonworking adults, and 26 percent are children.

A number of factors are responsible for the increase in uninsureds, including the erosion of Medicaid coverage for the poor, demographic shifts, more part-time workers, and a shift of workers to service industries that are less likely to offer health insurance.

LIFE INSURANCE

In addition to its involvement in the early development of group health insurance, Montgomery Ward & Co., Inc. also is credited as the originator of group life insurance. In 1910, the executives of Montgomery Ward were greatly concerned with the problems created by the deaths of employees who had made no provision for funds for their own burial or for the welfare of their families. Management, aware of the economies and advantages in the volume buying of merchandise, reasoned that the same principles could logically and effectively be applied to the purchase of insurance. The company, rejecting any thoughts of self-insurance, hired a consulting actuary to investigate the possibility of obtaining insured death benefits at low cost for all employees, regardless of age or physical condition. Inquiries were made to several of the largest life insurance companies of the time, but all of these insurers declined any consideration of such a revolutionary approach to the life insurance business.

In early 1911, however, a newly hired actuary of the Equitable Life Assurance Society of the United States, William J. Graham (the "father of group insurance"), came across the "dead file" containing the correspondence between Montgomery Ward and the Equitable. He had the vision to recognize the real possibilities in the discarded group idea. At his urging, negotiations were reopened with Montgomery Ward.

While Montgomery Ward was trying to decide if its original concept was a good one, a director of the Equitable, Eugenius M. Outerbridge, "jumped the gun" and purchased the first group life insurance contract in June 1911 for the employees of the Pantasote Leather Company, of which he was president. Several other small employers quickly followed suit. By the time the Montgomery Ward contract was issued on July 1, 1912, the company could claim only that it held the sixth group insurance contract written in the United States.

It is not difficult to imagine Mr. Graham's apprehension regarding the first year's loss experience calculation under the Montgomery Ward contract, but he had no reason for concern. The premium for the first policy year was almost $87,000; claims and total expenses amounted to less than $69,000. The experience continued just as favorably for the next five years; by that time the soundness of the principle of group insurance was well established and accepted.

Features of the first group life contract, still often included, are:

- Insurance is issued on a nonmedical, term insurance basis;
- The individual's amount of insurance approximates one year's salary;
- Premiums all are paid on a noncontributory basis by the employer;
- The policyholder has the right to a return of excess paid premium if claims are less than anticipated;
- Policies have a 30-day grace period for the payment of premiums due; and
- Policies have a conversion privilege.

DEVELOPMENT

Throughout the decade 1910 to 1920, group life insurance was the principal group coverage written. Since then, insurers have developed many group life insurance products, including:

- *Creditor Life (1926):* Group term insurance equal to an outstanding debt and payable to the creditor upon death of the debtor;
- *Paid-up Life (1945):* A combination of accumulating units of single-premium whole life insurance with correspondingly decreasing units of group term;
- *Dependent Life (1945):* Group term on spouse and children;
- *Group Ordinary (1959):* A combination of group term and individual permanent life insurance;
- *Survivor Income Benefits (1964):* Monthly income benefits, with payment contingent upon the existence of a qualified survivor after the death of the insured employee; and
- *Group Universal Life (1985):* A combination of group term life insurance with a cash accumulation feature.

CURRENT STATUS

Today, most of the population of the United States, including government employees and military personnel, are insured under or protected by some type of group life insurance. While some contracts are issued through unions, associations, and other groups (multiple employers), insurers still issue most policies to single employer-employee groups. The labor force is widely insured, and dependents of many working people are covered.

Starting with $13,000,000 of group life insurance in force at the end of 1912, the amount of insurance had grown to over $4 trillion by the end of 1991. Less than 500 master policies and 12,000 certificates of insurance were in force in 1912; by 1991, the number had grown to 697,000 master policies and 141 million insurance certificates. The following data, supplied by the American Council of Life Insurance, illustrate the growth

GROUP LIFE INSURANCE IN FORCE
In the United States (000 omitted)

Year	No. of Master Policies	No. of Certificates	Amount	Year	No. of Master Policies	No. of Certificates	Amount
1912	*	12	$ 13,000	1975	378	96,693	$ 904,695,000
1915	*	120	100,000	1976	404	100,138	1,002,647,000
1920	6	1,600	1,570,000	1977	437	105,649	1,115,047,000
1925	12	3,200	4,247,000	1978	495	110,445	1,243,994,000
1930	19	5,800	9,801,000	1979	559	114,893	1,419,418,000
1935	18	6,400	10,208,000	1980	586	117,762	1,579,355,000
1940	23	8,800	14,938,000	1981	631	122,611	1,888,612,000
1945	31	11,500	22,172,000	1982	636	124,279	2,066,361,000
1950	56	19,288	47,793,000	1983	635	126,628	2,219,573,000
1955	89	31,649	101,345,000	1984	634	127,405	2,392,358,000
1960	169	43,602	175,903,000	1985	642	129,904	2,561,595,000
1965	234	60,930	308,078,000	1986	612	135,157	2,801,049,000
1970	304	79,844	551,357,000	1987	672	136,006	3,043,782,000
1971	312	82,320	589,883,000	1988	625	138,071	3,232,080,000
1972	326	85,102	640,689,000	1989	701	141,556	3,469,498,000
1973	338	88,385	708,322,000	1990	707	140,966	3,753,506,000
1974	359	93,567	827,018,000	1991	697	141,086	4,057,606,000

of group life insurance in the United States.

In the United States, group life insurance has risen from 20.4 percent of all life insurance in force in 1950 to 40.6 percent of the total by the end of 1991.

FACTORS INFLUENCING THE GROWTH OF GROUP INSURANCE

Multiple economic, social, and political forces affected the growth of group insurance. By the beginning of the twentieth century, American society was becoming increasingly industrialized and urbanized; traditional family obligations to care for the old and the sick were weakening. Also, dissatisfaction with public measures for the relief of the ill, the old, and the destitute was growing. These general trends set the stage for development of group insurance.

Other factors responsible for the rapid and extensive growth of group insurance include:

- wage controls during World War II,
- union demands through collective bargaining,
- favorable federal tax treatment,
- social legislation,
- extension and refinement of the group insurance concept,
- the effect of consumerism,
- expansion of benefits,

- population demographics,
- the rising demand for, and cost of, medical care, and
- competition.

WAGE CONTROLS DURING WORLD WAR II

During World War II, the federal government imposed industrial wage and price controls in an effort to control inflation. Since fringe benefits, including insurance plans, were not controlled, employers turned to group insurance and pension plans to supplement wages as a means of attracting and retaining employees.

UNION DEMANDS THROUGH COLLECTIVE BARGAINING

The Wagner Act (National Labor Relations Act of 1935) gave employees the right to organize unions and bargain collectively with their employers over wages, hours, and other conditions of employment. However, the real impetus for negotiated employee benefit plans occurred in 1948 when the National Labor Relations Board ruled, in a dispute between the United Steelworkers' Union and the Inland Steel Company, that the term wages "must be construed to include emoluments of value, like pension and insurance benefits."

In upholding this ruling in its notable decision of 1949, the Supreme Court removed any doubt about the right of labor to bargain collectively over wages, hours, or other conditions of employment, including retirement and insurance plans. The decision clearly established that group insurance and other benefits are within the scope of collective bargaining, engendering much of the post-World War II growth of employee benefit plans.

Employers do not, however, have to bargain collectively with their nonunion employees—but most employers do extend the benefits negotiated for their union employees to their nonunion employees. Today, even nonunion employers recognize insurance benefits as an integral part of an employee benefits package.

FAVORABLE FEDERAL TAX TREATMENT

The premiums paid by an employer for employees' group insurance are deductible from the employer's gross income on the principle that they represent an ordinary and necessary business expense. The premiums paid by the employer do not constitute taxable income to the employees except under specific conditions for some amounts of life insurance.

Before the passage of the Tax Equity and Fiscal Responsibility Act of 1982 (TEFRA), only the employer's contribution to the cost of group term life insurance in excess of $50,000 from all sources was taxable income to an employee. As a result of TEFRA, however, effective for tax years after 1983, a qualification has been added. If a life insurance plan is considered to discriminate in favor of key (essential) employees, either as to eligibility or benefits, the key employees will no longer be eligible for the exclusion for the first $50,000.

An employee who itemizes federal income tax deductions may deduct contributions for medical and dental care expense insurance subject to the overall requirements for medical and dental expense deductions. Under the present federal income tax law, medical and dental care expense insurance is limited to coverage such as hospitalization, doctors' fees, and medicines. It does not include coverage for accidental death and dismemberment insurance or short-term and long-term disability income insurance.

SOCIAL LEGISLATION

Both state and federal legislation have had an effect on the group health insurance business. The enactment of certain state disability benefits and state health insurance plan legislation affected the growth of group health plans. The states and territories with compulsory nonoccupational temporary disability benefits legislation mentioned earlier permit health insurers to write short-term disability income coverage to meet the requirements of these laws (except for Rhode Island, which has a monopolistic state fund). California and New Jersey state funds, however, are conducted in a way that places insurers at a competitive disadvantage; therefore, state funds provide most of this coverage. Private insurers can provide statutory benefits and do compete with the funds in New York, Hawaii, and Puerto Rico, and sometimes in New Jersey.

Also, several states have increased the number of people with health insurance by enacting laws establishing comprehensive plans of medical care expense insurance for people who are uninsurable. In addition to the premium paid by insureds, these plans are sometimes financed through statewide pools to which all insurers operating in the state are required to contribute. Through this mechanism, premiums for individuals who are uninsurable and not eligible for group insurance are kept at affordable levels.

On the federal level, legislation such as Social Security disability benefits, Medicare, Medicaid, and the Health Maintenance Organization Act of 1973 has affected the growth of group health insurance and the design of products provided by insurers. For example, some long-term disability income insurance plans supplement the benefits available under the Social Security program.

EXTENSION AND REFINEMENT OF THE GROUP INSURANCE CONCEPT

Since World War II, group insurance has grown through many extensions of the group insurance concept. Amounts of group life and group health insurance on the lives of individuals have been increased, and the types of eligible groups to which the group insurance concept is applied have widened. Insurers have developed group plans for trade associations, professional associations, and multiple-employer trusts; residential mortgages under credit life and health insurance; the conversion of group medical care expense coverages to individual policies; and medical care coverages for retired persons and their dependents.

The refinement of group insurance procedures and techniques has been a strong contributing factor in the growth of group insurance. Sales and marketing approaches, as well as claim payment procedures, have been refined and broadened. For example, the direct payment of claims to hospitals and other providers results in more rapid payment of claims, decreases involvement of the policyholder in transactions, and improves the relationship between the patient, the provider of medical care, and the insurer. Furthermore, the development of computer programs and streamlined administrative procedures has reduced operating costs for group insurers and helped to provide products that comply with federal and state laws.

THE IMPACT OF CONSUMERISM

Consumerism, which has been a powerful influence since the 1960s, can be defined as a social movement seeking to increase the rights and powers of buyers in relation to sellers. Consumer advocates want buyers to have adequate information about a product or service, such as quality, quantity, advantages, disadvantages, guarantees, and prices. They also insist on the buyers' rights to additional protection against certain products and marketing practices.

The insurance industry has received the careful attention of the consumer movement. For example, there has been well-publicized concern over the availability and cost of automobile, fire, flood, glass, and theft insurance in the property and liability field to people living in certain areas of the United States. In addition, the National Association of Insurance Commissioners (NAIC), through NAIC task forces and insurance industry advisory committees, has studied appropriate methods of making valid cost comparisons of individual life insurance policies. It also has adopted model regulations dealing with complaints and the discontinuance and replacement of group insurance policies.

Reflecting consumer concerns, various states have legislated group health insurance coverage for alcoholism, drug addiction, home health care, mental and nervous disorders, newborn children, handicapped children, and continuation of survivors' health benefits. Insurers, too, are offering new benefits to address those concerns. Additionally, state legislatures have enacted laws mandating minimum health insurance benefits, confidentiality of medical care information, and the continuation of coverage for terminated employees.

It is natural that the insurance business should be subjected to consumer scrutiny, both because of the fiduciary nature of the business (the insurer is entrusted with the responsibility of acting in the interest of beneficiaries) and because it affects so many people in important and meaningful ways over long periods of their lives.

EXPANSION OF BENEFITS

One further factor in the growth of group insurance has been the expansion through the years of its benefits to solve various coverage and cost problems. For example, insurers developed dependent life insurance to pay for the expenses associated with the death of a spouse and dependent children, survivor income benefits insurance to provide income to surviving dependents for a period of time after the employee's death, and group paid-up and group ordinary life insurance to take care of the coverage and cost problems that arise when an employee's group term life insurance is either terminated or reduced because of age or retirement.

Along with developing new coverages to meet expanding needs, group health insurers continually revise and broaden existing coverages to keep pace with the increasing cost and scope of medical care. For example, the number of covered days for hospital confinements, originally about 31 days, may now range from 70 days to an unlimited number. Surgical schedules originally had $200-$300 maximums; they now offer $500-$1,500 maximums, or even higher. A typical overall maximum benefit under early major medical expense insurance plans was $5,000 or $10,000; these maximums now are $250,000, $1,000,000, or unlimited.

In life insurance, insurers currently are underwriting, without a medical examination, increasing amounts of group term life insurance—offering sums that equal two, three, or even four times annual earnings. In fact, on a medically examined basis, substantial amounts—$100,000, $250,000, or more—of supplemental group term life insurance can be purchased in addition to a basic plan.

POPULATION DEMOGRAPHICS

Most employee benefit plans were designed to meet the traditional family unit—a male employee with a nonworking wife and two or three minor children. Today's work force and population demographics make traditional forms of benefits inadequate for many persons.

In response to changing demography, group insurance has developed a number of new group benefits. Flexible (cafeteria) benefit plans allow participants to select some or all of their benefits from among those the employer will provide. Available benefit options may include life insurance, long-term disability, medical care, dental care, vision care, and dependent care.

Changes also include a population that is increasingly aging. A good part of the work force of many employers is or will soon be retiring. Therefore, many employers are adding post-retirement medical and life insurance benefits to group pension benefits. Group long-term care insurance products, too, are now being introduced in the workplace.

THE RISING DEMAND FOR, AND COST OF, MEDICAL CARE

The introduction and wide use of many highly effective drugs, advances in diagnostic services, and new lifesaving surgical procedures have greatly increased the use of medical care services and facilities. Increased demand is also a result of such factors as the greater availability and diversity of medical care services and facilities with widespread reimbursement for them by third-party payors, the change in the public image of the hospital from a place to die to a place to sustain life, and the more frequent use of the hospital for diagnostic and nonsurgical purposes.

A broader degree of health education through the use of mass media, the school system, medical societies, employers, labor unions, health insurers, voluntary agencies, and all levels of government also has served to expand public awareness of health matters, and, consequently, increased demand for medical care and treatment. Meanwhile, the more technical and highly specialized nature of medical care has resulted in increases in the price of that care. In fact, the medical care component of the Consumer Price Index has risen faster than the average of all goods and services.

This combination of greater demand and rising cost has caused a growing interest in managing health costs. In order to contain costs and reduce unnecessary utilization, employers' group insurers are establishing managed care programs such as Health Maintenance Organizations (HMOs), Preferred Provider Organizations (PPOs), and utilization review programs. For the first time, employers and insurers are involved in the provision of medical care, and thus have an interest in, and accountability for, the quality and quantity of medical care.

The cost of financing health care has had enormous impact on the health insurance industry. Employees are being asked to share in the cost of health insurance through use of deductibles and coinsurance. There has been an increase in the number of employer self-insured plans in the late 1980s. The number of uninsured persons also has grown. With cost shifting of nonreimbursed health costs to employers and insurers, payors are actively suggesting methods for a more equitable health delivery system.

Catastrophic illnesses such as AIDS also affect the life and health insurance industry. The use of managed health care concepts, such as medical case management, and support for research and education are two of the industry's responses to such illnesses. These responses encourage prevention, treatment, and humane, flexible benefits.

COMPETITION

In addition to the factors already mentioned, a highly competitive market also has influenced the development of group insurance. The group insurance market constantly changes because of rising costs and recognizing new insurance needs. New products, concepts in coverage, and funding vehicles are continually being developed. They provide, for the buyer of group insurance, alternatives in meeting specific objectives. A new type of contract or concept in plan design may be the deciding factor in competition until it becomes a part of the portfolio of most insurance companies.

The quality of service may be an

important factor in obtaining and retaining group insurance policyholders. The ability of the insurance company to communicate the plan effectively and to provide sound administration, computer capability, and prompt, accurate claim payments are all vital to the satisfactory operation of the group plan. Any of these factors may be an important determinant fr the buyer in selecting a group insurer. Also, effective communication of the financial operation and the annual rerating of the contract is a service that is essential to retaining policyholders.

Blue Cross/Blue Shield Plans are a competitive factor because they have been able to make arrangements for discounted contracts with hospitals and physicians. These concessions gave Blue Cross a distinct cost advantage over private insurers. Also, Blue Cross had provided full-benefit hospital plans and reasonable and customary surgical and medical plans. Today, private insurers provide full-benefit plans and have attempted to provide discounted plans, sometimes through their own PPOs.

In fact, competition from HMOs and PPOs became a factor for private health insurers. Today, a number of major private health insurers frequently control their own HMO or PPO benefit programs. For further discussion of HMOs and PPOs, see Chapter 2 in Part C.

Besides competition from alternate delivery systems, there is another competitive factor—the self-funded or partially self-funded employee benefit plan. The desire to improve cash flow and reduce tax liabilities has led many large employers to thc self- or partially self-funded approach to insurance. Thus, many private insurers have developed ASO services or partial risk assumption to provide services to large employers. ASO business has changed the relationship of insurers and large group employers.

The life insurance industry has been faced with a variety of competition that has also affected product development. The banking and financial services industries have created an environment in which life insurers must create new products, such as Group Universal Life, or develop more flexible and higher indemnity life benefit products.

SUMMARY

The contingencies of death, accident, and ill health could result in financial hardship to anyone at any time. Therefore, group life and health insurance has become a major consumer product, involving cooperative ventures among insurers, employers, employees, health care providers, and various other groups. The remainder of this text (together with Parts B and C) will assist you in an in-depth examination of the challenging and changing group insurance business.

KEY TERMS

Actuary
Administrative Services Only (ASO)
Adverse Selection
Baylor Plan
Cafeteria Plans
Claim Experience
Collective Bargaining
Contributory Plan
Cost Sharing
Establishment Fund
Evidence of Insurability
Group Insurance
Health Maintenance Organizations (HMOs)
Individual Insurance
Key Employee
Major Medical
Managed Health Care
Master Contract
Multiple-Employer Trust
Noncontributory Plan
Preferred Provider Organizations (PPOs)
Premium
Prepaid Plan
Risk
Self-Insured Plan
Underwriting
Workers' Compensation Laws

II

GROUP MEDICAL COVERAGES

INTRODUCTION

Operating in a competitive market, the private insurance industry has responded to continually changing social and economic conditions. Through the years, numerous forms of group insurance coverages have been made available to meet the changing insurance needs of the consumer.

The group coverages discussed in Chapters 2 and 3 are those most commonly offered by the insurance industry. Although many variations may be purchased, the characteristics described usually apply to the benefits offered by all insurers. Since most group plans insure employees of a single employer, the insurance described pertains to employees; however, the same concepts apply when the policyholder is other than a single employer, such as an association or labor union.

Group medical care expense insurance coverages provide full or partial reimbursement for various medical care expenses incurred by insured employees or by their eligible dependents. These coverages are being expanded continually as technology changes. Currently, the most common medical care expense benefits are:

- hospital expense,
- skilled nursing facility expense,
- home health care expense,
- surgical expense,
- physicians' visits expense,
- diagnostic x-ray and laboratory examination expense,
- radiotherapy expense,
- supplemental accident expense,
- pregnancy expense,
- vision care expense,
- prescription drug expense,
- hospice care expense,
- major medical expense,
- dental expense, and
- survivor health benefits.

HOSPITAL EXPENSE BENEFITS

Both inpatient and outpatient medical care expenses incurred in a hospital are reimbursed under this coverage.

INPATIENT BENEFITS

Hospital inpatient benefits can be divided into two broad areas:

- charges for room and board, and
- charges for necessary services and supplies, sometimes referred to as "hospital extras," "other hospital charges," "miscellaneous charges," or "ancillary services."

Most hospitals distinguish between these charges in their billings and usually itemize the services and supplies. Typical maximum periods of hospital confinement during which benefits are payable are 31, 70, 120, or 365 days.

Some hospitals do not itemize their charges but use an average daily charge called a per diem rate that includes room and board and all other services. Others charge a per diem rate but add an incremental charge for routine nursing care. In addition, under the provisions of the federally-sponsored Medicare program for the elderly and totally disabled, as well as formally under certain state programs, hospitals would charge using the diagnosis related groups (DRG) methodology. The DRG billing method resulted in fixed charges for combined hospital services under a schedule of costs and expected lengths of stay related to the patient's final diagnosis. Flat rate (per diem) and DRG billing methods have given rise to hospital benefit payment methods that reflect these characteristics.

CHARGES FOR ROOM AND BOARD

The room and board component of hospital charges covers the cost of the room, meals, and nursing services routinely provided to all inpatients. Hospital expense insurance benefits for room charges are usually expressed in one of two ways. One method is that of the specified maximum daily benefit, which states that reimbursement will be made for the room and board charge for each day of confinement, up to a specified daily maximum, such as $150. The specified maximum daily benefit usually is related to the most common semi-private room and board charges in the geographic area where the insured group is located. Since hospital charges vary greatly from one area of the country to another, larger groups with several geographic locations may have a different maximum daily benefit for each location.

The second method is the service-type benefit. This benefit provision has no specific room and board maximum, and the benefit payment equals the full charge for a semi-private room. For private room accommodations, frequently there is a stated maximum daily benefit limit. The private room benefit limit is usually equal to the most common semi-private room charge of the hospital, or the most common semi-private room charge plus a stipulated additional dollar amount such as $4, $5, or $10 per day.

INTENSIVE CARE

Hospital expense insurance plans may include an intensive care benefit that increases the daily room and board benefit when confinement in an intensive care unit is necessary. Intensive care and other special care units such as coronary care have special equipment and nursing staff to provide 24-hour monitoring and medical attention for critically ill patients. Many plans also either limit the number of days of reimbursement or reimburse up to an overall dollar maximum for an intensive care confinement. Some count each day of intensive care as two toward the maximum number of days for hospital benefits. Still others consider the part of the charge for an intensive care unit that exceeds a plan's maximum daily benefit as part of hospital extras or as special nursing services.

CHARGES FOR NECESSARY SERVICES AND SUPPLIES

The necessary services and supplies portion of hospital expense insurance commonly provides reimbursement for hospital charges such as drugs and medicines, diagnostic x-rays and laboratory tests, medical supplies, use of the operating room, and ambulance service of the hospital or other provider. Although charges for the professional administration of anesthesia and anesthesia materials are often reimbursable as part of the hospital benefit, it is also common to cover the professional component of anesthesia under the surgical benefit. This is true whether the anesthetist's services are billed by the hospital or an independent provider.

In most plans, charges for hospital extras are reimbursed in one of three ways, although other variations are possible:

1. A specified dollar maximum for

each confinement, which is usually a multiple of the room and board daily benefit (10 or 20 times the daily benefit). For example, if a policy has a $150 per day room and board benefit and a 20 times factor, then $3,000 is the maximum for necessary services and supplies.

2. A specified dollar maximum plus a certain percentage of charges in excess of that maximum. For example, the plan may pay the first $500 of charges in full, and a percentage of the next $3,000 of these charges. The use of this percentage technique is referred to as coinsurance—the sharing of the charges by the insured person and the insurance company. For example, an insured incurs hospital charges for necessary services and supplies amounting to $4,600. If the daily room and board benefit is $150 and the benefit for necessary services is 20 times $150, with charges over $3,000 subject to 75 percent coinsurance, the total benefit for necessary services and supplies would be:

20 × $150	$3,000
75% of $1,600	1,200
	$4,200

3. Full payment during the period for which room and board is payable.

OUTPATIENT BENEFITS

Hospital expense benefits also provide reimbursement for hospital outpatient services for the emergency treatment of an accidental injury if the services required are furnished within 48 hours following the accident, and for surgery.

Sometimes emergency care benefits also are provided for outpatient expenses incurred within 48 hours of a sudden and serious illness.

PREADMISSION TESTING (PAT)

Increasing use has been made of outpatient testing prior to prearranged hospital admission or scheduled surgery. This practice is called Preadmission Testing (PAT), and provides necessary presurgical x-rays and tests on a less costly basis than inpatient testing, because the patient does not incur a room and board charge.

Many insurers reimburse such outpatient procedures on the same basis as if they had been inpatient procedures, if they meet the following requirements:

- Tests are for diagnostic purposes in connection with a scheduled hospital confinement ("scheduled" would be interpreted to mean that a hospital room already had been reserved before the tests were performed);
- Tests have been ordered by the same physicians who ordered the hospital confinement;
- Tests are performed in the hospital where the confinement will take place and accepted by the hospital in lieu of the same tests made after confinement;
- Individual would have been eligible for benefits if such tests had been performed while the patient had been confined as an inpatient; and

- Tests are not for a routine physical check-up.

An administrative problem occasionally develops when a scheduled hospital confinement is canceled, either because of the results of the tests or for other reasons beyond the control of the physician, the hospital, or the patient. In these situations, insurers covering preadmission testing usually consider the expense an inpatient expense, subject to proof that the other conditions had been met.

For plans providing reimbursement of 80 percent for inpatient benefits, a policyholder may choose to provide a greater benefit, 90 or 100 percent, for preadmission testing as an incentive for employees to use outpatient testing services.

SUCCESSIVE PERIODS OF HOSPITAL CONFINEMENT

The hospital benefits described above apply to successive hospital confinements during any one continuous period of hospital confinement, unless a subsequent confinement is separated from a previous confinement by a return to active, full-time employment or arises from an entirely unrelated cause.

For dependents, successive confinements separated by less than three months are considered one continuous period of hospital confinement, unless the subsequent confinement arises from an entirely unrelated cause and begins after the covered dependent is discharged from the hospital for the previous confinement. Some plans also recognize "resumption of normal activities" after previous discharge to establish a new period for dependents.

SKILLED NURSING FACILITY EXPENSE BENEFITS

This coverage provides reimbursement for medical care expenses incurred when an insured individual requires ongoing active medical and skilled nursing care and is confined in an extended care facility (or skilled nursing facility) specializing in such care. The benefit permits the doctor to transfer the patient from the more expensive hospital room to the less expensive extended care facility when medical needs are almost exclusively for continued skilled nursing care.

Since this coverage is not intended to provide custodial care, the definition of an extended care facility is of extreme importance. Many insurers limit the benefits payable only to those institutions approved by Medicare as skilled nursing facilities. Other insurers specifically define the services that must be provided. Almost all definitions of extended care facilities include the following:

- The institution must be licensed in accordance with the applicable laws of the jurisdiction in which it is located.

- The institution must be engaged regularly in providing medical care and treatment of sick and injured persons at the patient's expense. Some insurers require continuous 24-hour skilled nursing care under the supervision of a licensed registered nurse or physician for the institution's care to be covered. In some cases, the person providing this supervision also may be required to be full time.

- The institution may be required to have a minimum number of beds.
- The institution must maintain daily medical records and require that each patient be under the care of a licensed physician. (Some insurers do not pay the benefit if the physician has a financial interest in the extended care facility.)
- The institution must not be a facility primarily for treatment of maternity, alcoholism, drug addiction, or mental illness, nor a rest home or residence primarily for the elderly or the physically handicapped.

DESCRIPTION OF BENEFITS

The amount and extent of available benefits vary among insurers. For example, there may be a total dollar limit for each day of confinement in an extended care facility; specific dollar limits for room and board and for necessary services and supplies, similar to a typical hospital expense insurance plan; or a daily limit that is expressed as a percentage (usually 50 percent) of the hospital room and board benefit available under hospital and/or major medical expense insurance coverages.

Plans normally are available ranging from 30 to 200 days per confinement in an extended care facility. When hospital and extended care facility benefits are fully integrated, the maximum number of days provided by the plan may allow two days of ECF care to equal one hospital day in counting the maximum number of days.

LIMITATIONS AND EXCLUSIONS

Extended care facility benefits are limited to individuals requiring continuous skilled nursing services, confined at the recommendation of a physician, and under the care of a physician while confined.

Although some insurers provide benefits for direct admission without prior hospital confinement, it is more common to require hospitalization for a period of three to five days prior to confinement in an extended care facility. It also is common to find plans requiring that the extended care facility confinement begin within a specific period such as 7 to 14 days from the date of discharge from the hospital for the same cause or disability. Custodial care is excluded. Most plans have a lifetime maximum limit, such as 365 days.

HOME HEALTH CARE EXPENSE BENEFITS

These benefits usually are written as a supplement to hospital expense benefits or major medical expense benefits. They provide reimbursement for a variety of types of skilled care while the individual is recuperating at home. The objective is to avoid prolonged institutional confinement when the services required by the patient can be provided more comfortably and less expensively in the patient's home.

DESCRIPTION OF BENEFITS

Plans typically provide payment for such home health care charges as:

- physical, occupational, or speech therapies,
- part-time or intermittent nursing care provided under the supervision of a registered nurse,
- part-time or intermittent services of a home health aide,
- medical social services provided under the direct supervision of a physician, or
- care provided by a hospital intern or resident in training under an approved hospital teaching program.

The charges may be made by a hospital-based or independently licensed home health care agency. Home health care usually begins within a specific number of days following hospitalization or confinement in an extended care facility for the same or a related disability. There is a trend, however, toward providing home health benefits without requiring prior hospitalization. Home health care services are covered if:

- prescribed by a physician in lieu of hospitalizing the patient,
- furnished under a plan established and periodically reviewed by the physician, and
- furnished on a visiting basis in the patient's home or in the outpatient department of a hospital, skilled nursing facility, or rehabilitation center.

Examples of controls that may be built into a home health care plan include a coinsurance factor or patient copayment (per visit) and a maximum number of home health care visits, such as 40 in a calendar year, or maximum dollar limit such as $2,000 per year.

LIMITATIONS AND EXCLUSIONS

Usually this coverage will not pay for any services provided when the insured is not under the regular care and treatment of a physician, for any services furnished by a person who ordinarily resides in the insured's home or who is a member of the insured's immediate family, or for any services included under other coverages. Types of expenses frequently excluded are custodial care, meals, general housekeeping services, companions, and personal comfort items.

SURGICAL EXPENSE BENEFITS

This coverage provides benefits for the cost of surgical procedures performed as a result of an accident or sickness. Payment toward the charges for administration of anesthesia for a surgical procedure is also often included as a surgical expense benefit. Most plans define the types of procedures that are considered as surgery, such as cutting operations, suturing wounds, and treatment of fractures.

TYPES OF PLANS

Surgical expense benefits may be provided on a scheduled or non-scheduled basis. Most are on a non-scheduled basis.

SCHEDULED

Under a scheduled plan, a specific allowance for each surgical procedure is listed on a surgical schedule. Every insurer has several different surgical schedules, the basic differences being:

- the amount that the schedule allows for each procedure,
- the overall maximum benefit for multiple procedures, and
- the relative or proportionate value of the procedures listed in the schedule.

The following are some of the allowances in a typical surgical schedule:

Procedures	*Maximum Payment*
Cardiac triple valve replacement	$4,000
Cutting into cranial cavity	1,400
Removal of lung	1,300
Removal of kidney	1,000
Hysterectomy	800
Removal of gallbladder	725
Appendectomy	475
Single hernia	450
Internal hemorrhoidectomy	350
Tonsillectomy—under 12 years old	200

A typical published schedule lists perhaps 100 operations that cover each of the important categories of surgical procedures, such as abdomen, amputations, breast, chest, genitourinary tract, or tumors. Operations for unlisted procedures are paid based on a master surgical schedule on a scale proportionate to the listed procedures.

NONSCHEDULED

Instead of a specific allowance, reimbursement of the surgeon's fees—and often the anesthetist's fee—is based on the usual and customary charge, usually on a percentage basis, such as 80 percent, 90 percent, or 100 percent of the usual and customary charge, for the procedure performed; there is no schedule of allowances.

A usual and customary charge is defined by each insurer based on the charges normally made by doctors for similar services and the amount most frequently charged by most doctors for comparable services in the locality where the service is received.

MULTIPLE OPERATIONS

Under most policies, multiple operations are reimbursed as follows:

- For two or more procedures performed at the same time through either the same incision or in the same operative field, the benefit payable is the larger amount of the two.
- For two or more surgical procedures performed at the same time through a separate incision or in different operative fields, the benefit is the amount with the highest payment

plus 50 percent of the amount for each other procedure.

- For two or more operations performed as a result of the same or related causes, but not during the course of a single operation, and not separated by (1) a return to active, full-time employment in the case of an employee, or (2) three months in the case of a dependent, payment will be made for each operation, subject to the overall schedule maximum.

SECOND SURGICAL OPINION EXPENSE BENEFITS

For patients who have been advised to have elective, nonemergency surgery, this surgical consultation benefit allows them to seek another professional opinion from a consulting surgeon, and to review the necessity and advisability of elective surgery. Reimbursement is provided for a second, and even a third opinion, and related x-rays or laboratory tests, and may apply to all categories of surgery or to a list of specific types of surgery. Obtaining a second opinion may be voluntary or mandatory.

Most medical care plans have incorporated second opinion programs for surgery. The benefit provided can be:

- full payment of expenses related to the second (or third) opinion;

- limited to usual and customary charges for surgical consultations, including additional necessary x-rays, laboratory tests, and other diagnostic studies (no deductible or coinsurance is applied to this benefit);

- same as above but subject to deductible or coinsurance provisions, or

- a fixed fee, such as $75, which is payable to the consulting surgeon if the surgeon agrees to accept the fee as payment in full. Charges for necessary x-rays and laboratory tests, up to a fixed limit, e.g. $150, will be reimbursed in addition to the fixed fee payable to the consulting surgeon. No deductible or coinsurance provisions are applied.

Even benefit plans not specifically providing second surgical opinion coverage may cover expenses for presurgical consultations. For instance, many major medical plans (to be explained later in the chapter) would consider second surgical opinions as a covered medical expense and would reimburse such expenses on a usual and customary basis, subject to deductible or coinsurance provisions.

Some plans require second surgical opinions before elective surgery. Under this mandatory approach, the plan may not pay the surgical benefit or may reimburse the surgical benefit at a lower level (e.g., 60 percent of the scheduled benefit or of the usual and customary charge) if the patient had elective surgery without seeking a second opinion. The requirement is only that another opinion be obtained prior to surgery. The decision to have surgery is made by patients and their physicians. Benefits are payable when a second opinion does not concur with the recommendation for elective surgery. Some will pay for a third opinion.

PHYSICIANS' VISITS EXPENSE BENEFITS

Often called medical expense insurance, this coverage provides reimbursement for physicians' fees for visits in cases of injury or sickness. The two types of plans commonly offered are in-hospital and comprehensive (in- and out-of-hospital).

IN-HOSPITAL PLANS

In-hospital plans pay physicians' fees for visits made while the patient is hospitalized as an inpatient. Benefits are subject to a specified maximum, such as $30 a day. The benefit period normally coincides with the benefit period for hospital expense insurance. For example, under a 70-day hospital expense insurance plan with a $30 daily in-hospital physicians' visits benefit, the maximum payment would be 70 × $30 ($2,100).

COMPREHENSIVE (IN- AND OUT-OF-HOSPITAL) PLANS

Comprehensive medical plans pay a specified maximum each day for the fees charged by a physician for home visits, hospital visits, and office visits. A plan, for example, may provide $20 for an office visit, $30 for a home visit, and $30 for a hospital visit, subject to an overall maximum of $500 for the care and treatment of one injury or sickness.

There may be a waiting period before benefits begin, such as with the second, third, or fourth visit. For hospital confinements and emergency care, a provision often is included for benefits to begin with the physician's first visit. Normally only one physician's visit per day is covered.

LIMITATIONS AND EXCLUSIONS

These plans normally do not cover visits after surgery if they are by a physician (or physicians) involved with the surgical procedure, since the surgeon's charge usually includes postoperative care. Other common exclusions are physicians' visits made for dental treatment and examinations for the prescription or fitting of eyeglasses or hearing aids.

DIAGNOSTIC X-RAY AND LABORATORY EXPENSE BENEFITS

This coverage provides reimbursement for diagnostic x-rays and laboratory tests when the insured is not hospital-confined. It complements other group medical care expense insurance coverages (such as hospital and surgical) that normally would not cover x-rays and laboratory analyses made in a doctor's office, an independent laboratory, or an outpatient department of a hospital.

TYPES OF PLANS

As with surgical benefits, diagnostic x-ray and laboratory expense benefits may be scheduled or nonscheduled. Most are nonscheduled.

SCHEDULED

Scheduled plans itemize the maximum allowance for each test as a dollar amount. Benefits typically are subject to a dollar maximum such as $100 to $300 either for all tests for one accident or sickness or for all accidents or sicknesses during a year. A two-part schedule commonly is used. The first part provides coverage for diagnostic x-ray and radioisotope images and sometimes is written as a separate coverage. The second part provides payment for diagnostic laboratory services and generally is written only in conjunction with x-ray services (the first part of the schedule).

NONSCHEDULED

Nonscheduled plans provide reimbursement for the actual fee charged, subject to a dollar maximum such as $100 or $300 either for all examinations in connection with one accident or sickness or in connection with all accidents or sicknesses during a calendar year.

LIMITATIONS AND EXCLUSIONS

Charges for x-rays and laboratory tests for dental treatment and services related to the prescription or fitting of eyeglasses or hearing aids are commonly excluded.

RADIOTHERAPY EXPENSE BENEFITS

Radiotherapy expense benefits cover the cost of radiological treatment, such as radium or cobalt therapy, and include:

- administration of the treatment,
- materials and their preparation, and
- the use of facilities.

Benefits frequently are provided through the use of a schedule with the maximum payment for all treatments during one day limited to the largest payment provided in the schedule. The total benefit for all treatments for the same or related injury or sickness is the overall dollar maximum, such as $400 in a calendar year.

SUPPLEMENTAL ACCIDENT EXPENSE BENEFITS

These benefits cover necessary treatment following an accidental injury which may include:

- treatment by a physician,
- hospital care,
- registered graduate nursing care (RN), or
- x-ray and laboratory examinations.

Usually the coverage applies only if these costs are incurred within three months of the date of the accident. Benefits are for medical care expenses that exceed coverage provided elsewhere under the basic medical care plan, and are subject to an overall maximum benefit for any one accident, such as $300.

VISION CARE EXPENSE BENEFITS

Unlike most medical care expense insurance coverages which focus on treatment of diseases or injury, vision care expense insurance is a coverage designed to provide benefits for routine preventive and corrective eye care. It usually is written to complement other basic coverages such as hospital, surgical, medical, or x-ray and laboratory benefits that cover expenses for a diagnosis and treatment of illness or injury of the eye. Its objective is to encourage regular or periodic eye examinations, so that appropriate corrective measures may be taken.

DESCRIPTION OF BENEFITS

Vision care expense insurance provides reimbursement toward the cost of eye examinations (including refraction) to determine whether the individual needs glasses and, if so, toward the cost of the glasses (frames and lenses of the type and strength required).

Single vision, bifocal, and trifocal lenses are almost always covered. Benefits also can be provided for contact lenses and other aids for subnormal vision (such as lenticular lenses). Since contact lenses are often selected by the individual for cosmetic reasons, payment may be limited to the allowance for single vision glasses except when correction to 20/70 in the better eye cannot be made with glasses but can be achieved with contact lenses.

Frames vary considerably in cost. Since selection of a frame is a question of personal preference rather than utility, insurance plans often place a significant dollar limitation on the amount payable for frames.

Under most vision care programs, the services covered require the authorization of an ophthalmologist or optometrist. Some plans simply provide a flat unallocated amount per individual, such as $50 toward all covered services provided in a calendar year; others provide coverage on a usual and customary basis. More often, however, the benefits are provided according to a schedule such as the example below. In any case, it is not customary to apply either a deductible or coinsurance.

SCHEDULE OF VISION SERVICES AND SUPPLIES
Maximum Amounts

Eye Examination, including refraction	$25.00
Lens, pair	
Single vision Rx	15.00
Bifocal Rx	20.00
Trifocal Rx	25.00
Lenticular	80.00
Contact	80.00
Frames	15.00

LIMITATIONS AND EXCLUSIONS

To avoid overutilization, vision care plans may limit coverage to only one examination and one pair of lenses in any 12 consecutive months and one pair of frames every two years. In addition, it is common to exclude medical or surgical treatment, sunglasses, tinted lenses, safety glasses, and duplication of existing lenses or frames because of breakage or loss. Although coverage for training for vision correction is often also excluded, some insurers offer it on an optional basis.

PRESCRIPTION DRUG EXPENSE BENEFITS

Prescription drug expense insurance covers drugs and medicines purchased on the order of a physician with very little, if any, cost to the insured. Because a large number of small expenses are involved, streamlined approaches to administration and claim processing are necessary.

TYPES OF PLANS

Prescription drug expense plans are available on both a reimbursement and a service basis.

REIMBURSEMENT PLANS

These plans rely on the individual to pay for the prescription drugs and to submit these expenses on a claim form completed by the pharmacist for the insurer. Reimbursement is made to the claimant on the basis of usual and customary charges.

The insured individual may also have to share some part of the charge. For example, the plan may provide for payment to be made based on the usual and customary charge less a specific amount, such as $2, for each prescription or refill. Using another method of reimbursement, a calendar year deductible, such as $10 or $25, may have to be satisfied before benefits are payable, and sometimes benefits are subject to an annual maximum limit, such as $250.

SERVICE PLANS

Generally, the term "service plan" refers to a system in which payment by the insurer is made directly to the provider of the service or product covered by the insurance policy. In the case of prescription drug insurance plans, however, because of the large number of small claims to be handled and the need for extensive networks of participating pharmacies, third-party administrative organizations have developed. These organizations are able to minimize costs through high volume and standardized forms and procedures. They assume the administrative duties of the insurance company including:

- enrolling participating pharmacies,
- claim processing and payment in accordance with the coverage established in the insurance contract,
- controlling claim costs, and
- developing statistical data.

This system relies substantially on an identification card that, when presented to the participating pharmacist, serves as a guarantee to the pharmacist that payment will be made under the plan.

A plan may include a copayment that is paid by the individual at the time of purchase of a prescription drug. The typical copayment is $2 to $10 per prescription. Copayments for generic drugs may be lower than copayments for non-generic drugs.

Mail order prescription drug programs also provide the insured the convenience of obtaining maintenance medication through the mail. These programs provide a 60- or 90-day supply of drugs and require the insured to make a copayment. Copayments for mail order plans are generally between $5 and $15 and are usually designed to encourage the use of this type of benefit.

Prescription drug insurance plans written on a service basis also provide for direct payment to the employee if the prescription is obtained from a nonparticipating pharmacy. Payment may be a percentage of usual and customary charges, or the same payment (or a percentage of the amount) that would have been made to a participating pharmacist.

LIMITATIONS AND EXCLUSIONS

The following charges are typically excluded:

- device of any type, such as a hypodermic needle or a syringe, and bandages,
- contraceptive drugs or devices, immunuization agents, sera, blood or blood plasma, dietary supplements, beauty aids or cosmetics,
- drugs that are dispensed while the individual is confined in a hospital or extended care facility, and
- a prescription that exceeds a specified number of days' supply of the drug, such as a 90-day supply if obtained from a participating mail order pharmacy and a 30-day supply if obtained from any other pharmacy.

HOSPICE CARE EXPENSE BENEFITS

The hospice concept involves a plan of care for the terminally ill patient and the patient's family. Its focus is on keeping the patient comfortable and free of pain (palliative care) as well as social support services, rather than the traditional curative approach to medicine. Hospice teams made up of trained medical personnel, homemakers, and counselors help the patient and the family cope with the social and psychological as well as the physical stresses of death and bereavement.

DESCRIPTION OF BENEFITS

Benefits are provided for usual and customary charges made by the hospice for the following:

- inpatient care services;
- physician's services;
- home health care services consisting of:
  1. part-time or 24-hour nursing care,
  2. physical therapy,
  3. use of medical equipment,
  4. rental of wheelchairs and hospital-type beds.
- drugs and medicines,
- emotional support services,
- homemaker services, and
- bereavement services.

Benefits are provided for a period before the death of the terminally ill patient and to the family for a period of bereavement after the patient's death. An overall benefit maximum, such as $5,000, generally applies to all covered expenses. Benefits may be provided on a first-dollar basis or may be subject to a deductible and coinsurance. Since some types of charges may be reimbursed under other parts of the medical care plan, coverage under this benefit is typically provided on a supplemental or an in-lieu-of basis to prevent duplication of benefits.

BENEFIT PERIOD

The benefit period starts when the attending physician certifies that the patient has a life expectancy of six months or less; it ends when the patient dies or at the end of a specified period, such as 6 or 12 months, whichever happens first. Successive periods may be established by recertification if the patient is still living at the end of the benefit period.

Daily maximums are often imposed in one of three ways:

- for inpatient services,
- for all services, or
- for inpatient services and a separate, and generally lower, daily maximum for outpatient services.

PERIOD OF BEREAVEMENT

This period begins when the patient dies and typically ends 6 or 12 months after the date of death. Benefits are usually limited to a specified number of counseling sessions for the surviving dependents. In some cases a dollar maximum per session also applies.

LIMITATIONS AND EXCLUSIONS

Benefits are not provided for services that have not been recommended by the attending physician or for those that an insured would not legally have had to pay in the absence of insurance. Some plans also exclude services by volunteers or other persons who do not customarily charge for services, such as family members or clergy.

MAJOR MEDICAL EXPENSE BENEFITS

Major medical insurance plans provide broad coverage and substantial protection from large, unpredictable, and therefore unbudgetable medical care expenses. They cover a wide range of medical care charges with few internal limits and a high overall maximum benefit.

Reimbursement for covered expenses may be provided in one of two ways:

- by first covering certain expenses with a basic plan of hospital-surgical-medical benefits, supplementing the basic plan with major medical coverage, or
- by using one reimbursement formula for total covered expenses without distinguishing between those expenses that would otherwise be covered under a basic plan and those expenses to be covered as major medical expense benefits.

The major medical portion of the first approach commonly is referred to as supplemental major medical expense insurance; the second and more frequent approach is known as comprehensive major medical expense insurance.

SUPPLEMENTAL MAJOR MEDICAL EXPENSE BENEFITS

A supplemental major medical expense insurance plan is superimposed on the insurer's own basic hospital-surgical-medical expense benefits or another basic plan, such as Blue Cross/Blue Shield. A claimant is reimbursed first for hospital and surgical charges, physicians' visits, or any other charges covered by specific reimbursement formulas in the basic plan. Certain covered expenses are not reimbursed under the basic plan, either because of limitations or maximums in the basic plan formula, or because they are outside the scope of the basic plan. These remaining expenses are subject to a deductible.

After satisfaction of this deductible amount, the supplemental major medical plan pays the remaining covered expenses, usually on a percentage basis, such as 80 percent. The total

MAJOR MEDICAL EXPENSE BENEFITS

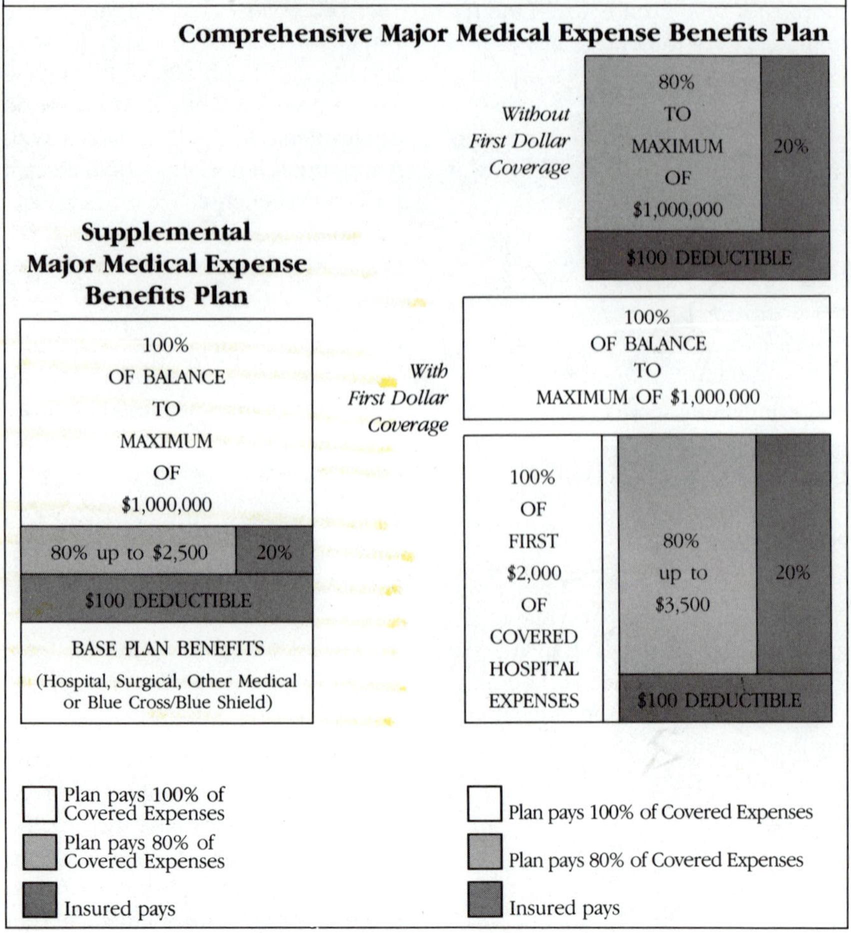

cost to the claimant, therefore, is the amount of the deductible plus the percentage of expenses not reimbursed under the major medical formula. A typical supplemental major medical plan is shown in the chart on page 36.

COMPREHENSIVE MAJOR MEDICAL EXPENSE BENEFITS

Comprehensive major medical expense insurance covers most types of medical care services and supplies in a single policy. A reimbursement formula is used for total covered expenses after a deductible. The deductible is referred to as an initial deductible since it applies before major medical benefits are payable. An example of the simplest form of these comprehensive plans provides for the reimbursement of 80 percent of all combined covered expenses in a calendar year, after a deductible of $100 to $300, up to a lifetime maximum benefit of $1,000,000.

The main features of comprehensive major medical are simplicity of plan design and avoidance of overlapping coverages and frequent plan revisions.

Some plans provide for first-dollar coverage, to this extent matching the alternative of basic plan with supplemental major medical. Often certain types of expenses are not subject to the deductible, such as hospital expenses, and no coinsurance is used on the initial hospital expenses, such as the first $2,000 or $5,000. Surgeons' fees may be treated in a similar manner, subject to the determination of usual and customary fees. The deductible and coinsurance features also can be waived and modified for other services such as physicians' hospital visits and pre-admission diagnostic tests, thus further matching the basic coverages plus supplemental major medical concept. The size, type, and application of the deductible; full coverage of certain expenses; and a dollar limit on out-of-pocket expenses to be borne by the insured are decided by the policyholder and the underwriting practices of the insurer. Diagrams of a comprehensive plan both with and without first-dollar coverage are shown in the chart on page 36.

FEATURES OF MAJOR MEDICAL PLANS

Both supplemental and comprehensive major medical have common provisions, such as deductibles, coinsurance, overall maximum benefits, and covered expenses.

DEDUCTIBLE

A primary purpose of the deductible is to lower premium costs by avoiding unnecessary utilization and eliminating small claims and the expense of handling them. In conjunction with the deductible, an accumulation period feature is included as a device to further ensure that only substantial claims will be covered. The accumulation period is the period of time during which incurred medical care expenses accumulate, sufficient to satisfy the deductible. The type and amount of the deductible and the way it operates, and the length of the accumulation period vary according to the needs of the policyholder and the underwriting requirements of the insurer. Common deductibles are the all cause, per cause, corridor, and integrated types.

All Cause Deductible. The all cause deductible includes all expenses incurred—regardless of the number of illnesses or accidents—that are accumulated to satisfy the deductible. Although it is possible to combine the all cause deductible with various accumulation periods and benefit periods, the calendar year is almost universally used for both. A typical example is a $300 deductible that applies to each calendar year benefit period and must be satisfied between January 1 and December 31.

The all cause deductible is also referred to as a calendar year deductible. Benefits are paid, following the satisfaction of the calendar year deductible, for expenses incurred during the remainder of the calendar year. Recognizing something of an inequity when some insureds incur expenses early in the year and others incur expenses late in the year, a carry-over provision may be included for the latter. Expenses incurred in the last three months of a calendar year, which accumulate toward satisfaction of the deductible for that year, are carried over to be used toward satisfying the deductible for the next calendar year. Currently, many insurers no longer offer the carry-over prevision, except under special conditions.

To reduce the financial impact of the deductible on large families, if several members have major expenses in one year, a "family deductible" provision waives the deductible for all family members after any two or three of them have individually satisfied their deductibles in the same year.

The most important advantage of the all cause approach is that it is simple to administer and is considered the easiest for the insured to understand.

Per Cause Deductible. All expenses incurred because of the same or related causes are accumulated to satisfy the per cause deductible. The benefit period for each cause starts with the first expense that is used to satisfy the deductible and normally either ends one to two years after the date it starts, or two years from the date the deductible was satisfied. When benefit periods longer than one year are provided, it is common to include an alternate cut-off date that terminates the benefit period. The cut-off date might occur at the end of a period of 60 or 90 days during which less than a certain amount of expenses (such as the deductible amount) is incurred. Once a benefit period ends, the deductible must be satisfied again to start a new one. An individual might have to satisfy two or more deductibles within one year if medical care expenses are incurred in several scattered episodes separated by more than 60 to 90 days.

The chief advantage of the per cause approach is that small claims for minor, unrelated illnesses can be eliminated. However, this approach can create administrative problems, since it often is difficult to determine whether various illnesses are related to the same cause. This is especially true in cases of chronic illness, diseases of advancing age, and diseases related to the immune system such as AIDS. The per cause deductible approach is not widely used today.

Corridor Deductible. The corridor deductible is used with supplemental major medical plans. Its name is derived from the fact that it operates as a "corridor" between the basic plan and the supplemental major medical plan. Medical expenses that exceed the amounts covered in the basic plan are covered under supplemental major medical after the corridor deductible is satisfied. Benefits paid under the basic plan are not counted toward satisfaction of the corridor deductible.

Integrated Deductible. Less common than the corridor deductible is an integrated deductible that is the greater of a fairly high amount, such as $1,000; or the basic plan benefits. For example, if the basic plan paid $1,250, a $1,000 deductible would automatically be satisfied and supplemental major medical benefits would be payable. However, if the basic plan only paid $700, $300 would be needed to satisfy the $1,000 deductible before supplemental major medical benefits would be payable.

Common Accident Provision. Most major medical plans have a special deductible modification, known as the common accident provision, which provides that only one deductible will have to be satisfied when two or more insured persons in the same family are injured in the same accident. A carry-over feature in a calendar-year type plan may also be included, in which case only one deductible applies to the total covered medical care expenses incurred as a result of the accident, both in the calendar year in which the common accident occurred and in the following calendar year.

COINSURANCE

Coinsurance is used to control plan costs, to retain the insured's financial interest in the cost of services, and to curtail unnecessary utilization of services. It sometimes is called percentage participation. Usually, for every dollar of covered expenses incurred beyond the deductible, the insured is required to pay 20 or 25 cents. However, many plans apply a dollar limit to the coinsurance amount to be borne by the insured, by eliminating coinsurance for the balance of the calendar year after the insured has incurred, for example, $2,500 in expenses paid out-of-pocket as the result of deductible and coinsurance application.

OVERALL MAXIMUM BENEFIT

Except for specifically identified coverage limitations, usual and customary charges for all eligible expenses are covered by the plan provisions up to the overall maximum benefit of the plan. Consistent with the application of the deductible, the overall maximum benefit may be written as lifetime (all cause) or per cause.

Lifetime (All Cause). The lifetime (all cause) maximum benefit applies to all covered expenses during the entire period of coverage. Also, a reinstatement provision is included to avoid penalizing insureds who have either partially or wholly exhausted their benefits, and have recovered to the extent of again being acceptable insurance risks. This provision might provide that after $5,000 or $10,000 in benefits are used, the maximum may be reinstated if the insured submits evidence of insurability satisfactory to the insurance company.

In addition, it is common to provide some form of "automatic" reinstatement. For example, benefits paid in amounts of $5,000 or $10,000 to as much as 10 percent of the full maximum, depending on the plan, may be reinstated automatically as of each January 1. Another approach reinstates some or all of the maximum if the insured does not incur medical care expenses of more than a specified amount, such as $500, during a given period, such as six months. Since it is not uncommon today to find lifetime (all cause) maximums as high as $1,000,000 and even unlimited benefits, the reinstatement provision has lost much of its significance.

Per Cause. The per cause overall maximum benefit applies to each cause, so for an insured who is receiving benefits under a per cause plan for the treatment of both diabetes and a heart condition, a separate overall maximum benefit would apply to each illness. A typical per cause reinstatement provision states that when a covered person has received benefits for any one accidental injury or any one sickness equal to the overall maximum benefit, major medical benefits for such injury or such sickness will terminate unless satisfactory evidence of insurability is submitted to the insurer. Termination of a covered person's major medical benefits for any one injury or sickness will not cause termination of coverage for other unrelated injuries or sicknesses.

COVERED EXPENSES

Major medical plans cover usual and customary charges incurred for the following types of medical care services, supplies, and treatments prescribed or performed by a physician and that are medically necessary. Although exact eligible charges and their description vary from plan to plan, the scope of covered expenses usually includes:

- professional services of doctors of medicine and osteopathy, and other recognized medical practitioners,
- hospital charges for semi-private room and board, and other necessary services and supplies,
- services of registered nurses and, in some cases, licensed practical nurses,
- physical therapy,
- anesthetics and their administration,
- diagnostic x-rays and laboratory procedures,
- x-ray or radium treatments,
- oxygen and other medicinal or

therapeutic gases and their administration,

- blood transfusions, including the cost of blood (when not replaced by blood donations),
- drugs and medicines requiring physician's prescription,
- local ambulance services,
- rental of durable mechanical equipment required for therapeutic use,
- artificial limbs or other prosthetic appliances, except replacement of such appliances,
- casts, splints, trusses, braces, and crutches,
- rental of a wheelchair or hospital-type bed,
- mammography screening,
- routine nursery care, and
- ambulatory surgical center services.

In addition, plans may provide coverage for confinements in skilled nursing facilities as well as coverage for home health care expenses and hospice care expenses.

GENERAL LIMITATIONS AND EXCLUSIONS

The following section presents some of the most common limitations and exclusions that are found in medical care expense insurance coverages and a brief statement of the reason for each.

CARE RECEIVED FROM ANY GOVERNMENT OR BY ANY GOVERNMENT AGENCY

Benefits are not paid for services and supplies furnished or provided by any government or government agency except (1) if covered by Medicaid; or (2) if furnished or ordered by the following (a) a Veterans' Administration Hospital or other military hospital for a veteran for a non-service disability; or (b) a Veterans' Administration Hospital or other military hospital for inpatient services provided to a retiree of the armed services or to a dependent of an active, retired, or deceased member of the armed services.

OCCUPATIONAL ACCIDENTS AND SICKNESSES

Benefits are not paid for medical care expenses resulting from an occupational accident, or from sickness for which a workers' compensation law or similar legislation applies. Workers' compensation benefits cover the medical care expenses of a worker for job-related accidents and sicknesses. An exception is that in some jurisdictions workers' compensation does not apply to business owners and partners because, by definition, they are not considered employees. In these cases, insurers may waive the exclusion and provide on-the-job coverage for such proprietors.

COSMETIC SURGERY

Elective cosmetic surgery is excluded. Such surgery is covered only if it is necessary to correct injuries caused by an accident that occurs while insured or to correct a congenital anomaly in an insured newborn infant.

PREEXISTING CONDITIONS

Because of the potential for selection against the insurer, preexisting conditions limitation allows for the payment of benefits only after certain requirements are met. For example, a preexisting condition's exclusion might read:

> "A preexisting condition is defined as a condition resulting from an injury or sickness for which a person has consulted a physician, received medical treatment, or has taken medication during the three months prior to the effective date of insurance. For such a condition benefits will be payable only (1) after the completion of a period of three consecutive months without medical services, treatment or medication; or (2) at the end of six months in which the insured employee was continuously insured and actively at work; or (3) after having been covered for major medical benefits for a period of one year."

A somewhat less restrictive provision covers preexisting conditions during the first year but only up to a specified dollar maximum such as $1,000.

DENTAL CARE AND TREATMENT

Care or treatment of teeth and gums is usually excluded, except for treatment required because of accidental injury to natural teeth while insured, removal of impacted teeth, and hospital confinement for an alveolectomy or a gingivectomy.

JAW JOINT DISORDERS

Treatment of temporomandibular joint (TMJ) disorders and all other craniomandibular disorders are generally limited to a specified dollar maximum such as $1,500 in each calendar year. Group dental expense insurance may provide such coverage, so provisions are made to avoid duplication of coverage (or coverage overlap) with medical care expense insurance.

EYE REFRACTIONS AND THE PURCHASE OR FITTING OF EYEGLASSES OR HEARING AIDS

These services are considered routine care and are not covered under Major Medical Plans. Coverage for eye refractions and eyeglasses are available through group vision care benefits. As is true of dental care, only eye diseases or accidental injury while insured are covered.

TRANSPORTATION EXCEPT FOR LOCAL AMBULANCE SERVICE

The intention is to exclude the costs of ambulance transportation, even if required by a doctor. It is common, however, for a plan to provide coverage for the cost of transportation by ambulance to the nearest hospital with care facilities appropriate for a particular illness, when the onset of the illness is sudden, or when hospitalization is due to an accident.

HEALTH EXAMINATIONS OR PERIODIC CHECK-UPS

As with other routine medical care services, it has been the responsibility of the insured to pay for non-illness related examinations or check-ups. However, plans may include benefits for preventive care as part of the basic coverage or under the major medical plan. If plans include such benefits, they will commonly include coverage for a physical exam at periodic intervals, up to a dollar maximum, such as $150.

MENTAL AND NERVOUS DISORDERS

Various limitations are applicable to mental and nervous disorders and chemical dependency, such as alcoholism or drug addiction. They are based on the concept that, while short-term therapy is beneficial, long-term treatment is often custodial in nature and not intended to be covered.

Inpatient benefits are usually provided on the same basis as any other illness, although some insurers limit inpatient coverage to a specific number of days each calendar year, such as 30 or 60. Outpatient benefits under major medical policies are usually 50 percent of the charges incurred, subject to a specific amount per visit, such as $30, and a total maximum amount each calendar year, such as $1,000. In addition, under major medical plans it is quite common to find a lifetime nonreinstatable overall maximum benefit, such as $25,000, for all mental and nervous disorders.

CUSTODIAL CARE

Since the purpose of health insurance is to provide benefits for the treatment of an injury or sickness, various exclusions and limitations are included to terminate benefits when institutionalization of the patient becomes custodial in nature, i.e., there is little medical care needed, and the patient primarily needs assistance with usual daily activities.

BODY MANIPULATION AND SUBLUXATION

These services to detect and correct body distortion are generally limited to a specified dollar maximum such as $500 in a calendar year.

Services or supplies for Experimental or Investigational Care and care not medically necessary are excluded from coverage.

USUAL AND CUSTOMARY CHARGES

Medical care expense insurance excludes charges that are not usual and customary. The purpose of this exclusion is to provide a reasonable benefit while excluding excessive charges. Usual and customary charges mean those charges that are the lessor of:

- the charge normally made by the provider for the medical care service; or

- the charge most other providers make for similar medical services in the same geographic area.

In applying this concept insurers do not try to set fee levels or interfere with the doctor/patient relationship. Rather, insurers establish a benefit maximum and the patient assumes the obligation to pay charges in excess of the insurer's allowed amount.

COORDINATION OF BENEFITS

In many households more than one family member is employed. Also, many people are covered by no-fault automobile insurance. As a result, a person may be covered for medical care expenses under more than one group insurance plan. This creates a situation where an insured may receive more in benefits than the actual expenses for medical care. This profit possibility for a few can hurt everyone concerned with obtaining good medical care at a reasonable cost and keeping the cost of group medical care insurance at affordable premiums.

A Coordination of Benefits (COB) provision is usually included in all medical and dental care insurance plans. The purpose is to give insureds all benefits to which they are entitled, but not more. COB applies if a person is covered under at least two group plans. The Order of Benefits Determination Rules will determine whether the benefits of one plan are Primary, that is, determined before those of another plan, or Secondary, after those of another plan. The Primary plan will pay its benefits as if there were no other coverage, but if a plan is the Secondary plan, the benefits payable under that plan will be reduced so that the sum of the benefits payable by all plans during a calendar year, will not exceed 100% of the allowable expenses the person incurs in that year.

ELECTIVE ITEMS

There are many services such as television and telephone charges, air conditioners, swimming pools, bath massagers, and trips to different climates that a patient can elect to use, which can relate to the illness or injury being treated, but which do not contribute materially to curing the patient. Charges for many of these items might be billed by a medical care provider, such as a hospital or a physician, or secured with a prescription. Because of the elective nature of these expenses, they are usually excluded.

WAR, DECLARED OR UNDECLARED, INCLUDING ARMED AGGRESSION OR RESISTANCE TO AGGRESSION

Injuries or illness from such causes are excluded from coverage because a substantial catastrophic risk is created that is beyond the scope of group medical care insurance.

MEDICARE AND MAJOR MEDICAL COVERAGE

The Tax Equity and Fiscal Responsibility Act of 1982 (TEFRA) amended the Social Security Act to make Medicare secondary to employer group health plans for active employees age 65 to 69 and their spouses in the same age bracket. TEFRA also revised the Age Discrimination in Employment Act of 1967 (ADEA) to require employers to offer active employees age 65 to 69 and their spouses the same health benefits as are offered to their younger employees. Neither provision affects employers with less than 20 employees. The law provided that both the employee and the employee's spouse had the option of rejecting the employer plan. In this case, Medicare would be the employee's or spouse's ONLY coverage.

Effective May 1, 1986, under the Consolidated Omnibus Reconciliation Act (COBRA), the age 70 cap was eliminated, and the employer's plan became the primary payor for all active, Medicare-eligible employees and spouses regardless of age.

Retired employees are not affected by this legislation. Group health benefits may be reduced when Medicare becomes primary.

When Medicare is the primary coverage, benefits under a group policy are commonly provided through one of two approaches, Coordination of Benefits (COB) or integrated plans.

COORDINATION OF BENEFITS

Under the COB limitation, when a claim is submitted the insurance company calculates the amount the claimant receives from Medicare and the amount payable under the full benefits of the group insurance plan. The claimant is then paid under the group plan the difference between the total allowable expense and the amount to be reimbursed by Medicare, but not more than the amount payable under the group policy. The claimant may collect from 80 to 100 percent of the allowable expenses from the combination of Medicare and the group policies under which he/she is insured, although there is also the possibility that there will be no payment of benefits by such policies. (See Appendix C.)

With the COB provision, the retiree medical plan will pay $1,350 because it is less than the $4,150 that would be paid in the absence of Medicare. The retiree will have no out-of-pocket expenses. Plans with relatively low deductibles and the COB provision will often cover all of the expenses not paid by Medicare, leaving the retiree with little or no remaining obligation.

When the insured collects from 80 to 100 percent of total allowable expenses under the plan with COB, the cost is higher than the cost of the integrated plan. This point is illustrated in the chart below.

	Medical Expense	*Medicare Reimbursed*	*Remainder*
Hospital	$3,000	$2,460	$ 540
Outpatient and Physician	1,500*	840	660
Prescription Drug Expense	150	—	150
TOTAL MEDICAL EXPENSES	$4,650	$3,300	$1,350
Plan Payments in Absence of Medicare	$4,150		

***We assume the Medicare Allowable Expenses on Outpatient and Physician is $1,125 of the $1,500.**

INTEGRATED (CARVE-OUT) PLANS

Integrated, or carve-out plans, are a generic term for many plans that coordinate with Medicare. A claim for benefits is calculated to determine the amount payable under the insurance company plan. The amount to be paid under Medicare is also calculated. The insured receives the amount payable under the group plan less the amount the Medicare plan will pay, thus collecting the same total dollars as is paid to an active employee under age 65.

An example best illustrates the carve-out method of coordination with Medicare.

Total Medical Expense	$4,650
Plan Payments in Absence of Medicare	4,150
Total Medicare Payments	−3,300
Retiree Plan Payment	850
Participant Payment ($4,650 minus $4,150)	500

With the increasing Medicare deductibles and reductions in benefits, the cost to the employer of integrated benefit plans is continually increasing.

DENTAL EXPENSE BENEFITS

This coverage provides reimbursement for expenses of dental services and supplies, including preventive care. The major classifications of dental services include:

- diagnostic,
- preventive,
- restorative (including fillings, inlays, and crowns),
- prosthodontics (installment and maintenance of bridgework),
- oral surgery,
- periodontics or endodontics (treatment of gums),
- orthodontics (straightening treatment), and
- miscellaneous.

Benefits may be provided through a plan integrated with other medical care expense insurance coverages, or a plan may be written entirely separate from other coverages (nonintegrated).

INTEGRATED PLANS

Dental expenses, under an integrated plan, are blended into the covered expenses of a major medical benefits plan. Generally, coverage is on a usual and customary or nonscheduled basis. The deductible may be satisfied each calendar year by either or both medical and dental care expenses. Usually the amount payable for dental and medical care expenses is subject to the same coinsurance percentage. Sometimes, however, when dental care expenses are separated into classes or categories of services (restorative prosthodontics, orthodontia, etc.) a different coinsurance level is applied to each class. Although the maximum benefit is most often a combined medical-dental maximum on a lifetime basis, there may be a separate calendar year dental maximum.

NONINTEGRATED PLANS

Dental expenses under a nonintegrated plan are covered separately on either a scheduled or a nonscheduled basis. Whether a nonintegrated dental plan is scheduled or nonscheduled, dental services often are classified so that different deductibles, coinsurance, and maximum benefits can be used for each class.

SCHEDULED

A schedule of dental services, similar to a surgical schedule, lists specific procedures. Reimbursement toward the dentist's charge is up to the amount specified in the schedule for each procedure. The maximum amounts in the schedule are varied to reflect the level of charges in different areas of the country, to avoid inadequate or excessive benefits.

NONSCHEDULED

Nonscheduled dental plans provide reimbursement toward the dentist's charge for all covered dental services on a usual and customary basis, similar to the integrated plan.

The following diagram describes a typical nonintegrated (nonscheduled) plan.

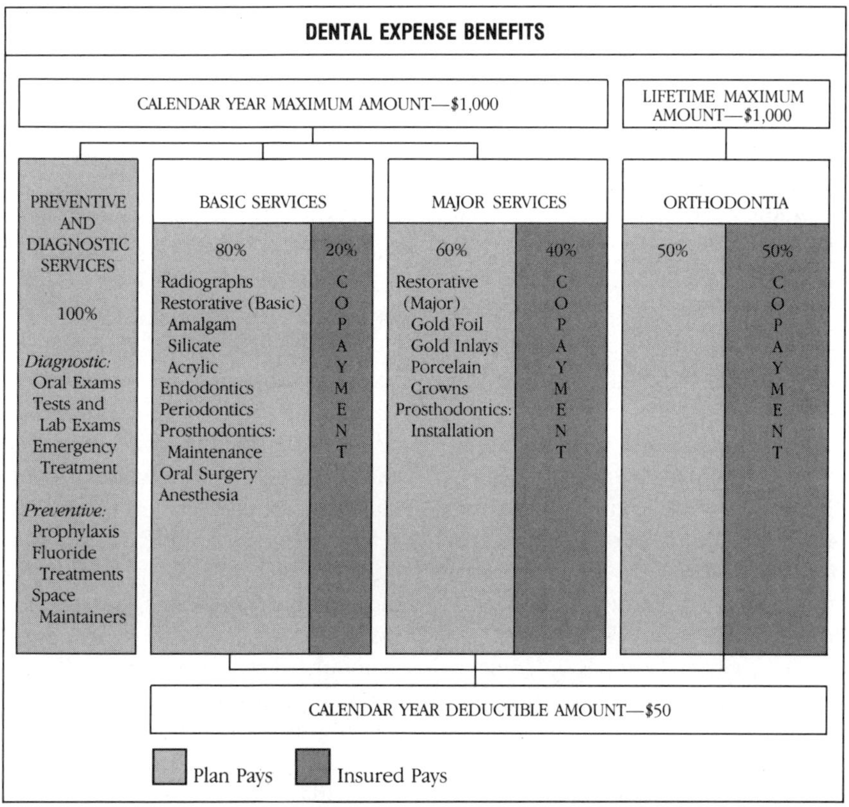

FEATURES OF DENTAL PLANS

Both integrated and nonintegrated dental plans have common provisions, such as deductibles, coinsurance, and maximum benefits.

DEDUCTIBLE

Some nonintegrated dental plans have no deductible. More often, they have a deductible of $50 to $100 to be satisfied by each individual during each calendar year. Frequently, to encourage preventive care, even if the rest of the plan has a deductible, it is not applied to preventive and diagnostic services. Sometimes a deductible applies to preventive and diagnostic services but needs to be satisfied only once during the entire period of coverage. To avoid severe hardship the same kind of family deductible and deductible carry-over provisions previously described as common to major medical plans may be included.

COINSURANCE

As with medical care expense coverages, most dental insurance plans are designed with some percent of the dentist's charge to be paid by the insured to maintain interest in the cost of service provided and avoid overutilization. In a scheduled plan, this often is built into the maximum amounts; in a nonscheduled plan the benefit for the dentist's usual and customary charge is subject to coinsurance. In either case, to encourage good dental health care habits and thereby reduce the need for corrective services, preventive care as well as diagnostic services may be covered at 100 percent of the dentist's charge.

Orthodontia, on the other hand, is a very high-cost service and benefit, and is therefore usually an option available to the policyholder. Because of the resulting severe danger of adverse selection, especially in small groups, it generally is classified separately with 50 percent or 60 percent coinsurance. The coinsurance on all other classes of dental care services may vary from 50 percent to 80 percent, the insured paying a greater percent of the cost of major procedures than the basic procedures.

Some so-called "progressive" or "incentive" coinsurance plans have been designed to provide an incentive for the patient to visit the dentist regularly with the expectation that more costly work at a later date will be reduced. These plans provide that in the first year of the program, an insured's basic dental care expenses will be reimbursed at a prescribed level, typically 70 percent. In each succeeding year the coinsurance payable by the insurance company for basic services will be increased by 10 percent, provided the insured has visited a dentist in the preceding year and completed the work recommended as necessary. In the fourth year and thereafter under such a plan, if the insured continually has satisfied the stated requirements, covered basic dental care expenses would be reimbursed at 100 percent. If during any year an insured fails to meet the stated requirements, the insurance company's coinsurance rate for the following year may be reduced by 10 percent, but never below the initial or first-year level (70 percent in this example). Major dental care services are not a part of the progressive coinsurance feature and usually are payable at 50 percent.

Although this type of plan has appeal and encourages regular dental care, there are some disadvantages. It produces considerably higher administrative costs and makes transfer to any other insurance company extremely difficult. Moreover, it may be confusing to the insured and increases the chance of claim payment error.

MAXIMUM BENEFIT

Some typical nonintegrated dental programs are designed with lifetime maximum for orthodontic benefits and include a calendar year or policy year maximum on all other dental care services. Some plans may also place a life-time maximum on periodontic care.

PRETREATMENT REVIEW

Pretreatment review may be incorporated in any dental care expense benefits program. It aims at providing quality care and service to the insured, at the same time attempting to avoid unnecessary or inappropriate dental treatment. Under its terms, if a course of treatment is expected to exceed a specified amount such as $200, a statement must be submitted in advance, for review by the insurance company, describing the planned treatment and expected charges. Customarily, diagnostic x-rays accompany the statement.

With the help of dental consultants, the insurance company verifies that the planned treatment is necessary and consistent with the diagnosis. Procedures that are covered, in accordance with the policy provisions, are identified; the amount of reimbursement allowed under the terms of the plan is specified in advance. This approach substantially reduces misunderstandings and financial concern on the part of both the patient and the provider by establishing the allowable reimbursement before the service is performed.

LIMITATIONS AND EXCLUSIONS

The frequency with which certain services will be provided under any dental care expense benefit plan is often limited. For example, typically no more than two dental prophylaxes and one fluoride treatment will be covered in any 12 consecutive months, and a bridge or denture will not be replaced within 5 years except under specific circumstances. Replacement of teeth missing prior to the effective date of the dental insurance may be excluded entirely or covered at a reduced coinsurance percent.

Services performed solely for cosmetic purposes are generally excluded, as are those considered experimental. No payment is made for charges for oral hygiene instruction, missed appointments, or completion of claim forms.

SURVIVOR HEALTH BENEFITS

This coverage may be an addition to many medical and dental care expense benefit plans. It provides that the medical or dental care insurance in force for dependents on the date of an employee's death will remain in force, usually without payment of premium, for some specified period of time ranging from six months to two years from the date of death. Coverage is terminated before the end of that period only if the surviving spouse remarries, in which case the coverage for all dependents terminates, or if any dependent becomes insured under another group insurance plan, becomes eligible for Medicare, or ceases to qualify as a dependent according to the terms of the contract.

MANAGING HEALTH CARE COSTS

In the early 1980s, employers and other sponsors of medical care plans became increasingly concerned about the cost of care. Medical care costs continue to rise at a rate far in excess of the general inflation rate; and, as a percentage of the U.S. gross national product, health care costs now account for over 13 percent of GNP. That figure is expected to rise in the future.

In response to these rising costs, insurance companies and employers have worked together to develop a number of approaches for managing health care cost. The next few pages will outline the various types of managed care programs that have been incorporated into health care benefit plans.

UTILIZATION REVIEW

Virtually all coverages are now affected by Utilization Review (UR). Utilization Review includes a number of services that help manage health care costs by attempting to improve care effectiveness and cost efficiency before providing the service. It is an attempt to reduce the number of unnecessary or inappropriate health care services. Various review processes for both inpatient and outpatient services are employed in order to ascertain covered benefits. Reviews may include preadmission review, concurrent review, discharge planning, and pretreatment review.

Preadmission review requires a covered person to obtain an authorization in advance from the review program for a hospitalization that is elective or non-emergency in nature. This review results both in greater assurance that the proposed treatment is customary for the diagnosis and that opportunities for treatment in a more cost-effective setting (such as a skilled nursing facility, or an outpatient surgical facility) have been identified. If a patient must be admitted to the hospital on an emergency basis, the Utilization Review program must be called within a certain period of time (e.g. 48 hours) to have the admission approved.

Concurrent review involves a monitoring of the patient's progress while confined in the hospital. During confinement, the Utilization Review administrator and physician discuss the patient's treatment and prognosis. The concept involves determining whether treatment and continued inpatient care during a patient's hospitalization are necessary and appropriate. Insofar as it can lead to a shortened length of stay, this procedure has the potential to produce cost savings.

The third phase of Utilization Review involves hospital discharge planning. For patients who have not fully recovered, but who do not require the acute care of a hospital, arrangements may be made for continuing care in a skilled nursing facility. The patient may not be well enough to return home but also does not require the acute care of a hospital. For these patients, continued care in a skilled nursing facility may be appropriate. This facility will provide the necessary level of care but at a cost less than a hospital stay. Discharge planning ensures that the patient receives the proper care in the most appropriate setting after a hospital stay.

Until recently, utilization review programs were directed at controlling hospital costs by eliminating unnecessary hospital admissions and minimizing the length of stay in the hospital. These programs brought a greater degree of control of hospital costs. However, this has resulted in significant increases in the cost and utilization of outpatient services since there was no system to monitor outpatient treatment.

Today, as more and more expenses are being shifted to the outpatient environment, it is critically important to effectively control outpatient expenses. Two strategies can be used to manage outpatient costs.

The first strategy is to implement a pretreatment certification program for certain high-cost, high-frequency procedures. This type of program, which operates similarly to inpatient utilization review, requires the patient or doctor to call the administrator prior to securing a particular medical service. The administrator will review the request based upon the patient's diagnoses and the appropriateness of the prescribed treatment or test. The administrator will either approve payment for the treatment or recommend alternative approaches.

A second strategy to managing outpatient costs is a retrospective review of utilization for a particular claim or group of claims. Under such a program, an administrator has determined the appropriate treatment for a given diagnosis in terms of tests required, office visits permitted, etc. As claims are received, they are reviewed against these treatment guidelines. Any treatment which does not fall within the guidelines must be justified by the physician or payment may be declined.

These services review and manage outpatient procedures in the same way they do inpatient procedures. Their objective is to manage and control health care costs by making sure suggested treatments or diagnostic procedures meet medical review criteria; that they are performed at the most appropriate, cost-effective site available; and that the health care services are medically appropriate and of the right intensity and duration.

For a more detailed explanation of the review process, see Chapter 2 of *Group Life and Health Insurance, Part C.*

NETWORK-BASED MANAGED CARE ARRANGEMENTS

Insurers have entered into a number of network-based arrangements with health care providers in an effort to manage health care costs. Insurers can promise to channel patients to participating providers in exchange for a reduction in providers' fees. Among the different types of network-based arrangements are Health Maintenance Organizations (HMOs), Preferred Provider Organizations (PPOs) and Point-of-Service (POS) programs. These arrangements differ based upon the amount of freedom that participants have in choosing doctors to provide care. By negotiating reduced prices from providers for their services and controlling utilization (that is, the number and type of services used), these programs can achieve significant savings for employer groups that use them.

Through HMO, PPO, and POS arrangements, the full range of health care services can be provided, including hospital, medical, surgical, and diagnostic services, and dental or vision services (although less common). Reimbursement of prescription drug expenses might be offered through prescription drug card programs.

HEALTH MAINTENANCE ORGANIZATIONS (HMOs)

An HMO is an organized system of health care delivery available to individuals residing in a specific geographic area. It provides comprehensive medical care, including preventive care, to a group of enrollees. HMOs are a prepaid form of health care in which the employer pays the HMO a set premium rate every month. Employees enrolled in an HMO will then secure all their medical care services from the HMO.

The main features of an HMO program are negotiated discounts with providers, along with aggressive utilization controls. These features give HMOs the ability to offer enhanced benefits over a typical indemnity plan or to offer equivalent benefits at a lower price.

In addition, many HMOs do not require that employees complete claim forms upon delivery of service, which is an added convenience to the employees. Due to these advantages, employers are offering a wide variety of HMOs to their employees.

The affiliation of hospitals and physicians that comprises the HMO assumes the responsibility of providing all of the health care services needed by the HMO membership. An HMO member is asked to select a primary care physician or dentist from among those participating in the HMO. The primary care physician supervises and coordinates all of the medical care the person receives, including the authorization of referrals to specialists or hospitals. Usually, most services are covered in full or subject to nominal copayments.

HMO participation provides services localized within the region served. There are limitations and restrictions on coverage outside of the geographical locale of the HMO, and also on medical treatment received from nonparticipating providers (nonparticipating hospitals or physicians), which may not be covered at all. Often, there are special waivers if the non-HMO care is received as the immediate result of an emergency involving accidental bodily injury, or because of the sudden, acute onset of life-threatening disease. For such emergency services, the HMO retrospectively reviews the services rendered outside of the network, and may provide equivalent coverage if the medical appropriateness of care can be verified. This restrictive nature of health care delivery allows the HMO to control utilization more tightly than a traditional indemnity program.

PREFERRED PROVIDER ORGANIZATIONS (PPOs)

Preferred Provider Organizations (PPOs) are groups of hospitals and physicians that contract with employers, insurers, third-party administrators, or other sponsoring groups to provide medical care services to subscribers (members or participants), and accept negotiated fee schedules as payment in full for services rendered in exchange for a higher volume of patients.

A PPO offers a provider network similar to HMO providers. For insureds, choosing a network provider reduces out-of-pocket expenses, while maintaining a certain amount of freedom to choose their own physicians and hospitals from among participating providers. However, insureds can also choose to receive care outside of the network, and to receive reimbursement at levels similar to traditional group insured coverages. For example, a network service may provide no deductible or lower copayment than traditional services. Non-network services may be subject to a deductible of $100 to $500 and higher coinsurance. Emergency care outside of the network of providers may be reimbursed at rates comparable to network services.

One of the key aspects of any preferred provider arrangement is to provide the necessary incentives such as lower deductibles or higher coinsurance levels to get individuals to use a preferred provider rather than using the normal plan. The chart below outlines different types of incentives that may be used to get patients to change from their current physician to a preferred provider.

PREFERRED PROVIDER ARRANGEMENTS PLAN DESIGN

Service	*Preferred Provider*	*Other Provider*
Deductible	$100/$200	$200/$400
Hospital Services	90%/10%	80%/20%
Surgery	90%/10%	80%/20%
Other Services	90%/10%	80%/20%
Out-of-Pocket Maximum	$1,000	$1,500

HMOs, PPOs, and other managed health care arrangements are covered in detail in Part C of this course.

POINT-OF-SERVICE (POS) PROGRAMS

POS programs are similar to PPOs. Typically, they are included as part of an employer's indemnity program with a distinction between in-network and out-of-network benefits (in-network benefits being paid at a higher level). Insureds are free to choose any doctor or type of service for out-of-network care. However, when accessing the point-of-service network, insurerds are required to coordinate care through their primary care physician (PCP). The PCP is viewed as the manager of care. For care to be eligible for consideration as in-network, it must be rendered by the patient's PCP or by another doctor based upon a referral from the PCP. This distinction brings a greater level of control in the utilization of medical care services and, as a result, is more restrictive than the preferred provider arrangement.

The key concept in POS programs (as well as in HMOs) is the use of the primary care physician. Functioning as a manager of the patient's care, the PCP can direct the patient to the ;most appropriate type of service for a given condition. Enrollment in a POS program, includes the selection of a PCP from the group of eligible network providers.

Point-of-Service programs have shown promise in their ability to control health care costs. They provide a good balance between the very restrictive HMO programs and the less restrictive PPO and traditional indemnity approaches.

As with PPO, POS programs require some plan design incentives to encourage participants to secure care from network physicians. The in network benefit levels are richer than those out-of-network.

CONCLUSIONS

Although HMOs, PPOs, and POS programs have been described above as if each type was clearly distinct, there are many varieties of each that often overlap. For example, many HMOs now offer POS plans, sometimes referred to as "opt out" programs. A member may receive benefits when using an out-of-network provider, but be required to pay a greater part of the cost for care received. This is much like a PPO with a gatekeeper or a POS plan as described. These plan designs continue to evolve with cost containment coupled with quality care as their goal.

LARGE CLAIM MANAGEMENT

Large claim management is one of the most important developments added to benefit plans to manage care. It is a method to control costs associated with care for patients with long-term or catastrophic illnesses. Large claim management programs attempt to control the cost of treating patients while ensuring that they receive appropriate and medically necessary care.

Large claim management programs that utilize a process called medical case management are used in those situations that are expected to generate significant medical expenses such as head and spinal cord injuries, AIDS, Crohn's Disease, severe strokes, and premature births.

The large claim management process begins with the identification of a potentially large claim and the assignment of an individual to manage the case. The case managers work with the patient, their families, and their physicians to develop a course of treatment for the patient. All treatment options are reviewed by the manager and the physician, and an overall course of treatment is developed. This plan is discussed with the patient or family before any treatment is implemented.

Once a course of treatment is implemented, it is periodically monitored and reviewed to determine if it is cost effective and appropriate for the patient. At any time, the plan can be changed or modified if the patient, physician, and case manager agree. Flexibility is a key factor in case management. Properly implemented and managed, large claim management programs can reduce an employer's cost for these potentially large claims while providing an appropriate course of treatment for the patient.

SUMMARY

The insurance industry has developed a variety of policies and approaches to meet society's need for protection against potentially high financial loss that accompanies illness or injury. As the health care scene and society's needs change, the insurance industry continues to respond to new challenges.

KEY TERMS

- Ancillary Services
- Coinsurance
- Comprehensive Major Medical Expense Benefits
- Coordination of Benefits
- Copayment
- Custodial Care
- Daily Rate
- Deductible
- Diagnosis-Related Groups (DRGs)
- Health Maintenance Organizations (HMOs)
- Home Health Care
- Hospice
- Inpatient Benefits
- Integrated (Carve-Out) Plans
- Intensive Care
- Large Claim Management
- Lifetime (All Cause) Benefit
- Maximum Daily Benefit
- Necessary Services and Supplies
- Palliative Care
- Per Cause Benefit
- Per Diem Rate (Flat Rate)
- Point of Service (POS) Programs
- Preadmission Testing (PAT)
- Preexisting Condition
- Preferred Provider Organizations (PPOs)
- Reinstatement
- Scheduled Hospital Confinement
- Service-Type Benefit
- Supplemental Major Medical Expense Benefits
- Usual and Customary Charge
- Utilization Reviews

III

OTHER GROUP INSURANCE COVERAGES

INTRODUCTION

Many insurers offer multiple lines of group coverage to employers or associations. In addition to group medical coverage, insurers will also contract to provide long-term care, group disability, life, and accident insurance. This chapter will describe the newest coverage of long-term care and common nonmedical group coverages.

LONG-TERM CARE BENEFITS

Long-term care insurance provides a specified dollar benefit or more commonly a percent of expenses charged if a covered person suffers a loss of functional capacity due to an accidental injury or sickness. Generally the insured must complete a waiting period, or a zero waiting period option may be purchased. Plans may cover adult day-care services.

Loss of functional capacity usually means a person needs human assistance to perform some of the following activities of daily living:

- *Mobility:* Walking or wheeling any distance on a level surface.
- *Transferring:* Moving between the bed and a chair or the bed and a wheelchair.
- *Bathing*
- *Dressing:* Putting on and taking off all necessary items of clothing.
- *Toileting:* Getting to and from the toilet, getting on and off the toilet, and associated personal hygiene.
- *Eating:* Getting food into the body.

These are by no means the only activities of daily living that insurers use. Cognitive impairment and combining mobility and transferring are two of several others.

A "functional loss" as to any activity of daily living means that without assistance of another individual, the person is unable to perform the activity at the appropriate time and place because of:

- physical incapacity resulting from disease or injury, or
- mental incapacity due to organic brain diseases.

Initial and ongoing certification of the qualifying loss are required by the insurer, who may also reserve the right to conduct on-site inspections.

Long-term care plans are generally provided on a fully contributory basis. The cost of a person's coverage is determined by his or her age on the date coverage becomes effective. The cost of coverage will not increase because a person is growing older, or because his or her health changes, although it may increase for other reasons. If such an increase occurs, it will affect all policyholders in the same class.

ELIGIBILITY

Long-term care is offered to active employees and spouses and to any two parents of an insured active employee and an insured spouse. Coverage may also be offered to retired employees and spouses. Most plans have an age limit requiring that each person be under age 80 on the date he or she becomes eligible.

EVIDENCE OF INSURABILITY

Employees who elect to participate in the long-term care plan within 31 days of their eligibility generally are automatically covered provided they are actively at work. Thereafter, employees are eligible to participate subject to evidence of insurability satisfactory to the insurer. The spouse of an employee and the parents of insured employees and insured spouses, and present retirees and spouses must provide evidence of insurability satisfactory to the insurer.

BENEFITS

Long-term care plans usually pay between $50 and $100 for each day of confinement in a nursing care facility and between $20 and $50 for each day of home health care.

A nursing care facility must be licensed or legally qualified and primarily engaged in providing nursing care and related services for sick or injured persons. Home health care must be provided through a home health agency and performed by a registered nurse; a licensed practical nurse; a licensed vocational nurse; a home health aide; a licensed, certified or registered occupational therapist; speech therapist; or a physical therapist. Home health care must be performed in the insured person's home, a private home, a facility for the retired or aged, or a licensed or legally qualified adult day care center operating with the purpose of providing nursing, medical, and health-related social services.

The overall maximum payment for all nursing care confinements and all home health care in an insured person's lifetime may be limited to a dollar amount or a number of years or both. Typical lifetime maximums run from $50,000 to $250,000 and from four to ten years. Reduced lifetime maximums are available for insured parents and retired employees and spouses.

Inflation adjustments may be provided by periodic increases based on changes in the Consumer Price Index or another reliable index. An alternative to an inflation adjustment is a provision that allows an insured to purchase additional limited insurance in years ending in zero and five at an age-related premium without providing evidence of insurability.

WAITING PERIOD

If a waiting period is required, generally long-term care benefits are payable after a waiting period of 90 consecutive days of continuous loss of functional capacity. Prior hospitalization or nursing home confinement is not required.

BENEFIT PERIOD

A benefit period begins on the first day following the end of the waiting period. It ends after the person no longer has a loss of functional capacity for a period of generally 60 days in a row.

Only one waiting period applies during any one benefit period.

At the close of any benefit period, benefits for any subsequent loss of functional capacity will not be paid until a new waiting period has been completed.

PREMIUM WAIVER

Premium payments are waived when benefit payments begin or after 90 days of benefit payments. Premium payments start again on the first premium due date following the end of a benefit period.

CASE MANAGEMENT

A medical care coordinator may be assigned to work closely with the insured and insured's physician to assess the specific situation, identify necessary services, develop a service plan, monitor, evaluate, and make changes to the service plan as necessary.

PREEXISTING LIMITATION

Any qualifying loss of functional capacity that is caused by a preexisting condition is not covered unless that loss begins more than 6 (or 12) consecutive months after the person was insured.

A preexisting condition is any injury or sickness which was diagnosed or treated during the 6 (or 12) months prior to the effective date of coverage.

OTHER LIMITATIONS

Other limitations specific to long-term care benefits include the exclusions of benefits:

- due to mental, nervous, or emotional disorders (This limitation does not apply to organic brain disease such as Alzheimer's disease.),
- on any day that person is confined in a hospital,
- due to alcoholism or drug addiction,

- due to self-inflicted injury or attempted suicide, and
- for benefits provided under a group medical expense benefits plan for confinement in a nursing care facility or for home health care.

DEATH BENEFIT

Some plans offer an optional life insurance benefit. If an insured dies prior to the attainment of a specified age, for example, age 70, the plan pays a death benefit equal to a percentage of the contributions paid for coverage of the deceased. The death benefit may not be available to an insured person once that person receives long-term benefits under the plan; or the death benefit may pay an amount equal to unused benefits.

PORTABILITY

Employees who leave an employer may continue long-term care coverage for themselves, spouses and others, when eligibility under the long-term plan terminates by continuing to pay their individual premium directly to the insurer.

DISABILITY INCOME INSURANCE

Disability income insurance insures an employee against the loss of a portion of income during a period of disability. The period during which benefits will be paid in the event of a continuing disability can be short-term—up to 13, 26, or 52 weeks (occasionally 2 years), or long-term—for a period of 5 or 10 years, or more commonly to the employee's normal retirement age.

SHORT-TERM DISABILITY INCOME INSURANCE

Partial income replacement is provided when employees become disabled due to nonoccupational accidental injuries or sicknesses and cannot perform the duties of their occupation. Sometimes occupational coverage also will be written to supplement workers' compensation benefits that are lower than the nonoccupational disability income benefits of the group plan. When this is done, the income replacement provided is the same in the event of either occupational or nonoccupational disabilities. The benefit paid under the plan usually is the nonoccupational weekly benefit less the workers' compensation benefit.

Since short-term disability income insurance is intended to replace a portion of lost income, it normally limits payments to a level that will discourage extended absenteeism which may occur if the amount of disability income is equal to or very close to an employee's normal take-home pay. A benefit plan that is too high in relation to take-home pay can be costly to the policyholder, not only because of claims but also because of prolonged absenteeism, since the incentive to return to work is lowered.

BENEFIT WAITING PERIOD

A benefit waiting period is used to eliminate small claims, to lower the cost of insurance, and to discourage short working absences for minor health reasons. Sometimes called the elimination period, the benefit waiting period is the time between the date of the disability and the beginning of the benefit payment period.

Short-term disability income plans frequently have no benefit waiting period or a shorter waiting period for disabilities caused by accidents than for those caused by sicknesses because absences for accidents are less frequent and not within the control of the employee. Most plans have at least a seven-day waiting period for sickness. If a plan has no waiting period for an accident and a seven-day waiting period for a sickness, claim payments would begin on the first day of an accident-related disability and on the eighth day of a disability due to sickness.

Group disability income insurance plans often are written to provide benefits that begin with the first day of hospital confinement if it occurs during the benefit waiting period. Some plans also will retroactively pay benefits during the benefit waiting period if the disability lasts for a specified period, such as three weeks.

Often the benefit waiting period is designed so that there will be a continuation of income after an employer's formal or informal salary continuance plan expires. For example, if an employer has a salary continuance plan that provides a 30-day extension of salary for disabled employees, the insurance program may have a 30-day benefit waiting period.

BENEFIT PAYMENT PERIOD

Benefits begin after the benefit waiting period. The usual benefit payment periods are 13, 26, and 52 weeks. Twenty-six weeks is the most common, although other benefit payment periods are available and may be chosen to provide income replacement after a salary continuance program ends and before the beginning of long-term income replacement benefits.

AMOUNT OF INSURANCE

The amount of insurance (weekly income benefit) can be a flat amount, such as $300 a week, or it may be based on earnings, which is generally considered to provide a more equitable distribution of benefits and therefore is more common. One design uses a schedule such as the following, which is directly related to earnings:

Weekly Earnings	*Weekly Income Benefit*
Less than $300	$200
$330 but less than $350	$225
$350 but less than $400	$250
$400 but less than $500	$300
$500 but less than $600	$350
$600 but less than $700	$425
$700 and over	$450

Equally effective, and most often used, is a weekly income benefit expressed as a percent of gross weekly income typically ranging from 50 to 70 percent, with 66⅔ percent being most common. An employee's gross weekly income usually is defined to exclude overtime pay, bonuses, or other supplementary compensation.

Payment for a disability that lasts or extends into part of a week can be based on either one-fifth or one-seventh of the weekly benefit.

A typical maximum weekly income benefit is $325, but it will vary based on the number of employees insured and the total volume of weekly income benefits in force on the effective date of the plan.

A less common approach is to base the amount of insurance on positions in the company.

DEFINITIONS

NON-OCCUPATIONAL COVERAGE

Weekly disability income benefits are payable to employees who are disabled by a nonoccupational accidental injury or sickness and thereby prevented from performing the duties of their occupation.

TWENTY-FOUR-HOUR COVERAGE

Twenty-four-hour coverage may be provided, as defined above.

SUCCESSIVE PERIODS OF DISABILITY

Successive periods of disability caused by sickness or related sicknesses, or any one accident, usually are considered to be one period of disability unless they are separated by, for example, a two-week resumption of continuous, active service on the job. This contractual provision precludes the possibility of a new maximum benefit period being established for the same disability by briefly returning to work. At the same time, it protects the employee who might have two or more unrelated disabilities within a short period of time. Successive periods of disability that are the result of unrelated causes and separated by a return to active service are treated as separate periods of disability.

LIMITATIONS AND EXCLUSIONS

Benefits are excluded if injuries are intentionally self-inflicted or if the disabled person is not under the care of a physician.

LONG-TERM DISABILITY INCOME INSURANCE

This coverage is designed to replace lost income when an employee is totally and continuously disabled by an accident or sickness for an extended period of time.

ELIGIBILITY

Long-term disability income insurance is generally written with eligibility requirements that are often different from those applicable to other group insurance coverages. Three- or six-month eligibility waiting periods are typical, and longer waiting periods may be required where there is high turnover. Some insurers have a rule requiring that employees have 30 days of continuous active employment before they can be insured.

BENEFIT WAITING PERIOD

As with short-term disability income insurance, the benefit waiting period is the period of time between the onset of the disability and the date on which benefits begin. The coverage is written so that there is no gap between the cessation of benefits under an existing short-term disability income insurance or salary continuance plan and the commencement of benefits under long-term disability income insurance. A benefit waiting period of at least three or six months is usually required.

BENEFIT PAYMENT PERIOD

There is a wide variation among insurers as to the maximum period of time for which benefits are payable. This maximum period most often is the same for both accident and sickness. Durations of two, five, or ten years are used, but the current trend in employee benefits is to the normal retirement age. A few plans may provide a lifetime benefit, usually limited to accident disabilities. Plans must meet the requirements of the Age Discrimination in Employment Act of 1978 (ADEA) and the Age Discrimination in Employment Amendments of 1986, which abolished mandatory retirement due to age for most workers, and removes certain references to "age 70" under ADEA.

A typical payment period, in compliance with the 1986 law, is illustrated below:

- Benefits if disabled before age 61: to age 65.

- Benefits if disabled on or after age 61:

Disabled at age	*Duration of benefits*
61	4 years
62	3½ years
63	3 years
64	2½ years
65	2 years
66	1¾ years
67	1½ years
68	1¼ years
69 or later	1 year

BENEFIT AMOUNT

Benefit levels must be high enough in relation to earnings to sustain an individual through a period of disability, but low enough to provide incentive for return to work. Plans typically are written to provide monthly income benefits that range between 50 percent and 66⅔ percent of gross earnings. A cost-of-living adjustment may also be included by changing the benefit payable once a year (typically January 1) based on the current Consumer Price Index. The increase or decrease is generally limited to a specified percentage of the previous monthly benefit, such as 3 percent.

A maximum monthly income benefit, such as $3,000, generally is based on the number of employees in the group and the total amount of long-term disability income insurance written for the group. While a schedule of benefits based on earnings classifications may be used, most plans express the monthly income benefit as a percentage of gross earnings for each insured employee. In some cases, particularly smaller groups, monthly income benefits may be subject to evidence of insurability. This is due to the potentially greater costs of long-term care.

INTEGRATION WITH OTHER INCOME

To avoid disability income benefits being higher than take-home pay, it is general practice to provide that income from other sources will reduce the benefits under the long-term plan. One method of accomplishing this is to simply total "other income" (as defined in the particular plan) received by the employee and subtract this sum from the plan's scheduled monthly disability income benefit. An alternate approach provides that the sum of (1) the benefits under the long-term disability income plan, and (2) all other income benefits will not exceed a reasonable, specified percentage of earnings, such as 70 percent.

"Other income" can be from:

- state or federal disability or retirement plans,
- Social Security benefits or any other group insurance plan that has a disability income feature, such as group life insurance with permanent and total disability income benefits,
- a salary continuance plan,
- rehabilitation employment remuneration, or
- a pension plan with disability benefits.

To help total disability income dollars keep pace with the rising cost of living, a provision known as the Social Security Freeze is usually included. This provides that increases in an employee's Social Security benefit after long-term benefit payments have begun will not reduce the monthly long-term disability income payments.

A guaranteed minimum monthly income provision is also part of most plans that require employee contributions. It guarantees that the monthly income benefit will not be less than a specified amount, such as $50, after integration with all other sources of income.

DEFINITION OF LONG-TERM DISABILITY

The most common definition is similar to that used in short-term disability income insurance: complete inability of the insured to engage in the duties of his or her occupation. For long-term disability, however, after the first year or two of disability a more stringent test is used. Commonly, this test is complete inability of the insured to engage in any gainful occupation for which the person is, or may become, reasonably fitted by education, training, or experience.

SUCCESSIVE PERIODS OF DISABILITY

Most policies provide that successive periods of disability separated by less than three (or six) months of continuous, active full-time employment will be considered one continuous disability unless the subsequent disability arises from a cause or causes unrelated to that of the previous disability and begins after the insured has returned to work as a regular employee.

REHABILITATION PROVISION

Recognizing that it is mutually beneficial for the disabled individual, for the employer, and for the insurance company to encourage the employee to return to work as soon as possible, insurers have adopted various approaches to promote this objective. Disabled employees who are able to return to their jobs on a part-time or intermittent basis usually are not considered totally disabled. When a partial return to work is part of an attempt to rehabilitate the disabled employee, most insurers will continue to pay partial benefits during the rehabilitative period. Some insurers include a specific rehabilitation provision in the group policy while others prefer to work out such arrangements for specific situations outside the terms of the policy.

A typical rehabilitation provision states that the plan will continue a specific level of benefit payments when the employee who has been totally disabled and receiving benefits returns to work in rehabilitative employment. For example, an employee engaged in rehabilitative employment would receive the regular monthly benefit less 50 percent of the income received from rehabilitative employment for up to 24 months.

Rehabilitative employment is defined as an occupation or employment for wage or profit for which the employee is reasonably fitted by training, education, or experience and that is performed while unable to perform the full duties of his/her regular occupation.

This rehabilitative provision will not, of course, extend the benefit payments beyond the policy maximum.

SURVIVOR BENEFIT

A survivor benefit is sometimes included as a part of a long-term disability income plan. It provides a continuation of income during a period after the death of a disabled employee, thereby helping to preserve the proceeds from life insurance on the employee. The monthly benefit payable to an eligible survivor is a percent, such as 66⅔ percent, of the employee's net monthly benefit payment after integration with other benefits as determined by the last monthly benefit payment prior to death. An eligible survivor commonly is defined as the spouse of an employee or, if there is no surviving spouse, the employee's unmarried children under age 21. Survivor benefits usually will be paid for up to 24 months following the death of the employee or until there is no eligible survivor, whichever comes first.

PENSION SUPPLEMENT

A significant gap in an employee's coverage under the employer's pension plan can occur if the employee becomes disabled before becoming eligible for the pension plan or if the pension plan does not provide for continued accumulation of pension credits during disability. Since monthly income benefits under a long-term disability income insurance program usually have been paid out by "retirement age," some plans attempt to fill the pension gap by continuing the disabled employee's contributions that would have been made to the pension plan had the employee remained in active service. Therefore, the value of the pension benefit for the employee is maintained when retirement age is reached.

LIMITATIONS AND EXCLUSIONS

Most policies limit or exclude psychiatric disorders, alcoholism, and drug addiction, except that some insurers provide coverage when the insured is confined in a hospital or an institution specializing in the medical care and treatment of such disorders. Other policies may limit the duration of benefits for these conditions to two years, for example. In addition, most insurers write their long-term disability income plans on a 24-hour basis, integrating them with workers' compensation benefits. If the policyholder wants the benefits limited to non-occupational disabilities, an occupational exclusion is used.

A preexisting conditions limitation is included in most long-term disability income plans. It is designed to protect the insurer from the adverse selection that can occur if an employer establishes a group plan that may provide benefits for a known potential disability, or if an employee elects to participate in the plan for the same reason. It is particularly important to include this limitation if the group is small—fewer than 100 insured employees—since the risk of adverse selection is greater when small numbers of employees are covered under the plan. A typical preexisting conditions limitation provides that there will be no benefits for a disability that begins within one year of the date the employee becomes insured if the disability is because of an accident which occurred or a sickness that commenced during the year prior to the date of becoming insured.

Group plans transferred from another insurer may waive this preexisting conditions provision for individuals who were insured under the prior insurer. They may also modify it to provide the same benefit otherwise payable without the limitation except that the duration of payments for a preexisting condition may be limited to, for example, 12 months.

In addition, benefits generally are excluded under long-term disability income plans for:

- intentionally self-inflicted injuries,
- participation in a felony, or
- any act of war, declared or undeclared.

Although conditions resulting from pregnancy also have commonly been excluded in the past, federal and state legislation requires that employers provide the same benefits for pregnancy, childbirth, and related medical conditions as for any other sickness or injury.

CREDIT HEALTH INSURANCE

Similar to credit life insurance, credit health insurance (often called group creditors disability insurance) is insurance designed to assure repayment of a loan. In the event the debtor becomes totally disabled, the insurer will pay to the creditor the amount of the debtor's monthly installments. The type of loans covered may be:

- secured or unsecured personal loans,
- direct loans made to purchase goods, such as motor vehicles or furniture, and
- loans made on an installment basis through a dealer.

In certain instances, credit health insurance also will cover budget fuel plans, mortgage loans, and home improvement loans.

DESCRIPTION OF BENEFITS

The benefit provided in the policy usually is payable on a monthly basis and typically equals the monthly loan installment. Benefits normally begin after a benefit waiting period, such as 14 or 30 days. Some contracts are written so that benefits are retroactive to the first day of disability after the benefit period has been satisfied. Payment normally is a daily benefit that equals 1/30th of the monthly benefit, but if the debtor remains continuously disabled, monthly payments will be made until the expiration of the loan, or the length of the benefit period. This generally will not run beyond five years although plans covering first mortgages may run longer.

LIMITATIONS AND EXCLUSIONS

Group credit health insurance policies may contain age limitations, and require that the debtor be actively at work on a full-time basis. Usually excluded are disabilities resulting from pregnancy, intentionally self-inflicted injury, or accidents and illnesses that occur outside the continental United States.

GROUP LIFE INSURANCE

The purpose of group life insurance is to provide financial assistance to the beneficiary of a deceased employee. Thus if an employee dies from any cause while insured, group life insurance pays the amount of coverage provided by the plan of benefits to the beneficiary or beneficiaries designated by the employee. There are several types of group life insurance plans available, and these are described below.

TERM LIFE INSURANCE

Most group life insurance is term insurance that provides coverage at the lowest current cost, by only insuring the possibility of death during the term period. Group term life insurance should be viewed by insureds as a type of insurance that has limited guarantees of permanence and few living benefits, since it has no cash values, no savings features, and provides no emergency funds on which to draw.

In establishing a group life plan, the policyholder and insurer agree on a benefit schedule that stipulates the amount of insurance provided for each person. The benefit schedules for most plans are based on earnings or positions.

GROUP LIFE BENEFIT SCHEDULES

Several types of group life schedules are used to establish a group term life plan. The most common schedules are listed below.

Earnings Schedule. The life insurance earnings schedule approach is based upon individual earnings. Two methods may be used: a Percentage of Earnings Schedule and an Annual Earnings Schedule. Typically, under a Percentage of Earnings Schedule the amount of group life insurance for each insured employee is a percent of the employee's annual earnings rounded to the next $1,000 to a maximum benefit of $100,000. For example, a 100 percent schedule of $26,500 in earnings would provide a $27,000 benefit.

An Annual Earnings Schedule is illustrated below:

Annual Earnings	*Life Insurance*
Less than $20,000	$ 20,000
$20,000 but less than $30,000	$ 30,000
$30,000 but less than $50,000	$ 50,000
$50,000 but less than $75,000	$ 75,000
$75,000 and over	$100,000

Employers can use an annual earnings schedule when they wish to provide a higher proportionate benefit to higher salaried employees. Annual earnings typically do not include overtime, bonuses, and other supplemental income.

Positions Schedule. A less common approach is the Positions Schedule—similar to the Annual Earnings Schedule except that it establishes amounts of insurance based on the employee's job classification.

A Positions Schedule is most appropriate when employee earnings are not constant. Typical examples are salespersons' incomes that vary year to year based on sales, or employees for whom income largely is based on bonuses resulting from production or profits.

Flat Benefit Schedule. All employees are insured for the same amount of coverage, for example:

Classification	Life Insurance
All Employees	$20,000

There are three situations in which a Flat Benefit Schedule is usually provided:

- Employer wishes to provide only a minimum benefit for all employees, perhaps for economic reasons;
- Employees are hourly-paid employees who may be unionized. In this case, wages of hourly-paid employees working for the same employer or in the same industry often do not vary greatly; or
- Employer does not want to discriminate among employees.

Other Schedules. A group policyholder may request a different schedule based on a special need or desire. Although not as common as the schedules described above, two other types of schedules are used in group term life insurance plans. One provides a benefit related to an employee's contemplated pension: for example, the amount of group life insurance for each employee is equal to 100 times the monthly income that will be payable to the employee at age 65 under the employer's pension plan, up to a maximum amount of insurance of $75,000.

Another type of schedule is based on length of service. When group life insurance plans became popular, length-of-service plans were common because the group insurance was looked upon as a means of rewarding the employee for long and faithful service. However, this type of plan is now less common.

MULTIPLE SCHEDULE PLANS

The various schedules outlined above would apply to specific classes of employees. Many employers use more than one type of schedule in their policies, based on location, type of work, collective bargaining agreements, etc. For example, an earnings plan could apply to the salaried employees of a particular employer while a flat benefit plan would apply to the same employer's hourly paid employees.

To select the types of schedules desired, it is a rule (required by law in many states) that individual employees cannot choose an amount of life insurance for themselves. A specific schedule must apply to all employees in a class; however, an employer may provide different schedules for different classes of employees, as illustrated in the chart at the top of the next page.

OPTIONAL PLANS

In addition to their basic term life plans, some employers make optional life insurance plans available to give employees more flexibility in choosing coverage to suit their needs. Two such plans are the Basic Plus Supplemental and Voluntary Life Insurance.

Basic Plus Supplemental Plan. Basic Plus Supplemental plans are one or more separate plans offered to employees by class on an optional basis. The number of options available are based on the underwriting requirements of the insurer, the desires of the policyholder, and statutory requirements. Below is an illustration of a Basic Plus Supplemental Plan.

Plan	*Amount of Life Insurance*
■ Basic Noncontributory Insurance	$20,000
■ Additional Supplemental Contributory Insurance	One year's annual earnings, up to a maximum of $100,000

In this example the employer provides a basic benefit of $20,000 for all employees that is noncontributory—the employer pays the entire cost. The employee who has a need for additional coverage may purchase the supplemental plan on a contributory basis—the employee pays part or even all of the cost of the insurance.

Voluntary Life Insurance. Voluntary Life Insurance provides employees the option of choosing coverage in incremental amounts, generally of $5,000 or $10,000, up to a maximum based on the employee's earnings (e.g., three times salary). In addition, an overall plan maximum from $100,000 to $300,000 often applies. These amounts usually supplement a basic amount of insurance that is provided by the employer on a noncontributory basis.

The following describes some of the kinds of special provisions often included in Voluntary Life Insurance plans:

Classification	*Life Insurance*
■ All salaried employees	100 percent of the employee's annual earnings, rounded to the next higher $1,000, to a maximum benefit of $100,000
■ All commission salespersons	$25,000
■ Employees in job classifications under a collective bargaining agreement based on basic hourly wages:	
Less than $10 per hour	$10,000
$10 or more per hour	$15,000
■ All nonunion hourly paid employees	$10,000

- Any increased amount is subject to evidence of insurability unless the increase is associated with a salary increase of not more than 10 percent.

- Late enrollees are subject to evidence of insurability unless they enroll as of the policy anniversary or other specified time.

- Evidence of insurability is waived under certain conditions, such as a change in marital status or an increase in the number of the employee's dependents.

BENEFIT REDUCTIONS

Many group life insurance plans contain provisions that start the reduction of benefits for active employees at a certain age, normally age 65. These provisions are aimed at stabilizing costs, since term insurance at higher ages becomes expensive. The need for insurance at higher ages is usually reduced, since financial plans have often been established, and beneficiaries may be eligible for Social Security benefits and often for pension benefits.

In addition, reductions may be an underwriting requirement of the insurer, that may not want a large portion of the insurance in force on older persons. As a result of legislation, the usual practice is to reduce the amount of group term life insurance for employees after a certain age, such as age 65, provided the reduced amount to older employees is equal to the cost of providing the full amount to younger employees.

A typical benefit reduction in compliance with the law is illustrated below:

Reduction of up to:
35% at age 65
55% at age 70
70% at age 75
80% at age 80

Employers, subject to an insurer's underwriting practices, may continue life insurance for retired employees.

ACCELERATED DEATH BENEFIT

This benefit is available as a provision of a group term life policy. It is intended to provide to an insured who is terminally ill a payment that will allow for unexpected personal expenses, medical expenses not covered by insurance, and income replacement not covered by insurance. There are, however, no restrictions on the use of the benefit payments. The purpose of this type of benefit is to help relieve some of the financial burden that is associated with a terminal illness.

Accelerated Death Benefit represents an advance payment of a portion of the face amount of life insurance due to a qualifying event. A qualifying event may be defined as one or more of the following:

- A medical condition which would result in a drastically limited life span as shown in the group contract, for example, twenty-four months, twelve months or six months; or

- A medical condition which has required or requires extraordinary medical intervention, such as major organ transplant or continuous artificial life support, without which the insured would die; or

- Any condition which usually requires continuous confinement in an eligible institution, as defined in the group contract, if the insured is expected to remain there for the rest of his or her life; or

- A medical condition which would, in the absence of extensive or extraordinary medical treatment, result in a drastically limited life span. Such conditions may include coronary artery disease resulting in an acute infarction or requiring surgery, permanent neurological deficit resulting from cerebral vascular accident, or end stage renal failure, Acquired Immune Deficiency Syndrome, or other medical conditions approved by a State Insurance Department.

Most plans allow an accelerated benefit of 25% to 75% of the death benefit payable in a lump sum. Prior to the payment of the accelerated benefit, any assignee or irrevocable beneficiary must submit to the insurer a signed acknowledgment of concurrence for the payout.

The insurer must also disclose that receipt of accelerated benefits may adversely affect the recipient's eligibility for Medicaid or other government benefits or entitlements and that receipt of an accelerated benefit may be taxable.

SURVIVOR INCOME INSURANCE

Survivor income insurance is normally written to supplement a basic plan of group term life insurance, Social Security survivor benefits, death benefits under pension plans, personal insurance, and personal savings and investments. It is unlike group term life insurance in two important respects. First, the benefit is payable only if there is a qualified survivor at death and only for as long as that survivor lives. Second, there is no lump-sum death benefit; the benefit is always paid in monthly installments.

The purpose of a survivor income plan is to provide coverage for the employee with a family; this coverage is in addition to the clean-up fund—the insurance needed at death to take care of burial expenses, final medical care expenses, other debts, etc. In normal insurance planning, first consideration is given to the clean-up fund. Even the single employee has a need for a clean-up fund; for this reason most survivor income plans are not written alone but are provided in addition to a basic term life benefit, or a minimum death benefit applicable to all employees.

Survivor income plans are used infrequently, since they are very expensive compared with other benefit plans.

DEPENDENT LIFE INSURANCE

The law in most jurisdictions permits group policyholders to extend group term life insurance to the employee's spouse and eligible children. The amounts of dependent life insurance are usually small in relation to the amount of insurance on employees.

Some states have legal limits on the life insurance benefits for dependents. These limits usually restrict the amount of insurance on the spouse to a maximum amount (from $2,000 to $100,000), and often provide that in no event will the spouse receive more than 50 percent of the benefit provided to the employee. Children's benefits are also restricted in some jurisdictions. State statutes often contain a limit as to the maximum age of the children, maximum amount of insurance, and require certain benefits for children under six months of age.

The following is an example of what a group life insurance plan with dependent coverage might provide:

Age Bracket	*Amount*
2 weeks and under 6 months	$ 100
6 months and under 2 years	200
2 years and under 3 years	400
3 years and under 4 years	600
4 years and under 5 years	800
5 years and under 19 years	1,000

Specific dependent life maximums and age limits may be required by law in the state of issue.

PLAN PROVISIONS FOR CONTINUING PROTECTION

Many group term life insurance policies contain various provisions for continuation of coverage in cases where an individual's employment has been terminated or the individual is totally disabled. The most common provisions are described below.

CONVERSION PRIVILEGE

When an employee's life insurance ceases because of termination of employment, termination of membership in a classification(s) eligible for coverage, or retirement, that person may convert all or part of the group term life insurance to an individual permanent life insurance policy (excluding disability or supplemental benefits) without having to submit evidence of insurability. The employee must apply to the insurer in writing within 31 days of termination and pay the premium in relation to attained age, the type of insurance, and the class of risk involved.

THIRTY-ONE-DAY CONTINUATION OF PROTECTION

This provision gives a terminated employee an additional 31 days of protection while evaluating whether or not to apply for the conversion privilege.

DISABILITY BENEFITS

Most plans contain a total disability benefit that allows employers to continue insurance in force on disabled employees, at least for a limited period of time, by continuing to pay premiums, whether or not the employees are still employed or terminated. The benefit is usually in one of three forms, or a combination thereof:

Waiver of Premium Benefit. In life insurance plans containing a total disability benefit, this is the most common provision. Under a typical waiver of premium benefit, the life insurance remains in force without premium payment if:

- the employee is under a specified age (usually age 60) at the date of commencement of total disability,
- total disability commences while the employee is insured,
- total disability is continuous until the date of death, or
- proof of total and continuous disability is submitted annually to the insurer.

In many plans, life insurance continued on disability will reduce and terminate in the same way as for non-disabled employees.

Extended Death Benefit. If the employee is totally disabled, life insurance coverage is continued during the disability for a maximum of one year but not beyond age 70. Group life plans containing a waiver of premium provision for disabilities commencing before age 60 may also contain a one-year extended death benefit for disabilities commencing between ages 60 and 70.

Total and Permanent Disability Income Benefit (Installment Payment Benefit). Popular before 1950—when other disability income benefits were not common—but not seen often in current plans, this total disability benefit provides that the employee's life insurance amount is paid in income installments, usually monthly for 60 months, during a period of total disability. To eliminate minor claims, it is often stipulated that total disability must exist for a specific period of time, such as six months, before the monthly income installments begin.

CREDIT LIFE INSURANCE

Group credit life insurance is designed to assure repayment of a loan if the debtor dies, under a policy issued to a creditor (lender) insuring persons who have borrowed money from the creditor, or made a purchase on credit. The group policyholder may be a bank, finance company, savings and loan association, credit union, retail sales outlet (e.g., appliance dealer), or credit card company.

Most insured loans are repayable on a monthly basis. The amount of insurance on these loans is the outstanding balance of the loan at the date of death; therefore, the insurance benefit is reducing-term insurance. Some group credit life insurance policies insure short-term loans where the loan is repayable as a lump sum at the end of the loan period. In these situations the amount of insurance at death is the face amount of the loan plus accrued interest.

For short-term loans, coverage is usually automatic with no special policy restrictions or requirements. For long-term loans, such as mortgage repayment, some form of evidence of insurability is often required as a condition for becoming insured. Long-term loan policies often contain a conversion privilege that permits the mortgagor to convert to an individual life policy if the credit insurance terminates.

To assure adequate participation and spread of risk, the group credit life insurance policy normally requires that a minimum number of new debtors (at least 100) become insured each year. Coverage may be provided for all debtors of the creditor or certain types of loans may be excluded. For example, a policy issued to a bank may cover all direct automobile loans made by the bank but exclude indirect loans, such as those originally made by an automobile dealer that are subsequently transferred or sold to the bank.

There are other forms of life insurance benefits, including Group Universal Life. This subject is covered thoroughly in Part C of this course.

ACCIDENTAL DEATH AND DISMEMBERMENT INSURANCE

Accidental death and dismemberment insurance (AD&D) is a benefit payable if an employee dies, loses the sight of one or both eyes, or loses a hand or a foot, directly and solely as a result of an accidental bodily injury. Although this coverage can be written on a non-occupational basis only, it usually is written as 24-hour coverage.

DESCRIPTION OF BENEFITS

The typical benefit provision reads that if, as a result of an accidental injury, an employee incurs, directly and independently of all other causes and within 90 days of the injury, one of the following losses, the insurance company will pay the amount of the individual's insurance, often called the principal sum, or part of it, as follows:

- For loss of life, the full principal sum is payable;
- For severance of a hand or foot at or above the wrist or ankle, one-half of the principal sum is payable;
- For irrecoverable loss of sight of one eye, one-half of the principal sum is payable; or
- For more than one of the losses described above, the full principal sum is payable.

MULTIPLE BENEFITS

Multiple benefits in excess of the full principal sum are not payable as a result of any one accident, regardless of the extent of the loss. For example, if the insured loses both a hand and the sight of both eyes as a result of the same accident, only the principal sum would be payable. Also, benefits are paid separately for each accident as it occurs. Thus, if an employee dies as a result of an accident, the beneficiary would be entitled to the principal sum even though a dismemberment claim might already have been paid as a result of a previous accident.

The amount of insurance usually is payable in a lump sum to the designated beneficiary for accidental death. For other losses, payment is made to the employee. An accidental death claim may be paid in installments at the request of the beneficiary.

LIMITATIONS AND EXCLUSIONS

Benefits are not payable for any loss that results directly or indirectly, wholly or partly, from any of the following:

- disease or bodily or mental infirmity or their medical or surgical treatment,
- ptomaine or bacterial infection, except infections occurring through an accidental cut or wound,
- suicide or intentionally self-inflicted injury,
- war or any act of war, or
- drugs, unless taken as prescribed by a doctor.

If benefits are provided only on a non-occupational basis, as is common in the more hazardous industries (e.g., explosives manufacturing, logging and lumbering), injuries arising out of or in the course of employment, or where the employee is entitled to benefits under a workers' compensation act or similar legislation, are excluded.

TYPES OF AD&D PLANS

There are four main types of AD&D plans: Group Life Supplement, Voluntary, Business Trip, and Dependent AD&D.

AD&D AS A GROUP LIFE SUPPLEMENT

When included as part of a plan that includes group life insurance, the AD&D principal sum is usually the same as the amount of the group life insurance. However, if life insurance is continued after retirement, accidental death and dismemberment coverage normally terminates at that time.

VOLUNTARY AD&D

Since accidental death occurs infrequently, the premium is low. Because of the lower premium there is a demand for higher amounts of coverage than usually are provided under basic group life and AD&D plans. An elective benefit that is not a part of a group life insurance program is available, called "Voluntary AD&D." Employees pay all or almost all of the premium, and the employer uses the payroll deduction facilities for collecting the employees' contributions.

Description of Benefits. The benefits of Voluntary AD&D insurance are essentially the same as those of basic AD&D, the most significant differences being in the substantial amounts of coverage available—as high as several hundred thousand dollars on a single individual—and the employee's privilege of selecting the amount of coverage. While some plans may provide a predetermined amount by using a schedule with broad categories, more often, when the law allows, the employees choose their own amounts in $5,000 or $10,000 units, within the specified minimums and maximums. Five times the salary is common.

Special Features. A number of factors contribute to the willingness of some insurance companies to offer voluntary AD&D insurance without the usual 75 percent minimum enrollment requirement and allow the employee to select the amount of insurance. The nature of the benefit—payment in the event of accidental death or injury—does not influence the prudent average individual to take risks that might not have been taken in the absence of insurance. In addition, voluntary accidental death and dismemberment insurance includes the following general features, each of which helps to lessen the risk:

■ *Crew Member and Special Aircraft.* Exclusions parallel those used in the AD&D benefits written in conjunction with group life insurance, i.e., disease, bodily or mental infirmity, suicide, war. Also excluded is private flying as a pilot or crew member and flying in certain types of aircraft, such as experimental planes, or planes used in high-risk occupations, such as crop dusting.

■ *Late Enrollments and Class Changes.* Plans usually permit insurance for late enrollees, and increases because of class changes, to become effective only on a specified date. After the initial amount of insurance is selected the employee may increase or decrease the amount only at a specified time, usually the policy anniversary date. This provision is included to prevent the employee from increasing protection when a need is anticipated.

■ *Common Accident.* Some plans may include a common accident limitation. This means that the total amount payable for all deaths or injuries resulting from one accident is fixed in advance and may be less than the combined principal sum amounts for all employees killed or injured in the accident. In these cases, the amounts payable are pro-rated. For example, if the policy provides a common accident limit of $1,000,000 and the total principal sum for all employees killed in the accident is $1,250,000, each beneficiary would be paid 80 percent ($1,000,000/$1,250,000) of the employee's principal sum.

Statutory Restrictions. Several states have minimum initial enrollment requirements for voluntary AD&D plans. In several other states, only plans providing amounts of insurance based on a fixed schedule may be written and individuals may not select their own amount of coverage.

Because of such statutory restrictions, voluntary AD&D insurance is not offered in all states.

BUSINESS TRIP AD&D

This coverage, sometimes called travel accident insurance, is designed for employers who wish to provide supplementary accident protection for their employees while they are traveling on company business. The cost of this coverage is usually paid entirely by the employer.

Description of Benefits. The schedule of business trip AD&D benefits is essentially the same as for basic

AD&D: benefits are payable for death or dismemberment caused by an accident and occurring within a specified number of days, while the employee is on a business trip. Employees usually are considered to be on a business trip while they are on an assignment authorized by the employer, at the expense of the employer, and engaged primarily in furthering the employer's business. Three types of business trip accident plans are offered:

- *Comprehensive or All-Risk Plans* provide 24-hour protection from the time the employee leaves home or place of business until the return from a business trip.

- *Common Carrier Plans* cover accidents only when the employee is traveling on business in, boarding, alighting from, or struck by a specified type of vehicle, such as a public conveyance that is licensed and being used for the transportation of passengers. Company- or personally-owned vehicles are excluded.

- *All Conveyance Plans* include coverage while traveling on business in, boarding, alighting from, or struck by a motor vehicle, airplane, or other conveyance including personally owned or company owned vehicles.

In all three business trip accident plans, individual maximum amounts of insurance are high, often $100,000 or more, and are usually based on an earnings schedule. The common accident provision, explained under voluntary AD&D, frequently is included to lessen the risk of insuring several people who may be involved in the same accident.

In addition to providing benefits for losses because of death and dismemberment, group business trip policies also may include short-term disability income benefits and medical care expense benefits for accidents occurring while traveling on business.

Sometimes, for cost purposes or for clarification of what constitutes a business hazard, these policies stipulate that coverage is only applicable while traveling on a common carrier, thus eliminating the possibility of covering a death while employed at the regular business location.

DEPENDENTS AD&D

AD&D for dependents may be provided under a plan covering employees. It is written on a 24-hour basis, regardless of how the coverage is provided for employees. Eligible dependents include the employee's spouse and unmarried children, up to a specified age. Generally a minimum enrollment, such as 75 percent, of the employees with eligible dependents is required and an employee must insure all eligible dependents.

The amount of insurance for each dependent is a percent of the scheduled amount of the principal sum for the employee, typically 50 percent for the spouse and 20 percent for the children. Benefits are paid to the employee in a lump sum.

SUMMARY

Today's insurance industry offers numerous forms of nonmedical group coverage to employers or associations. Employers frequently use these coverages to attract and retain employees. These employee benefits are usually part of a total compensation package that helps to protect both employees and their families.

KEY TERMS

Accelerated Death Benefit
Accidental Death and Dismemberment Insurance (AD&D)
Adult Day Care Center
Age Discrimination in Employment Act (ADEA)
Annual Earnings Schedule
Basic Plus Supplemental Plan
Benefit Amount
Benefit Payment Period
Benefit Reductions
Benefit Waiting Period
Business Trip AD&D
Case Management
Clean-Up Fund
Continuation of Coverage
Conversion Privilege
Cost of Living Adjustment
Dependent AD&D
Dependent Life Insurance
Disability Benefits
Disability Income Insurance
Elimination Period
Extended Death Benefit
Flat Benefit Schedule
Functional Loss
Group Life Insurance
Guaranteed Minimum Monthly Income
Home Health Agency
Home Health Care
Length-of-Service Schedule
Long-Term Care Benefits
Long-Term Disability Income Insurance
Loss of Functional Capacity
Medical Care Coordinator
Multiple Schedule Plans
Non-occupational Coverage
Nursing Care Facility
Other Income
Percentage of Earnings Schedule
Portability
Positions Schedule
Preexisting Conditions Limitation
Principal Sum
Rehabilitation Provision
Short-Term Disability Income Insurance
Successive Periods of Disability
Survivor Income Benefit
Term Life Insurance
Thirty-One-Day Continuation of Protection
Total and Permanent Disability Income Benefit
Twenty-Four-Hour Coverage
Voluntary AD&D
Voluntary Life Insurance
Waiver of Premium Benefit
Weekly Income Benefit

IV

Marketing

INTRODUCTION

Marketing formerly was considered synonymous with selling. Many considered it to be concerned only with the seller's actual sales plans and the methods used to convince the consumer to buy the product offered for sale.

This concept has been expanded and broadened in recent years. Insurers now realize that every facet of their business process ultimately affects the successful sale of their products.

Marketing the group insurance product is complex and highly technical. It includes identification, evaluation, and selection of markets; thorough development of appropriate products; and planning, promotion, and controlled distribution of the product. And, since nothing happens until something is sold, it needs a well-trained and professional salesforce.

Specific marketing activities for group insurance may involve one insurer department or be assigned to more than one department within the corporate structure. Interaction involves specialists from other business functions—actuarial science, underwriting, administration, and sales, for example—and facilitates the marketing process.

INTERACTION WITH OTHER INSURER FUNCTIONS

ACTUARIAL SCIENCE

The actuarial function plays an important role in the evaluation of markets, development of products and pricing, and the company's profit objectives for the various group products. It also contributes directly to the sales effort by providing experience refund projections, special rate calculations, answers to technical questions that often appear in bidding specifications, and personal contact as required on prospective or in-force business.

UNDERWRITING

Group underwriters contribute to marketing through the evaluation and selection of markets in general and the achievement of profit goals on specific cases and classes of business. Underwriters also maintain a group underwriting manual for salespeople, evaluate new prospects, provide field assistance in special situations, and help prepare proposals for new prospects and benefit improvements for policyholders.

ADMINISTRATION

Group administration plans and provides for the on-going service required for the successful operation of group plans at an expense level that will permit the insurance company to achieve its profit objectives. It also assists the group sales department by providing service to policyholders, doing cost containment studies, developing administration manuals for policyholders, installing sold cases, offering special claims and administrative services, and responding to bidding specifications on new case activity.

SALES

At the "front line," if you will, of all these activities are the men and women who interact with prospects, brokers, consultants, and policyholders. These are the people who use the marketing services of insurer units and who, because of external interactions, provide input to insurer units on marketing strategies and tactics.

OTHER FUNCTIONS

Various departments within or outside the group insurance department may be called on because of their expertise in specific areas. For example, the insurer's advertising, sales promotion, communication agency, data processing, legal, medical, and claims departments all may have special input in a marketing process.

GROUP INSURANCE MARKETS

Insurers categorize group insurance markets primarily by size, type of group, and certain common characteristics. The following paragraphs describe these basic categories.

MARKET CATEGORIES BY SIZE

Approximately 80 percent of all insured groups have fewer than 100 lives. Generally, contracts for these smaller groups provide standardized benefit structures and are administered by the insurer. The primary purchasing considerations in this market are price, ability to buy the same kinds and quality of benefits that are available to large employers, and simplified administration.

The second category consists of groups of 100 to 500 lives, which accounts for about 10 percent of all group contracts in force. Greater flexibility in benefit design and administration characterize plans in this market. Both individual sales insurance agents and brokers/consultants actively sell to this market, with the insurer's group field sales representative frequently involved directly in the sale and service to the policyholder. Particular purchasing considerations in this market are net cost, plan design flexibility, and quality of service.

Groups of 500 or more lives, although they account for over half of the total premium dollars, make up only about 10 percent of all group insurance contracts in force. Insurers often tailor benefits to the specifications of the buyer and modify administrative procedures to suit policyholder needs. Insurers usually sell these contracts through brokers/consultants or directly, with the interests of the buyer represented by an employee benefit consultant. Both situations involve the insurer's group field sales representative or home office sales personnel. The common purchasing considerations are net cost (retention), cash flow arrangements, tailored administrative systems, claim processing and cost control systems, and other special services.

TYPES OF POLICYHOLDERS

It is well established that an employer, to acquire and retain employees, must provide not only a fair wage but also a package of insurance benefits to offset the expense and economic loss resulting from death, disability, or medical treatment. This reality leads to the purchase of group insurance by various policyholders.

SINGLE EMPLOYERS

A single employer, private or public, may provide insurance coverage for employees through purchase of a group policy. The employer may be a sole proprietor, a partnership, a corporation, or a number of entities (such as subsidiaries) insured through a common owner. Single employer contracts compose by far the largest share of the group market, with about 90 percent of all group policies in force.

For smaller employers the group insurance plan may obtain attractive benefits at lower cost, and on a tax-favored basis for the owners and their employees.

Single employer groups receive the greatest concentration of sales effort by agents and brokers. Often, unions influence the benefits, even though the employer is the policyholder. Employers may pay all premiums, or the employer and employee both contribute to the amount. In addition, state insurance laws and regulations may affect minimum requirements regarding group size, employee eligibility, life insurance maximums, and requirements for health insurance coverage of these groups.

LABOR UNIONS

A labor union—national, regional, or local—may provide coverage for its members under a policy issued to the union. In these contracts the union pays premiums through its dues structure or member contributions.

Most state insurance statutes permit the issuance of such policies. However, a state may have minimum size requirements and may require approval of health insurance contracts by its insurance department.

Only a small number of all group contracts in force, however, are issued to unions. This market is diminishing in importance, as unions prefer to obtain their benefits through collective bargaining. Perhaps the only reason for the purchase of group insurance under a contract issued to a labor union is to provide an additional membership benefit, such as a death benefit that serves as a burial fund. The union also might serve as a policyholder to provide medical care benefits, if it is unable to negotiate these benefits through the employer.

MULTIPLE-EMPLOYER GROUPS

Multiple-employer groups involve union/management trusts, groups combining several employers, professional organizations, and creditor arrangements.

Negotiated Trusteeships (Taft-Hartley Groups). Negotiated trusteeships involve a trust established under the authority of the Labor Management Relations Act of 1947 (the Taft-Hartley Act). Composed of one or more unions and one or more employers, the trust provides coverage for union members engaged in activities that affect interstate or foreign commerce under a group contract issued to the named trustees. These contracts, established as a result of a collective bargaining agreement between the union(s) and the employer(s), account for about 2 percent of all group insurance contracts in force. Although, usually funded solely by employer contributions, the trust may involve employee contributions. Typically, the plans written are large group plans, motivated by considerations similar to those of a large single employer and handled through brokers or consultants. Policyholder administration typically is handled by a third-party administrator. These contracts, permitted by the group insurance statutes of most states, may be subject to minimum size and eligibility factors.

When a union negotiates to provide group insurance benefits for its members, a joint labor-management trust often is established as the vehicle for providing the benefits, if more than one employer or union is involved. Lower cost and improved plan design may result from the large size of the group. Other results of participation in the trust may include standardization of benefits, administration procedures, and premium costs among different unions and different employers. Even if only one employer is involved, the trust may be used to assure the union of an equal voice in the management of the plan.

Multiple-Employer Trusts (METs). METs involve the participation of single employers, usually in the same or related industries, brought together by an insurer, agent, broker/consultant, or administrator. The purpose for uniting these employers is to provide insurance for their employees through a master contract issued to a trustee under a trust agreement. In this way employers provide benefits, usually available only to big companies, at low cost for the small employer.

The MET trustee often is a corporate entity, such as a commercial bank; the administrator may be an insurer or a third-party administrator (TPA). When established by a broker or administrator, it is not uncommon that the MET is noninsured—that is, a self-funded plan without the services of an insurance company.

Trade Associations. Single employers, bound together by membership in a trade association, may provide insurance for their employees under a contract issued to the association. This type of contract accounts for less than 1 percent of all group contracts in force.

An association which establishes a group insurance plan is usually motivated by the need to attract, retain, and involve members in a closer relationship with it. Members can obtain broad benefits at low cost through the greater purchasing power of the association. Among associations of employers, these plans also may be a response to a common collective bargaining agreement.

The statutes in some states do not provide for group contracts to be issued to a trade association of employers in the same industry. Most of these states, however, do permit group contracts issued to the trustees of a trust established by two or more employers in the same industry. These trust arrangements accomplish essentially the same objectives as plans established directly by the association of employers. Again, specifications such as minimum size and eligibility of employees may be considered in establishing this type of group insurance plan.

The premium may be paid by the employer or by both the employer and employee. Sometimes the benefits are established as a result of union negotiations. These are usually large group plans handled through brokers or consultants and administered either by the association or a third-party administrator.

Professional and Other Individual Membership Associations. Individuals in various professions—law, medicine, engineering, and education, for example—can provide coverage for themselves and sometimes their employees through a contract issued to an association or to a trust formed to administer the insurance. These professional associations, employee associations, and other individual membership groups (associations of people of the same occupation, college alumni groups, veteran, and fraternal groups) compose a small part of all group contracts in force. The premium for insurance coverage in these groups ordinarily is paid by the association member.

Typically these are large group plans, established on a statewide, regional, or national basis, and sold through highly specialized broker-consultants. Although the plans may be administered by the insurer or the association, they are frequently administered through third-party broker-administrators who specialize in the sale and service of such plans.

Established for the same reasons as described above for trade associations, these plans may be affected by state laws that specify the types of organizations that may contract, minimum size of the group, and eligibility specifications.

Creditor Groups. A creditor institution, such as a bank or finance company, may contract to insure its debtors to provide for payment of a debt if a debtor dies or suffers a period or periods of disability.

Among the legal considerations in establishing these plans are minimum size requirements, eligibility of loans, periods of coverage, amounts of coverage and premium rates paid by the debtor.

The premium under these contracts may be paid through the creditor institution by the debtor. This cost may or may not be identified in the overall cost of the loan. The coverage may be voluntary—if the premium is identified—or automatic, if it is not included as an identifiable amount in the cost of the loan.

Such life and accident and health plans benefit the creditor policyholder by securing the repayment of the indebtedness. They may also be viewed as an additional service to the borrower and may help to attract customers to the creditor institution.

PRODUCT RESEARCH AND DEVELOPMENT

The potential for new products or improvements to existing products is limited only by imagination and creativity. In order to be effective, however, insurers expect research and development activities to directly support insurer goals.

THE PRODUCT DEVELOPMENT STATEMENT

To achieve its goals, most insurers prepare a carefully designed product development statement. This statement targets specific customers and defines the degree of risk the company is willing to undertake and the financial objectives of product development efforts.

THE PRODUCT DEVELOPMENT PROCESS

The product development process has seven basic stages:

1. *Idea Generation.* Idea generation usually starts with some specific input either from the field, the home office staff, or senior management.

2. *Market Research.* Market research involves analysis of competition, analysis of market needs, market penetration studies, office location studies, and detailed analysis of sales results.

3. *The Product Outline.* The product outline includes a general statement of the target market (group size and type, geographic area, industry, socioeconomic group, etc.), the essential distinguishing characteristics that differentiate the product from others, a preliminary estimate of the cost of developing the product, and a list of potential benefits to be derived from its development.

4. *Market Analysis.* Market analysis examines whether a product is compatible with the product development statement and if it relates to other products and services the insurer sells. It assesses the expertise and ability required to support devel-

oping the product and considers whether its current distribution and administration systems can handle the product. Also, very important here is the influence of external factors—consumers, providers of health care, the government, competitors, group representatives, and producers.

5. *Detailed Design and Development.* Detailed design and development involves a number of steps:

- creation and filing of the contract with the state insurance department,
- development of rates and commission schedules,
- setting of underwriting limits, requirements, and guidelines,
- writing of underwriting manuals, field releases, field training programs, and marketing brochures for producers, employers, and employees, and
- data processing systems modifications and administrative processes (proposing, rating, issuing, billing, accounting, benefits processing, and ongoing administrative maintenance). Data processing capabilities are especially important at this stage. During development, input also is sought from field sales staff in whatever manner is appropriate so that changes to the original design can be incorporated before the product is actually implemented and sold.

6. *Product Introduction.* After completion of all the detailed design and development tasks, the insurer actually offers the product to prospective purchasers, and

7. *Sales Monitoring and Review.* Sales monitoring and review include analysis of sales results, analysis of a number of quotes, and direct input from the sales staff and agency force. Considerations of monitoring and review requirements are taken up as early as the market analysis phase in order to build in any needed procedures.

ORGANIZATION OF ACTIVITY

Every insurance company writing group insurance is involved in product research and development (R&D) activities to some degree, but the organization of these efforts vary. The research and development responsibility is delegated either to an R&D department or to a specially appointed ad hoc committee. Experts from various insurer departments will probably be consulted.

RESEARCH AND DEVELOPMENT DEPARTMENT

When established as a formal department, the R&D department (sometimes an ad hoc committee or task force) conducts a continuing program in research and development and works on specific projects such as the development and introduction of a new product or existing product enhancement. How an R&D department might operate in developing and introducing a new product or product enhancement is outlined below.

- The product being proposed for

development or enhancement is reviewed and approved by the heads of all interested departments.

- When the project is undertaken, each department assigns a coordinator to work with the project manager of the R&D department.

- These coordinators (who usually represent the actuarial, administration, claims, contracts, data processing, sales, and underwriting departments) see to it that the particular interests of their own department are satisfied, keep their department heads informed on the status of the project, and obtain needed approvals from their department heads as the project progresses.

- The project manager works with the coordinators to develop the framework of the product under consideration. This framework is built from conclusions drawn from analyses of market needs and competitors' products, detailed proposals from other functions as to benefit provisions and limitations, administrative and claim procedures, data processing applications, compensation plans, sales aids, and marketing plans.

- The project manager identifies all tasks to be accomplished, establishes deadlines, schedules the entire project, and coordinates the activities of the individuals responsible for carrying it out. It is the project manager's job to see that the project is done correctly and on schedule.

EXTERNAL INFLUENCES

Health insurance is a complex product that affects, and is affected by, forces outside the insurance industry. Consumers, health care providers, government, producers, and competition are some of these external factors.

CONSUMERS

Insurers are keenly interested in the number and kinds of groups who buy group insurance, the reasons for the purchase, and the manner in which the insurance benefits are used after purchase. Policyholders' attitudes, too, influence the revision of existing products and the creation of new products. In addition, overlaps and gaps in coverage, as well as high cost brought to light by policyholders, may be important in the revision of present policies and creation of new products.

PROVIDERS

Private health insurers are vitally interested in decisions that hospitals, doctors, and other providers of health care make. To illustrate, the decisions of providers to revise and expand the scope of hospital and medical care have had important influences on the development of insurance for new care concepts such as home care, preventive care, preadmission testing, second surgical opinions, hospice care, freestanding birthing centers, and ambulatory surgery.

GOVERNMENT

Government programs and legislation at the state or federal level influence private insurers' decisions concerning group life and health insurance products. Tax regulations, workers' compensation laws, Social

Security, statutory disability laws, the Equal Employment Opportunity Act of 1964, Medicare, Medicaid, ADEA, Health Maintenance Organization (HMO) legislation, the Mandatory Retirement Act, the Employee Retirement Income Security Act (ERISA), and TEFRA are examples of government influence requiring product research and development. In addition, many laws have been enacted at the state level in recent years concerning areas such as small group reform mandatory insurance coverage, and conversion benefits. These laws generated considerable R&D activity in the design of new coverages. Public opinion probably will continue to be reflected in state and federal legislation and be an important factor in the design of new life and health insurance products and enhancements.

PRODUCERS

Because of their close contact with clients and potential buyers, agents, brokers/consultants, and group representatives are excellent sources of information regarding buyer needs. This information can be the determining factor in deciding whether to market a revised or a new life and health insurance product. These are also the people who must be trained and informed as to new offerings in order to be effective in the marketing of new products, systems, and ideas.

COMPETITION

A private insurer, like any member of the free enterprise system, must cope with the actions and decisions of competitors. Competition is intense among private insurers, other types of insurance carriers such as Blue Cross/ Blue Shield, health care delivery systems, and self-funded plans. It centers on factors including the technical aspects of plan design, cost considerations, and administrative services.

The group insurance market is constantly changing because of rising costs and new insurance needs. New products, concepts in coverage, and funding vehicles continually are being developed. They afford, for the buyer of group insurance, alternatives in meeting specific objectives. A new type of contract or concept in plan design may be the deciding factor in competition until it becomes a part of the portfolio of most insurance companies.

Perhaps the most significant factor, however, in competition among insurers is the cost of the group program. The prospect usually reviews coverage proposals from several insurers and places a great deal of significance on comparative costs. On small groups the cost comparison is limited to premium rates. On large groups insurers prepare net cost illustrations based on certain assumptions about future claim experience and the services to be provided to the policyholder. By comparing these illustrations, the policyholder can evaluate the potential net cost of the program after taking account of any experience refunds.

The quality of service also may be an important factor in obtaining and retaining group insurance policyholders. The ability of the insurance company to communicate the plan effectively, to provide sound administration, and prompt, accurate claim payments, may all be determinants. In the large group market, claim processing, claim analysis reports, and claim cost control capabilities (cost containment techniques) have become a major competitive factor. Effective communication of the financial operation and the annual rerating of the contract, too, are services essential to retaining policyholders.

In addition, various cash flow concepts, alternates to conventional funding, have become factors in competition among group insurers, along with product, service, and price. These cash-flow arrangements influence the cost of the insurance program by making available for the use of the policyholder money that would otherwise be paid or retained under the insurance contract. To the extent that policyholders gain the use of money that normally would be tied up in the insurance contract and earn income from the available funds, they may realize savings in the net cost of the insurance program.

Another competitive factor in the group insurance marketplace is the self-funded (noninsured) or partially self-funded employee benefit plan. A growing understanding and identification of risk and the desire to reduce tax liabilities and improve cash flow have caused many large employers to reevaluate the role of the traditional fully-insured contract in their group insurance programs. The insurance industry has responded with a number of modifications to the standard group contract. The modified contracts compete with the self-funded concept by providing improved cash flow to policyholders and by reducing the amount of risk assumed by the insurer.

SALES PERSONNEL

Often a separate insurer department, although obviously allied with the marketing effort, the group sales function plans, coordinates, and supervises policy sales and service through both home office and field sales office personnel.

THE SALES FORCE

Home office salespeople (the executive in charge, his/her staff, and others) support the field sales offices by product promotion and development, training, and administrative and national account services. In the group field sales offices are group representatives and a staff responsible for sales and service through agents and brokers within a defined geographic area. Each field sales office also has a manager who reports to a regional vice president or regional manager located in the field or home office.

An insurer with a group operation too small to have a group field sales force usually delegates sales and service responsibilities to general agents and brokers. Regardless of the size and organization of the group sales operation, however, the sales and service activities generally are the same.

Most insurers conduct marketing activities involving policyholder contact through their group representatives and through group producers—insurance agents, brokers, and consultants. A few insurers, known as direct writers, solicit business directly from prospective policyholders. They employ salaried representatives to obtain group business, rather than work through commissioned agents or brokers.

GROUP REPRESENTATIVES

Group representatives are insurance company employees trained in the techniques of selling and servicing group insurance plans. Because of the different skills required, some companies employ both group *sales* representatives and group *service* representatives. Their important responsibilities are:

- working with agents and brokers in developing group prospects,
- securing data and submitting them to the insurer's home office with recommendations for a proposal,
- preparing field group proposals and presenting group proposals to prospects,
- assisting in the closing of group sales,
- assisting in the enrollment of employees under new group plans,
- setting up administrative procedures for new policyholders,
- making regular service calls to assist in administration and plan modernization,
- "selling" rate increases and retaining present policyholders, and
- keeping the home office informed of competitive developments in the group field.

Insurers generally compensate group representatives by a salary or by salary plus an incentive bonus for exceeding goals or quotas. The importance of bonus compensation varies from insurer to insurer; a few provide no bonus, while others use a bonus as the principal form of compensation.

Bonuses are a percentage of premiums—first-year premiums or both first-year and renewal premiums. The percentage may be weighted to give special emphasis to the sale of specific products or to certain markets. Typically, bonus payments may range between 10 and 50 percent of a group representative's salary, sometimes with a maximum payout limited to an amount equal to the salary. The bonus may count along with salary as total compensation and be used to determine the amounts of company fringe benefits (group life insurance and pensions) due the "group rep."

Some compensation plans increase or decrease compensation based on results in persistency and profitability.

GROUP PRODUCERS

Although insurers use several types of group producers, they all perform three basic activities: locate the prospect, secure information and data regarding the prospect, and call on insurers' group representatives for technical assistance in selling, installing, and servicing the group program.

Agents. Generally, agents of a group insurer are under contract to sell its full line of products and are a primary source of small- and medium-size group sales. On these smaller cases, the agent may work without the assistance of a group representative, thus providing valuable personal service to clients.

In addition to receiving compensation for the sale and service of a group plan, insurance agents take an active part in group selling for two principal reasons. First, the group business is an excellent source of prospects for other business insurance or personal lines. Group insurance also complements other lines in the portfolio, enabling the agent to offer a complete range of products and service to business clients.

Brokers. Brokers, individuals or business firms that represent the policyholder in placing coverage with an insurer, are the principal source of large group sales and a secondary source of smaller group cases. For some insurers, brokers are the primary source of group business of any size.

Although business written by individual and small brokerage firms accounts for a significant portion of the market, the largest percentage in terms of premium is controlled by specialized group brokers (or consultants) and by the larger brokerage firms with specialized group departments. Their contacts with top management for general insurance lines (property, casualty, and fire) are helpful to them in handling group insurance for larger accounts. In addition, these specialists have both technical insurance knowledge and knowledge of the policyholder's operations. Since the largest brokerage and consulting firms have nationwide organizations with offices in principal cities throughout the country, they are able to serve the needs of large clients with geographically widespread organizations.

A broker also may act as a third-party administrator (TPA) handling the administration of one or more group plans, including premium accounting, maintaining lists of employee eligibility, and claims.

Employee Benefit Consultants. Individuals or firms that specialize in the design, sales, and service of employee benefit plans are known as Employee Benefit Consultants. Because they may deliver the same services as the larger brokerage firms, it is difficult to distinguish between consultants and brokers. The consultant, however, is less likely to be involved in the placing of coverage with an insurer, but rather make recommendations to the policy holder. Consultants are usually paid a fee by the policyholder rather than commissions by the insurance company.

PRODUCER COMPENSATION

Group producers usually are compensated for group sales and services by commissions for business that they personally sell. Two types of commission schedules are in general use: the high-low schedule and the level commission schedule.

COMMISSION SCHEDULES

The high-low commission schedule provides higher commissions the first year and lower commissions in renewal years. The level commission schedule provides the same total commission dollars each year (assuming the same premium each year) and is becoming the most common schedule. Over a ten-year period either schedule usually will produce the same commissions (assuming the same premium each year and that the group stays with the same insurer for those ten years). Persistency fees may be paid for business continuing beyond the tenth policy year.

The table below illustrates a typical high-low and level commission scale for each sale.

Although insurance company practices vary, the agent or broker may sometimes choose either the higher first-year commission schedule or the level schedule. However, insurers or regulators in some states require a level schedule when cases are:

- transferred from another insurer—far more common today than groups being insured for the first time,
- reinstated,
- set up for participants to pay all the premium,
- judged by the insurer to have a high chance of lapse, or
- negotiated with unions.

Insurers commonly combine the premiums from both life and health insurance coverages when calculating the commission, although practice varies. Some insurers accelerate the payment of commissions to the agent by advancing substantially all the first-year commissions in one sum as soon after the sale as possible.

Commissions for groups of less than 25 employees may be paid at a slightly higher scale in the first year and later years because the agent may be expected to do much of the work connected with selling, installing, and servicing the small group case.

OVERRIDE COMMISSIONS

Since a general agent or agency manager who is an experienced group producer can provide assistance to

COMMISSION SCHEDULE

	High-Low Scale Percentage Commission		*Level Scale Percentage Commission*
Annual Premium	*1st Year*	*2nd through 10th Year*	*1st 10 Years*
First $ 1,000	20.0%	5.0%	6.5%
Next 4,000	20.0	3.0	4.7
Next 5,000	15.0	1.5	2.85
Next 10,000	12.5	1.5	2.6
Next 10,000	10.0	1.5	2.35
Next 20,000	5.0	1.5	1.85
Next 200,000	2.5	1.0	1.15
Next 250,000	1.0	.5	.55

the writing agent that the insurer would otherwise expect to provide, insurers will sometimes agree to pay an additional commission called an "override commission." This payment is in addition to the commission paid to the selling agent or broker, which is produced by the high-low schedule or level schedule. A typical override schedule is illustrated in the chart below.

VESTING

Vested commissions grant writing agents, or their estate, ownership of renewal commissions, whether or not the agent remains with the insurer. Vesting practices differ among insurers, but the general trend in group insurance is away from this concept. Commissions generally are paid only when continuing service is provided to the policyholder by the writing agent who remains under contract with the insurer.

OTHER COMPENSATION ARRANGEMENTS

Sometimes group producers may negotiate a fee arrangement directly with clients according to the services provided, based on some measure other than premium. For example, they may negotiate a flat monthly or annual fee or a "per employee per month" charge. These arrangements are most common with producers who are either acting as third-party administrators or representing large clients.

SELLING THE PRODUCT: THE SIX-STEP PROCESS

The sales process involves initial and continuing sales effort, which can be divided into at least six distinct steps:

- prospecting,
- proposal preparation and plan design,
- presentation of the proposal,
- closing the sale,
- employee enrollment and plan installation, and

OVERRIDE COMMISSION SCHEDULE

	High-Low Scale Percentage Commission		Level Scale Percentage Commission
Annual Premium	*1st Year*	*2nd through 10th Year*	*1st 10 Years*
First $ 1,000	4.0%	1.0%	1.3%
Next 4,000	4.0	.6	.94
Next 5,000	3.0	.3	.57
Next 10,000	2.5	.3	.52
Next 10,000	2.0	.3	.47
Next 20,000	1.0	.3	.37
Next 200,000	.3	.13	.15
Next 250,000	.2	.10	.11

■ service and conservation of business.

PROSPECTING

Group representatives generally prospect for new group insurance clients through agents and brokers and devote considerable time and effort to developing them as sources of business.

The group representative may take a comprehensive approach to the development of group prospects among the full-time agents of the insurance company in a given area by participating periodically in agency meetings, conducting training sessions for groups of agents, and distributing sales and informational bulletins. The most effective development of group prospects usually occurs, however, when the group representative is able to establish a close working relationship with an agent and educate and motivate that agent to prospect regularly. General insurance brokers may be developed and cultivated in much the same way as individual insurance agents. One-on-one motivation and training of the individual broker are the keys to the successful development of group prospects.

Group representatives prospect somewhat differently in dealing with large, specialized brokers. Through establishing a close working relationship, "group reps" attempt to demonstrate their own abilities to the broker and to motivate the broker to place group insurance with a particular insurer because of its products and capabilities. The development of group business through employee benefit consultants is similar to the methods used with large brokers.

The group representatives of some insurance companies may prospect for buyers directly. Also, it is common for group representatives to make direct contact with a large employer and attempt to secure its group business.

Regardless of the methods employed in prospecting for group insurance, an essential element of a successful effort is the securing of information necessary for plan design and the proposal preparation.

PROPOSAL PREPARATION AND PLAN DESIGN

To prepare a proposal, an insurer must evaluate the prospect's needs, design the benefit plan, underwrite the plan, calculate the rates, and arrange all plan aspects into an attractive sales proposal.

NEEDS EVALUATION

Preparing a proposal requires certain information regarding the prospect, including an employee census, a description of the present and proposed plans, and claims and premium experience of the present plan.

The employee census usually provides data regarding age, sex, income, family status, occupation, and geographic location for all eligible persons. A description of the present plan will be in the master contract and in the employee certificates or announcement booklets. The claim experience for any in-force plan usually includes paid premium, paid or incurred claims, premium rates and enrollment for each line of coverage (for example, life, disability income, and medical care).

Among the other items of information that may be considered are the business of the prospect, any collective bargaining agreements affecting the coverage, trust agreements, objectives of the client, and a statement of financial condition.

PLAN DESIGN

For prospects submitted by agents and small brokers, the final plan design may combine the client's expressed desires with recommendations based on an evaluation of the client's needs by the agent or broker and the group representative. Smaller groups are limited in the variety of plan designs that may be available.

On larger cases and those submitted by larger brokers and employee benefit consultants, fairly rigid specifications may govern the submitted request for proposal. The development of plan specifications varies according to the preferences of individual brokers or consultants. Some design their specifications to be more effective in specific markets, such as negotiated trust funds, or professional or trade associations. Others prefer to use a standard format for all markets. Whatever the format selected, the main purpose of plan specifications is to give the client a basis for comparing "apples to apples," and to establish, as objectively as possible, which insurer can best administer the program at a competitive net cost.

A typical set of specifications consists of a cover letter from the broker (on behalf of a client) and a series of exhibits that serve as the basis for the insurer's offer and rate estimate. These specifications are mailed either directly to the insurer's home office or to the insurer's nearest local group insurance office.

The local group representative's recommendation is always a strong factor in an insurer's decision to submit a quotation on a case. The "rep" must feel the prospect meets the insurer's underwriting standards and that there is a reasonably good chance of making the sale before the insurer proceeds. The development of home office quotations from specifications is a costly procedure that demands considerable expertise, particularly in the sales, underwriting, and actuarial areas. Often there are difficult rate questions to resolve, and always there is the problem of meeting tight deadlines.

Although specifications frequently stipulate that quotations must be mailed rather than hand-delivered, few sales are consummated without a personal interview with the prospect and the local group representative or someone from the home office.

UNDERWRITING THE PROPOSAL

Underwriting of the proposal normally is done in the insurer's home or regional office. The underwriter evaluates the data, approves or modifies the benefit plan, and reviews the group's previous claim history, if any. If the prospect is already insured—the usual situation—the "new" insurer evaluates the claim experience of the present insurer in detail and makes cost projections to establish the proper rate levels to be charged for the types of benefits proposed. The insurer then specifies any special conditions pertaining to the case.

For smaller groups, it is a common practice for group representatives at the field office nearest the prospect's location to do the initial underwriting, price the benefits, and prepare the proposal. However, whether underwriting is done in the field, in the home office, or jointly, prospective clients are screened carefully by the field people according to the insurer's underwriting standards.

RATE CALCULATION

The field office usually completes rate calculations for most groups, based upon rate levels provided or approved by home office underwriters. However, rate computations for large groups are often completed by the home office in order to compile and process computerized census data.

FORMAT

The proposal format for large group prospects usually includes the following information:

- brief description or outline of each coverage included in the benefit package,
- schedule of the rates and premiums quoted for each coverage,
- underwriting assumptions and requirements related to the proposed program of benefits,
- a net cost illustration of the program (usually covering a three- or five-year period), and
- information regarding the insurer's financial strength and accomplishments together with a list of its well-known group policyholders.

Proposals for small groups usually include the above items, except the net cost illustration. They also generally include a complete description of eligible employees and dependents to be insured under the proposed plan.

Most salespeople consider that a carefully prepared, well-designed, and attractive proposal is a valuable and essential tool in the selling process.

PRESENTATION OF THE PROPOSAL

Employee benefit consultants and large brokers usually want proposals submitted directly to them for analysis and recommendation to the client. This also is true of some smaller brokers; however, many smaller brokers and agents encourage direct participation by the group representative in presenting the proposal to the client.

General considerations in the final evaluation of the proposal are the insurer's capabilities, experience, and reputation. Specific considerations are the insurer's constructive plan design, suggestions and degree of compliance with plan specifications, and the competitive position of the insurer's rate quotation and net cost illustration. Net cost illustrations usually are not made for smaller groups because the individual claim experience of such groups does not entitle them to an experience refund. When net cost illustrations are used, the prospect must be cautioned that experience refunds are merely illustrative of results that *may* be achieved under the insurer's refund formula, providing all assumptions are realized. The illustration may not show the considerable variations possible in the range and quality of service from one insurer to another.

CLOSING THE SALE

Whether the group is large or small, this part of the sales process is completed with a signed application and receipt of the first month's premium from the new policyholder.

EMPLOYEE ENROLLMENT AND PLAN INSTALLATION

The process is somewhat different for new and existing plans.

NEW PLANS

When a group plan is being offered for the first time, or a line of insurance (such as dental insurance) is being added to an existing plan, the next step after closing the sale is the presentation of the plan to the employees. The enrollment must be properly planned and executed if it is to be satisfactory—particularly when employees will contribute to the plan cost. The most essential element is the active support of the employer and the use of key personnel in securing the signed employee enrollment cards. After the insurance company prepares an announcement letter or booklet for use in explaining the plan to the employees, the employer arranges for employee presentation meetings, distribution of employee enrollment cards, and key employees' follow-up to obtain the signed cards.

Even when the employer pays the entire cost of the plan, the plan requires proper presentation to secure maximum employee understanding and appreciation. The group representative and agent or broker play an important role in this service.

EXISTING PLANS

If an existing plan is awarded to a new insurance company, re-enrollment may be conducted even though no new line of insurance is added and the existing lines remain unchanged. This re-enrollment might be done for a number of reasons:

- to improve employee awareness of the plan,
- to make the employees comfortable with the new insurer,
- to ensure adequate participation when employee contributions are increased, or
- to obtain new life insurance beneficiary designation forms.

Upon completion of the enrollment process, the group or service representative sends the signed application, the enrollment cards, and the first month's premium to the insurance company home office or group field office for final acceptance and issuance of the master policy, individual certificates, and administrative material. Thereafter, this material is sent to the representative for installation of the program. The representative, usually accompanied by the agent or broker, delivers the material to the client and thoroughly reviews all aspects of the plan's administration, including premium billing and accounting, claim procedures, and benefits. For smaller groups, the installation may be made by the agent alone.

Proper installation is most important to the future success of the group plan and to the relationship among the insurance company, client, and broker or agent.

SERVICE AND CONSERVATION OF BUSINESS

The group or service representative makes periodic service calls on the policyholder to assist in the proper administration of the plan. It is customary to use a check-off type form as a guide in making a thorough review of all administrative practices and to check on the status of various aspects of the case. This form generally is then used as a service report to the home office of the insurer.

Persuading the policyholder (and often the broker) to expect and accept rate increases is an important part of the service function. The conservation problems caused by group health insurance rate increases are best met by frequent service, resulting in proper education of, and close contact with, the client.

Good service contributes greatly to increased policyholder satisfaction and lessens future conservation problems. Poorly serviced plans are prime targets for sales efforts by other insurance companies and brokers. One very important advantage for the group representative who gives regular and efficient service is the opportunity to sell expanded or additional group coverages to the client. Good service also helps maintain good broker relationships.

OTHER SALES-RELATED ACTIVITIES

There are a number of activities performed by the sales function in addition to the actual sale of the product.

RECRUITING AND TRAINING

Many companies recruit recent college graduates for entry level sales positions while others prefer people who have had one or more years of general business or sales experience. Recruiting may be done by the home office or delegated to the field office group manager or regional manager.

Continuing training is essential for an insurer's sales force. Formal training may be done in different ways:

- The home office may run training programs periodically, either before or following on-the-job training in the field offices;
- The trainee may spend time in each of the home office group-related departments before assuming field sales responsibility; or
- The trainee may use self-study programs (such as HIAA).

On-the-job training may precede or follow the formal training and is often supplemented by various educational programs available from industry organizations. Under all types of training programs, the subjects generally emphasized are:

- company organization and objectives,
- prospecting, sales and interview techniques,
- description of the insurer's products,
- benefit plan design and financial arrangements,
- explanation of the insurer's underwriting rules,
- proposal preparation and presentation,
- rate calculations,
- enrollment and installation of new plan,
- administration and claim payments, and
- policyholder service and renewal responsibilities.

Continual training is necessary to keep pace with both technical advancements and the changing selling environment.

STRENGTHENING AGENCY RELATIONS

Most companies offer a variety of programs aimed at increasing agent technical knowledge and selling skills while building their confidence in the company's products and services.

To meet these objectives, the home office may conduct formal conferences and seminars, release regular and special bulletins, and develop promotional items and articles for the insurer's in-house publications.

In the field the group representative may promote sales through periodic presentations at agency meetings, the release of promotional and informational bulletins, and one-on-one promotion and training efforts with selected agents.

BROADENING SALES THROUGH BROKERS AND CONSULTANTS

Group representatives develop and maintain relationships with broker and employee benefit consultants to persuade them that their clients will be well-served by the insurer's products and services. Insurers encourage group representatives to call on these producers regularly to present ideas, to attract new business, and to conserve existing accounts. The home office may assist the group field salespeople by making available information about changes in products, underwriting, statutory requirements, and other matters that affect the group business.

ADVERTISING AND SALES PROMOTION

Advertising and sales materials promote a good corporate image and inform buyers, brokers, and employee benefit plan consultants of the insurer's products, services, and benefits.

The group sales department collaborates with the marketing, advertising, and public relations or communications areas to develop general and specific advertising copy. The advertising department prepares copy, layouts, and media recommendations; the sales department specifies objectives and contributes sales content.

The group marketing and/or sales department usually creates and develops sales promotion material and point-of-sale literature. (Other times this may be the responsibility of a product development unit.) These items include pre-approach letters, mailers, folders, sales brochures, and other materials designed to inform and motivate prospects during an interview. When prospects, such as trade or professional associations, are solicited by mail, special sales kits are designed to explain the plan details and enrollment procedure.

In addition, attractive sales aids enhance the ability of the group representative and producer to present and explain the insurer's products and services and to motivate the prospect to buy. Such aids include brochures describing available products or services, listings of prestigious cases, flipcharts, and proposals—as well as training material, such as do-it-yourself sales kits, interview guides, competitive analyses, and compensation plans.

SERVICING LARGE CASES

Some insurers have field or home office specialists with direct responsibility for service who assist the group representative on large or unusual cases. Also, for certain national or prestigious groups, insurers may use home office group account executives in the field either to assist the "group rep" in sales and service activities or to represent the insurer directly to the client.

REWARDING SUCCESSFUL PRODUCERS

Most insurers use some program of personal recognition and financial reward to stimulate the sale of their group product line by their group representatives, full-time agents, and brokers. Personal recognition programs include sales achievement awards, awards for meeting sales quotas, sales contests for group representatives, agents, or brokers, and allowing group sales to count toward agent qualification for an insurer's sales club. Financial reward programs for group representatives may include a sales bonus (above base salary) for production that exceeds established goals. Indirect financial rewards, such as insurer-paid trip to a sales meeting or conference, also may serve as an incentive for group representatives, agents, or brokers.

CONDUCTING CONFERENCES AND SEMINARS

Most group sales departments conduct an annual or biannual sales conference for all group field sales representatives. These meetings, which usually last three or four days, ordinarily include:

- an analysis of past and current sales results,
- a discussion of future expectations, developments, and trends in group insurance,
- introduction of new products,
- technical training,
- marketing presentations,
- problem-solving forums, and
- presentation of sales honors and awards.

Home office group insurance officers, certain other key insurance company officers, selected home office technical group personnel, and representatives of general agents and agents' groups are generally present at these sales conferences.

Also, selected group sales department personnel usually attend and participate in the insurance company's conference for general agents or agency managers and the leading insurance salespersons.

PERSISTENCY

Persistency of group life and health insurance refers to the extent to which insured groups continue their coverage with the same insurer. Simply stated, an insurer enjoys good persistency when its policyholders continue coverage in force over a sustained period.

Good persistency is essential to a successful group insurance operation. Except for benefit payments, the costs of acquiring and issuing new group contracts are among an insurer's largest items of expense. Usually initial acquisition expenses are not charged entirely against the group contract in its first year; instead, they are amortized or charged off over several years. An insurer, therefore, must keep new contracts in force over a long enough period of time both to recover the initial expenses and to profit from underwriting the business.

REASONS FOR PERSISTENCY PROBLEMS

Certain characteristics of the group insurance contract underlie the general problem of persistency. Although a contract continues, the insurer usually reviews it periodically with the right to change premium rates after a designated time. Furthermore, the contract generally may be terminated by the policyholder on any monthly premium due date by notifying the insurer. As a result, each rate increase produces a potential problem in conserving business, since the policyholder must be convinced that the increase is justified and that it is in the best interest of the group to continue the contract with the current insurer. In a period of rising medical care costs "selling" of the rate increase becomes an increasingly difficult and important marketing challenge.

Because of the importance of a high rate of persistency in achieving satisfactory financial results, every group insurer is concerned about the reasons why groups terminate, the factors that affect persistency, and the methods of developing more quality business. In general, most groups transfer their coverage to another insurer for one or more of the following reasons:

- lower cost for the same or better coverage,
- availability of improved benefits or new coverages,
- policyholder dissatisfaction with service or administration,
- consolidation of several coverages of the policyholder with one insurer,
- business reorganization or merger, or
- loss of control by the salesperson (agent, broker, or group representative).

Therefore, attaining good persistency involves the continued and effective use of various techniques designed to reduce or eliminate these conditions. Techniques include a careful initial selection of prospects, the manner in which the salesperson makes the initial sale, sound underwriting practices, and effective service and conservation methods.

IMPORTANCE OF POLICYHOLDER SERVICE

Good policyholder relations contribute to conserving business. Conservation is accomplished by constant service and attention to policyholders and is the result of good teamwork by the home office, the general agent or agency manager, the agent or broker, and the personnel in group sales and claim offices. It begins when the initial sale is made and continues throughout the entire life of a group case.

A good installation by the group representative is of prime importance in providing effective policyholder service. Satisfactory operation of the group plan depends in part on the policyholder's personnel having a sound understanding of the coverage, the claim payment process, and the general administration methods. A thorough installation helps to eliminate policyholder dissatisfaction arising out of misunderstanding of administrative and claim procedures.

Throughout each policy year the insurer's group representative and service personnel are on call at any time by the policyholder. This means not only visiting the policyholder to solve problems when so requested but also being able to anticipate such requests by reviewing copies of important home office correspondence that usually come from administrative or claim personnel. Most often, administrative and claim personnel are the first to be aware of any problems or dissatisfaction of the policyholder, and they are invaluable in alerting the group representative.

In addition to being on call, the group representative or service representative also schedules visits to the policyholder or broker. The frequency of visits depends upon the size of the group, its accessibility, and the requests of persons administering the employee benefit plan. These periodic service calls are made for many purposes, such as:

- to determine the effectiveness of the plan administrator in administering the plan,
- to discuss the adequacy and cost effectiveness of present benefits, benefit trends, and suggested plan changes,
- to prepare the policyholder for the annual rerating and to obtain the data needed by the underwriters to complete the annual underwriting review, and
- to present the rerating action.

Also, the service calls may be used to diagnose claim or administrative problems, to build permanent relationships while stressing the benefits and services relating to the plan, and to keep the policyholder or broker informed of changes in laws and practices that may affect the plan.

Most service calls involving routine administrative matters, claim procedures, and the collection of data required by the underwriters may be made by the group representative or the policyholder's administrative personnel. Calls that concern new or revised benefits, dividends, and rate increases usually are made by the group representative with the agent, broker, or consultant. In such instances contact within the policyholder is made with a person in a decision-making capacity.

IMPORTANCE OF THE RERATING SALES CALL

Unquestionably the most important service call made by the group representative and the agent or broker together is the "sale" of the renewal premium rates. Many conservation techniques may be found in the effective selling of higher premium rates, some of which are as follows:

- The group representative informs the policyholder and agent or broker of any possible rerating action to be taken by the insurance company well in advance of the actual group policy date. The final action will be more readily accepted if good, early groundwork has been undertaken. It is not conducive to persistency if a policyholder is informed of a premium increase very close to the rate change date.

- A general knowledge of the methods used in pricing group health insurance benefits is important to the policyholder's understanding of the insurer's rerating action with respect to adjusting present rates. The group representative emphasizes the effects of those items that cause uncontrollable cost increases, such as increased ages of the insureds, changes in salaries and wages, and the rising cost of medical care and treatment. Benefit changes or changes in insurance amounts also affect cost.

  On plans where the group's own experience significantly affects premiums, the group representative reviews claims, reserve requirements, and other pertinent factors. On plans where the group's own experience has little or no effect on rates or other renewal actions, such as for a smaller group pooled arrangement, the group representative knows that experience data often can confuse the issue and gears the discussion to general trends in medical care costs, disability incidence, or mortality.

- At least once a year, regardless of any pricing actions, the group representative and agent or broker review the benefit structure with the policyholder relative to adequacy, local conditions, competition, and the current economic situation. If a bargaining agreement is pending, the insurer's representatives often can suggest benefit changes and offer to obtain cost estimates of alternative benefit designs. If such an agreement is already in existence, with a considerable time to run, they can advise the policyholder on cost controls and other details in the administration of benefits.

- The value of a permanent relationship is stressed with particular emphasis on the benefits and services being provided. The payment of dividends or retroactive rate credits also cements relationships and provides an excellent opportunity to make recommended plan changes.

- In the development of a rerating

presentation the group representative analyzes all pertinent reports, correspondence, and figures, including employee census data taken during the policy year, current data, service call reports, claims incurred by individual claimants, current year and accumulative experience summaries. Where problems exist or might arise, the group representative recommends corrective measures, such as plan changes, elimination of "first-dollar" benefits, increased deductibles or coinsurance, or inclusion of needed contractual limitations.

- If consideration is being given to transferring the group to another insurer, the group representative emphasizes the potential shortcomings of such action with the policyholder. For example, the high cost of acquisition must be incurred again; rarely, if ever, does the policyholder get exactly the same coverage. Also, some employees may lose benefits in the transfer due to changes in benefit limits and new plan provisions.

SUMMARY

The marketing of a group insurance product or product line involves a number of insurer personnel with diverse, but interrelated, responsibilities. Knowing the market and its needs, developing appropriate products, and maintaining sound business relationships are key elements of an insurer's marketing strategy.

KEY TERMS

Ad Hoc Committee
Agent
Broker
Commission
Commission Schedule
Compensation
Competitive Factor
Conservation
Consumer
Direct Writers
Employee Benefit Consultant
Group Representative
Installation
Market Analysis
Market Category
Marketing
Needs Evaluation
Net Cost Illustration
Override
Persistency
Plan Specifications
Policyholder Service
Producer
Product Development
Product Development Statement
Product Research
Proposal
Prospecting
Rerating Sales Call
Research and Development (R&D)
Sales
Sales Promotion Material
Sales Representative
Servicing
Vesting

V

Basic Underwriting

INTRODUCTION

In general, the term "underwriting" identifies that process by which an insurer determines if it will accept an application for insurance. In individual insurance, medical factors customarily determine whether each applicant is accepted or declined. Insurers underwrite group insurance, however, on a different premise—that any large group of individuals will have only a few persons who, because of severe and frequent medical problems, are either substandard or noninsurable risks. Except in very small groups or where high amounts of group life insurance are involved, individual health conditions usually are not of concern to the group underwriter. What is important is a wide spread of risk—a high percentage of eligible employees and their dependents participating in the plan. This spread creates a good chance that persons in the group are generally healthy.

THE GROUP UNDERWRITER'S JOB

The group insurance underwriter selects risks whose characteristics, plan design, and supporting data will meet the standards established by the insurer. Other functions include:

- identifying exceptions to standard underwriting rules,
- analyzing past experience,

- projecting claims,
- determining administrative costs,
- underwriting new and existing groups, and
- reviewing policy revisions and evidence of insurability applications and modifying where appropriate.

Groups have many similarities, but the group underwriter is concerned mainly with analysis of the characteristics that distinguish a particular group. The underwriter determines if a group falls within the parameters set by the insurer for acceptable groups. Problem characteristics of a group often are not immediately obvious, but show up as potential problems as the underwriter examines the prospective group.

This selection process includes a number of steps:

- analyzing each group's underwriting characteristics—type of group, industry, size, eligible lives, participation, and financial considerations,
- evaluating the characteristics of the group, such as sex, age, occupation, geographic location, income, employee turnover, administrative facilities, and employee contributions,
- determining that the contract applied for can be legally issued in the jurisdiction where it will be written,
- ascertaining that the prospective plan can be administered satisfactorily by both the policyholder and the insurer,
- determining the credibility of past claims experience or health history for a small group policyholder, and
- establishing premium rates that can be expected to produce a reasonable contribution to surplus or profit.

Special underwriting situations arise. For example, a group underwriter, asked to duplicate a benefit plan that a large group has with another insurer, may find that the plan does not conform to the requirements of the underwriter's insurance company. Because of the highly competitive nature of the group insurance business, insurers allow considerable flexibility in designing and underwriting prospective plans, particularly to duplicate existing benefits. Also, the underwriter often suggests alternative benefits, provisions, or methods of funding as a solution to a problem in underwriting a particular group. If an analysis of outpatient claims shows an abnormally high incidence of questionable claims in a group, the underwriter might suggest contractual limitations on this coverage to avoid unnecessary utilization of benefits.

When rating a plan, an insurer's basic rate manual provides for general statistical variations (sex, age, and earnings) of a group's employees. For larger risks, insurers typically use an experience rating formula to adjust their manual rates for prior claims experience. On very large accounts, insurers give full credibility to actual claims experience. Additionally, certain types of industries produce losses so materially in excess of those anticipated by the manual rates that insurers set up for them substandard or unacceptable risk classes and will not accept them under standard rating procedures.

In summary, the group insurance underwriter's primary functions are to examine the characteristics of the group's plan, weigh the variables, and then determine if a plan is acceptable as submitted or as modified to conform to the insurer's standards. If the group is not acceptable and no modifications seem to exist that will make the plan reasonably compatible with the insurer's standards, the insurer declines the group. If the group is acceptable, the underwriter determines the cost of the plan of benefits to be written and the services to be provided, including the methods for funding claims, reserves, and administrative expenses.

CHARACTERISTICS OF ACCEPTABLE GROUPS

Previous chapters presented the various types of groups: single employers, labor unions, trade and professional associations, multiple-employer groups, and creditor groups. The following information, although discussing the underwriting considerations applicable to single-employer groups, also applies to the other types of groups.

What constitutes an acceptable group is determined by the underwriting standards of the insurer and the statutory definition of group insurance, if any, in the state, province, or territory in which the group is located. Generally, acceptability depends on the following characteristics:

- permanency,
- reasonableness of the benefits,
- adequacy of the enrollment,
- centralized administration facilities,
- substantial employer contribution,
- automatic collection of employee contributions (if any),
- no obvious adverse selection, and
- satisfactory credit.

PERMANENCY

Permanent cohesive groups are characterized by a strong, mutual, continuing interest in more matters than insurance. The proposed policyholder must be legally authorized to fulfill its contractual obligations and to act for the group on a continuing basis.

Insurance available to a group should be a natural outgrowth of the relationship of the members of the group to one another, through employment, association membership, and the like; the insurance benefits resulting from this relationship should be incidental. Otherwise, the group will attract a disproportion of poor risks, will not be held together as a cohesive unit, and will be inefficiently administered. Also, the healthy employees will lose their enthusiasm for enrolling or continuing in the group, resulting in deterioration of the group itself.

Seasonal businesses, subject to

long layoffs, shutdowns, or high labor turnover, and firms organized to perform but one or two contracts and then dissolved, often contain unsatisfactory underwriting elements. The elements include marginal levels of benefits, minimal policyholder contributions, low participation and the need for costly resolicitations, high administrative expenses, large numbers of unskilled workers, poor policyholder-employee relations, malingering, and duplication of coverage.

REASONABLENESS OF THE BENEFITS

Reasonable benefits are adequate, but not disproportionate, to the insurance needs of a group. Group life insurance amounts should relate to earnings. Group medical care expense benefits should be written with limits appropriate for avoiding overutilization or abuse and with deductibles and coinsurance features to help contain costs.

ADEQUACY OF THE ENROLLMENT

The relationship of the policyholder to the persons eligible for insurance must provide a ready means of obtaining and maintaining a substantial enrollment. At least 75 percent of the employees eligible must enroll, for example, if the plan is contributory. To stay within predicted claim levels and attain desired profitability and persistency, a consistently high level of enrollment with a steady flow of newly hired or eligible persons into the group is necessary. Otherwise, as the average age of the group gradually increases, the average cost of the insurance also will increase.

CENTRALIZED ADMINISTRATIVE FACILITIES

A group plan requires a single, centrally-located administrator, able and willing to assume specific responsibilities—enrollment of newly hired and eligible employees, collection of contributions, remittance of premiums, keeping of records, and assistance with claims.

SUBSTANTIAL EMPLOYER CONTRIBUTION

When an employee's portion of the cost of group coverage is low compared with other benefit plans and is not subject to wide fluctuations, participation is encouraged. The employer usually pays a significant portion of the premium and absorbs cost fluctuations without substantial increases in the employees' contribution rates. In this way the cost to employees is kept low and the benefit plan is more attractive. As the cost of providing a quality health care program continues to spiral, however, employers are beginning to have their employees pay a higher percentage of the total premium.

AUTOMATIC COLLECTION OF EMPLOYEE CONTRIBUTIONS

Under a contributory plan where the employer and employees share the cost, the insured employees' contributions usually are collected by payroll deduction. The contribution thus becomes simple and routine.

POSSIBLE ADVERSE SELECTION

Some elements in the makeup of the group as a whole, such as poor health of several employees or late entrants to the plan, can result in selection against the plan, sometimes called adverse selection. This selection can produce loss experience not anticipated in the rates.

Therefore, eligibility requirements and benefits are formulated on the basis of uniform conditions pertaining to employment. This process precludes individual selection of amounts or benefits and inordinate concentration of risk in a few classes or a few individuals.

SATISFACTORY CREDIT

Employers maintain a good credit standing by meeting premium payments and other funding requirements as they become due.

SOURCES OF UNDERWRITING INFORMATION

For the analysis of the acceptability of a risk, the underwriter has a variety of information sources, discussed below.

THE REQUEST FOR PROPOSAL

Besides identifying the applicant, the Request for Proposal and accompanying forms provide underwriting information, including employee data and claim history. For example, they give the number of employees eligible, which is useful for determining if there is adequate participation in the plan. Also, identifying excluded classes helps to determine if there is adverse selection against the plan.

The Request for Proposal also usually provides prior insurance history, which helps the underwriter determine the stability of the risk. High first-year expense in the sale and issue of a group case compels the insurer to look for groups that can be expected to remain insured for a number of years. A Request for Proposal that shows the group has changed insurers several times in recent years indicates a lack of stability, which may result in early termination of the group plan.

ENROLLMENT CARDS

These cards usually provide underwriting information as to age, sex, earnings, dependent status, and occupation.

INSPECTION REPORTS

On smaller groups (less than 50 lives), a few insurers use commercial investigating companies that supply underwriting information about the applicant. Representatives of these investigating organizations visit the employer's business, report on any adverse working conditions, and help verify the eligibility information supplied by the employer in the Request for Proposal.

FEDERAL DISCLOSURE INFORMATION

Employers with 100 or more insured employees are required under ERISA to distribute annual plan experience reports to their employees and file similar information with the U.S. Department of Labor. Underwriters often secure copies of these reports to verify experience information supplied by the applicant.

AGENT OR BROKER INFORMATION

For new groups, insurers usually require the agent or broker to get information from the policyholder about past experience, benefits, and rates. This detailed information is given to the group representative or home office of the insurer.

GROUP REPRESENTATIVES

The sale of a group plan often involves the visiting of the employer's premises by the insurer's group representative to discuss the plan of benefits. The group representative can, therefore, present the underwriter with first-hand information for an objective analysis of several aspects pertaining to the employer and the employees.

UNDERWRITING NEW BUSINESS

SELECTION FACTORS FOR SINGLE-EMPLOYER GROUPS

When evaluating a new group (often a case transferred from another insurer), the underwriter assimilates and considers all relevant information, particularly the following selection factors:

- size of the group,
- industry,
- composition of the group,
- location of the group,
- plan of insurance,
- cost sharing,
- policyholder's administrative facilities,
- previous coverage and experience, including changes in benefits or rates during the rating period,
- commission arrangements,
- expected persistency, and
- ability to meet financial obligations (particularly true on larger accounts).

SIZE OF THE GROUP

The larger the number of individuals insured, the more accurately the level of claims can be predicted. In a comprehensive medical care plan a large group will by itself produce year-to-year a credible claim experience pattern.

A principal concern, however, in underwriting larger groups is the availability and accuracy of prior experience patterns for establishing initial premium rates. A small group with a 10 to 20 percent increase in claim experience from that anticipated in the rates would have no significant effect on the insurer's overall operation, since results could be averaged out by another small group with a similar percentage decrease in claims. The same deviation, though, in a very large group could produce a loss to the insurer running into hundreds of thousands of dollars—a significant amount for even the largest of insurers.

To safeguard against such deviations, most insurers will not underwrite a very large group at manual rates. Instead, they will require prior experience and establish premium rates adjusted for prior experience deviations. Of course, if actual claim experience shows that the initial rates were too high, they can be adjusted by the experience refund formula and prospective rate reductions.

Groups under 50 lives have different underwriting problems. Many insurers issue policies to groups with as few as two employees. Because expenses in small groups are high in relation to the premium charged, insurers usually limit available benefit variations to keep administrative costs down. Additionally, because of the limited spread of risk in each small group, claim experience generally fluctuates widely. These claim loss fluctuations lead most insurers to pool the experience of their small groups. The total premiums and total claims for such groups are combined into categories, with all groups in each category treated as a single risk for rating purposes.

A specific hazard in underwriting small groups is the possibility that key persons in a small firm might purchase or substantially increase group insurance benefits because they or a family member have a physical impairment that will result in an immediate or substantial claim. This, together with the normal claims of the entre group, would place the insurer in a precarious loss position if it did not apply more restrictive underwriting requirements to small groups than those used for large groups.

Most insurers attempt to control hazards inherent in small groups by using special underwriting rules, such as:

- limiting the benefits available to standard plans,
- applying preexisting condition limitations or exclusions which restrict coverage during some period, usually one year, for a condition treated immediately prior to coverage being effective, or
- requiring medical evidence of insurability of the individual employees (and perhaps their dependents) for very small groups (for example, less than ten persons).

INDUSTRY

Since group life insurance covers death resulting from occupational hazards, many insurers include industry-related life rate adjustments, both increases and decreases, in their rate manuals. These adjustments reflect anticipated mortality differences because of insuring specific industries or occupations. Health insurance, on the other hand, generally provides benefits on a non-occupational basis, because the occupational hazard usually is covered by workers' compensation laws.

Persons employed in certain industries, however, may develop health problems that are not considered occupational in origin. Group plans usually cover these secondary health conditions that result from the physical environment in which the employees work. Employees working in a very hot area (foundry, for example) are more susceptible to respiratory ailments than those working in normal temperatures and may have unusually high claims for these conditions. Too, sedentary (sitting) occupations can result in back problems that are not directly attributable to the job itself.

Other businesses, such as restaurants and parking garages, present a different underwriting problem. A substantial number of employees receive low pay and need little or no training. Individuals who cannot meet the health standards of more selective employers might be forced to find employment in these marginal occupations, and their physical conditions would result in a much higher-than-anticipated health claim loss ratio. For these reasons, certain industries are either not acceptable for health insurance or are classified as substandard and written at higher rates.

COMPOSITION OF THE GROUP

Certain variables in the characteristics of employees can affect the claim experience of a group. These variables, discussed below, usually are compensated for by specific adjustment factors in the rate structure.

CLASSES OF EMPLOYEES

Generally, an underwriter desires to cover all full-time employees who are actively at work, since a large spread of risk can reduce selection against the insurer and lower the expense rate per insured employee. Part-time, seasonal, and temporary employees often are not covered or are covered in a way different from full-time employees. Their occupations may show frequent turnover, and administrative expense may be high. Hourly-paid employees also are sometimes excluded because many of them are insured for benefits under a separate collective bargaining agreement. Exclusion of the hourly workers generally does not create an underwriting problem, provided the remaining eligible employee group is sufficiently large to meet the insurer's minimum requirements.

However, the underwriter will be cautious if the policyholder elects to exclude all employees except executive and key personnel. Duplicate coverage or selection against the insurer is a possibility in this situation, since the insurer may find itself covering mainly a specific health condition of one of the executives or a member of the executive's family.

AGE DISTRIBUTION

Most insurance companies have an automatic adjustment for age in their rate structure. Older individuals have a higher mortality rate and larger disability income and medical care claims than younger employees. Even though this adjustment factor automatically will modify rates, the age distribution will be analyzed for deviations from norms. For example, an older group would have not only much higher mortality and morbidity rates, but also might indicate, because of few young entrants into the group, financial difficulties of the employer's business. If a group is losing its younger members continuously, initial rates, based on the ages of the original members of the group, soon will become inadequate. Also, a younger group possibly could indicate high turnover, which would entail high administrative costs.

SEX DISTRIBUTION

Life insurance rates reflect the fact that women live longer than men; health insurance rates (except for accidental death and dismemberment insurance) show that women generally have a higher incidence of health claims than men. A survey conducted by the U.S. Department of Health and Human Services over a period of years has shown that female employees have 25 percent more disabilities than male employees. Women are more likely to have frequent, short-duration disabilities during their younger years, with the frequency decreasing, but duration increasing, as they reach the 40- to 50-year-old range.

DEPENDENT DISTRIBUTION

Where there is a high percentage of married women in a group, the percentage of employees carrying dependent coverage may be well below the 75 percent enrollment participation required, because their husbands have coverage with their own employers. However, when a spouse has an existing health condition, the employee usually elects duplicate coverage because of the high probability of a claim. The underwriter is then faced with the possibility of selection against the insurer if only a few employees choose to insure their spouses.

Certainly, employees whose dependents have existing significant medical impairments will elect coverage even if it represents duplication of benefits. Where there is low dependent participation, insurers may make inquiries into the dependent status of all employees, both men and women, to determine what other coverage is in effect. The risk generally will then be accepted if there is adequate enrollment participation—that is, 75 percent of those with dependents who do not have other coverage.

Traditional dependent distributions have also changed because of the increase in the number of single-parent households and fewer children in most families.

EARNING DISTRIBUTION

The earnings of employees in a group may affect the underwriting of the risk in several ways. Individuals with higher-than-average incomes generally seek more frequent and higher-priced medical care. This results in higher utilization of medical care services and expenditure of more claim dollars available under the program. A group consisting primarily of low-income employees may have significant underwriting implications, such as an undesirable type of work or working conditions or a substandard risk because of work location. These situations might lead to difficulty in obtaining and maintaining the proper participation required under the plan if it is written on a contributory basis.

LOCATION OF THE GROUP

Life insurance mortality rates for groups that are otherwise acceptable are not significantly affected by geographic location, but medical and dental morbidity vary materially by geographic area. On the average, hospitals in the Southeast United States charge less than those in the Northeast. Since rate manuals adjust for these differences by use of area factors, geographic location is not a problem in rating.

The underwriter also must consider the location of the group in relation to the insurer's service facilities. Many employers insist on local insurer representation to assist in day-to-day problems. Solicitation, installation of the group, and handling policyholder questions make it desirable for the insurer to have service facilities within a reasonable distance of the policyholder, especially when the agent or broker expects local support. The underwriter may, therefore, be reluctant to accept a group that has a substantial number of employees at a location where the insurance company has no service facility.

PLAN OF INSURANCE

The basic elements of a plan of insurance are eligibility and benefit structure. Eligibility for insurance determines who will be insured; the benefit structure determines the coverage that will be provided.

ELIGIBILITY

Employee eligibility for group insurance is based on conditions pertaining to employment. If only certain classes of employees are to be insured, eligibility cannot be determined by age, race, or sex, since these are not conditions of employment.

In addition to the insured employee or member, the group insurance plan usually will cover dependents for medical care benefits. Dependents usually are the spouse of the employee and the unmarried children under 19 years of age. Many policies provide coverage for children who are beyond age 19 if they are unmarried full-time students, usually with a maximum age limit between age 23 and age 26. Many insurers continue medical care coverage of handicapped children beyond the normal termination age if they are incapable of self-support.

A probationary (waiting) period, usually one to three months, may be included in the plan. This period, the length of time an employee must be employed before becoming eligible for insurance, is included in the program to eliminate the cost of maintaining records for employees whose employment may terminate quickly. The probationary period must be long enough to cover the usual period of time when quick turnover may occur, but not so long as to prevent a continuing flow of new entrants into the group.

BENEFIT STRUCTURE

Although insurance company underwriting rules usually establish standards for minimum and maximum benefit structures, the underwriter takes special note of any prospective plan in which the benefits are either minimal or overly liberal.

Minimal benefits can be indicative of policyholder financial problems. Also, if a program is inadequate, many employees will secure additional coverage by purchasing individual policies and thus present a problem of overinsurance. This overinsurance problem cannot be prevented in most instances because the Coordination of Benefits (COB) provision in most group plans does not coordinate benefits with individual policies.

An overly liberal program, on the other hand, can indicate selection against the insurer, especially for a smaller risk where the choice of such a plan may be prompted by the need to provide broad benefits for an existing disability of a key employee. In addition, a liberal plan that requires heavy employee contributions may lose continued employee participation because of its high cost.

COST SHARING

As already explained, premium payment may be contributory with the insureds paying some or all of the cost, or noncontributory with the employer paying all of the premium.

Contributory plans have a variety of combinations:

- Employees pay a specific percentage of the cost for their own and their dependents' coverages;
- The employer pays the employees' cost and the individual contributes all or part of the cost of dependent coverage; or
- The employee pays the entire cost of benefits (fully contributory).

From an underwriting viewpoint the noncontributory plan is preferable. First, it assures full participation in the program and simplifies administration by eliminating the requirement that late entrants submit evidence of insurability. Second, insurance companies sometimes require that certain groups be written on a noncontributory basis as a condition of issuing the policy. In very small groups (for example, fewer than ten lives), noncontribution by employees may be required to assure participation. Third, if the policyholder's employees are distributed at a number of locations, the noncontributory approach may help simplify administration where local facilities are not adequate.

The underwriting rules of most insurance companies prohibit fully contributory health insurance programs except in certain special circumstances and only in locations where they are legally permitted. There are reasons for this:

- Requiring full contribution could indicate a lack of employer interest in the program resulting in poor administration and lack of cooperation with the insurer;
- The full cost of an adequate medical care expense insurance program may be more than the average employee can afford;

- Requiring employees to pay the total premium will cause a lack of initial participation; or
- Problems may occur in resolicitation and maintaining participation because a required rate increase will be passed on entirely to the employees.

Because of these negative factors, insurers offer fully-contributory plans only as an opportunity for the insureds to purchase additional benefits to meet their needs under special circumstances, such as:

- long-term care insurance,
- benefits with low cost such as voluntary accidental death and dismemberment insurance, and
- supplemental group life insurance where the rate is extremely attractive to the group.

Even in these circumstances, however, insurers have some minimum participation requirements.

POLICYHOLDER'S ADMINISTRATIVE FACILITIES

Responsibility for administering the group life and health program lies with an employee or staff of people employed by the group policyholder. Administrative responsibilities may consist of:

- preparing premium statements,
- processing enrollments and terminations,
- issuing certificates of insurance,
- certifying eligibility for coverage when there is a claim, and
- processing claims for medical care benefits in some cases.

If an employer has several locations, an administrator of the group plan at each location is responsible, at least, for the enrolling of new employees and the reporting of terminations and additions.

Most group plans cover employees automatically if they join the plan within 31 days of their eligible date. Without proper policyholder administration, employee additions may not be made on time and, as a result, new employees would be required to furnish evidence of insurability because they were enrolled as late entrants. In addition, terminations may not be properly recorded, and premium billings would have to be adjusting continually for debits and credits because of poor reporting by the policyholder. Also, not enrolling newly hired and usually healthy employees results in selection against the plan and consequently higher loss ratios (claims to premiums).

PREVIOUS COVERAGE AND EXPERIENCE

It is not unusual for employers to transfer their benefit plans from one insurer to another. In some cases the transfer is for administrative reasons—poor service, unsatisfactory claims handling, or difficult administration— but most transfers are because of cost, especially when the present insurer requires an increase in rates. An insurer asked to quote on a group being transferred from another insurer reviews rating, claims history, the prior benefit structure, and the history of changes in insurers.

The review of the rating basis evaluates the risk and establishes proper premium rates. For larger groups rate review is important because past claims experience indicates future results. On the other hand, with small groups—those under 100 lives—claims experience may be high, and the insurer's underwriting policy may be to ignore the prior claims experience entirely.

If a small group case has large individual losses, the underwriter usually will examine individual claims. This examination determines the nature of the claims: Are they for accidents that probably will not recur or do they indicate a chronic condition that automatically will present a continuing claim under the risk, causing high loss ratios? (Occasionally, these same concepts apply to prior group life insurance experience, but usually not with the same significance as for health insurance.)

In groups whose rates are based on their own prior experience, insurers may require special underwriting consideration for the larger individual claims. For example, if a dependent had a very large major medical claim and subsequently died, the underwriter may eliminate a substantial part of that particular loss in evaluating the acceptance of the risk, considering it nonrepetitive. On the other hand, if the dependent is still insured and the condition is chronic, the underwriter may assume that the claim for this particular condition will continue, and will not eliminate part of it.

In addition, when evaluating a group's past claims experience, insurers desire information by line of coverage for the past three years. In this case the competing insurer determines what its renewal rating would be if it had the same claims experience on the same plan of benefits. For larger risks, insurers use a formula similar to their renewal formula in determining the rates to be charged, based on the group's prior experience.

Finally, the new insurer carefully reviews the benefit structure of the previous group plan, since it may reveal areas of possible abuse that might have led to unfavorable loss ratios. In such cases, the insurer would take corrective action by suggesting benefit modifications.

PREVIOUS GROUP INSURANCE PLAN

To do a complete underwriting analysis, the underwriter secures as much information as possible about the previous group insurance plan. As a general rule, the underwriter prefers the contract, but a copy of the employee booklet or certificate of insurance usually will suffice. There are a number of reasons why an insurer needs information about the present plan of benefits.

First, the underwriter uses it to determine if there are any provisions in the previous plan that are not essentially the same as, or equal to, the insurer's standard contract. This enables the underwriter to be certain the policyholder understands that the new insurer's group contract might contain different provisions for some coverages. Also, if the group is large enough to warrant special plan design, the insurer can consider the inclusion of broader benefits in the rate-making process—after the underwriter has determined that the insurer can handle these benefits from both an administrative and claims standpoint.

Second, the underwriter is concerned with the effect on existing claims if the policy is transferred. If the group is located in a state that has adopted some form of group insurance replacement (no loss-no gain) regulation, the new insurer may have to assume substantial existing liabilities. These regulations, stipulating that no employee shall suffer a benefit loss in the event of a policy transfer, typically (1) limit the use of requirements that the employee be actively at work and dependents not be hospitalized, and (2) prohibit preexisting condition limitation clauses for individuals insured under the employer's prior group plans as the basis for denying or reducing a claim that is otherwise payable under the policy. In these cases the individual must be guaranteed the old policy's benefit, unless the new policy would have paid less, even if it did not have the preexisting condition limitation. The no loss-no gain terminology is misleading, since benefits can be lost if the new policy limits or excludes the condition regardless of when it occurs. If the underwriter is requested (or compelled by statute or regulation) to cover preexisting conditions, the insurer may then ask the employer about known conditions, larger claims, and employees who are not actively at work, to assess this aspect of the risk.

Even if not legally required, the employer may ask the insurer to pick up existing health conditions and to waive policy requirements limiting preexisting conditions on the initial group. In these cases, to eliminate possible duplicate coverage, the underwriter must review the present policy to determine what benefits the policy provides on termination of the contract—for example, the continuation of coverage for some period of time in the event of existing total disability.

Third, the underwriter wants to identify any benefit provisions in the present plan that could have caused the problems that motivated the policyholder to change insurers. If any are found, the underwriter can require certain plan changes for acceptance of the risk.

PRIOR CLAIM EXPERIENCE

The new insurer uses the group's past claim experience, one of the most important considerations in analyzing a transferring risk, to determine the acceptance or declination of the group and often to establish the premium rates to be charged. Although reliable past claim loss experience is not always available, an underwriter would be unwise to ignore the possibility that the transfer is being sought because the group's present insurer has or is about to raise rates as a result of an unsatisfactory claims record. Also, renewal action of the present insurer may have involved plan changes, such as increased deductibles or additional contract limitations, that attempted to solve specific claim problems. The new insurer analyzes these suggested revisions to determine if they are needed in its contract.

On smaller groups (generally fewer than 100 employees), experience information has only partial credibility. An unusually high claim level may indicate the existence of a large claim for which the new insurer will be expected to pick up any continuing liability. On larger cases, as experience becomes more credible, if claims information cannot be obtained from the policyholder, most underwriters either will refuse to quote rates on the group or will include in their quotation a substantial safety factor to guard against unrevealed situations. Whether or not prior claims experience may be considered reliable depends on many factors, four of which are:

- Is the length of time covered by the statistical data sufficiently long to reduce chance fluctuations and reflect a true loss trend?

- Is the unfavorable experience the result of many claims of minor severity (to which the underwriter usually gives heavy credibility) or is it the result of only a few claims of major proportion that are not likely to recur, and which might be discounted in the rating process?

- Is the group so large (such as 1,000 lives depending on the coverage) so that its loss experience is statistically fully credible, or is it so small (such as 10 lives) that its past losses may reflect chance fluctuations and are not fully statistically credible?

- Is more than one year of experience available in order to determine if the most recent year's experience is typical, abnormally high, or abnormally low?

Obviously, there are no exact answers to the problems that arise in establishing the credibility of claims experience. Each underwriter makes decisions based on his/her own degree of experience and the insurer's standards for writing quality business at adequate rates.

PREMIUM RATES TO BE CHARGED

An insurer carefully determines the rates to use for a transferred group. It may include all risks of a certain size, (for example, under 50 lives) in a general rating pool. The underwriter may not be permitted to adjust rates to reflect prior experience for these risks, but only to decline or accept them at current manual rates. If a rate adjustment can be made, the underwriter usually develops initial rates using the same approach he/she would use in developing renewal rates; or, after developing rates for the present plan, suggests revisions in plan benefits at better rates.

No answer to these questions exactly fits all situations. Underwriters examine each alternative solution together with other factors, including the insurer's underwriting philosophy.

POSSIBLE ADMINISTRATIVE PROBLEMS

As the last general underwriting consideration in transferred business, the underwriter determines if the policyholder has or expects special administrative handling. When transferring a risk, a policyholder usually expects that both its administrative work and the services of the new insurer will be comparable to those of the former insurer. The policyholder may expect the new insurer to continue using the special enrollment and administrative procedures of the former administrator. For example, the new insurer may be asked to use all existing records and beneficiary designations where appropriate. The policyholder also may expect to make greater use of the insurer's administrative facilities than the insurer is prepared to provide.

Additionally, if the policyholder has various locations throughout the country, the new insurer must determine whether special administrative facilities have been established.

- Are separate billings required for each location?

- Will the new insurer be expected to maintain separate records at each of the policyholder's locations and have local service offices deal directly with these locations?

- In handling claims, will the new insurer be expected to provide local claim service for each of the branch locations, or will the branches process all claims through the policyholder's home office?

- Will billing procedures cause a problem?

- If the policyholder presently gets a list billing that names each employee and shows each employee's amount of coverage and premium, will it accept self-billing, which requires the policyholder to keep all records and report only totals each month?

The underwriting of transferred business requires more extensive and detailed consideration than does the underwriting of new risks because of the need to analyze the past experience. To perform the essential analysis properly, group representatives and underwriters must work closely together and have sufficient time prior to the contemplated date of transfer to examine all pertinent data.

COMMISSION ARRANGEMENTS

Many insurance companies use a level commission scale on both transferred business and new business, thus spreading the usual high first-year commission over a period of time. The underwriter may make the level scale compulsory as a condition for accepting the risk—particularly in situations where there is some uncertainty about the rates and the underwriter wants to add some additional cost margins to the plan. The level scale helps keep the policyholder's first-year cost low.

EXPECTED PERSISTENCY

There are substantial costs, usually referred to as acquisition expenses, incurred by an insurer when underwriting a new group. Such costs include field sales, new business underwriting costs, and case issue expenses. The underwriter looks for some assurance that, barring special circumstances, the new business will remain "on the books" for a reasonable period (certainly not less than three years) so that these expenses can be recovered in the renewal rates. Toward this end the underwriter tries to avoid businesses that:

- may be temporary in nature, that is, established for a specific project,
- have a history of frequently changing insurers, or
- are in financial difficulties.

Any one of these conditions may cause the insurer to decline the business.

UNDERWRITING OTHER GROUPS

LABOR UNIONS

Today, insurers issue few policies directly to labor unions, as most unions have their benefits provided through collective bargaining under the provisions of the Taft-Hartley Act. Most plans issued directly to a union are issued on a member-pay-all basis. The union plan, therefore, presents the underwriter with the participation problems inherent in all fully contributory plans—keeping the plan of benefits and its cost at a level that encourages and maintains initial and continuing high participation (75 percent of the eligible group).

When the plan is noncontributory (the union paying the entire premium), the underwriter expects that the union has the financial ability to maintain the necessary dues, that membership in the union is compulsory, and that the union does not exist principally to create a collective group for providing insurance benefits. If membership in the union is not compulsory, and even though the plan seems to have 100 percent participation, the participating union members may be principally the impaired risks, with the better risks having chosen not to join the union.

Eligibility Requirements. Most employer-employee contracts stipulate, as a condition for insurance eligibility, that the employee be actively at work on a full-time basis. In many union groups, however, being a member in good standing in the local is often the sole test of a member's eligibility. Being a member in good standing often may not require that the individual be actively at work, full-time or otherwise. In fact, if the members of a union are in an industry subject to strikes or seasonal or cyclical fluctuations, many members may experience long periods of inactivity but continue to pay dues. In such cases, many individuals may have other employment during the strike or cyclical period, and thus present a problem of coverage duplication.

Besides the fact that unions prefer to obtain their benefits through collective bargaining, many insurance companies do not offer coverage on labor unions because of the difficulty of evaluating the factors that complicate the underwriting.

MULTIPLE-EMPLOYER GROUPS

Negotiated Trusteeships (Taft-Hartley Groups). In underwriting negotiated trusteeships, the underwriter analyzes a number of factors:

1. *Size.* Of concern to the group underwriter is the number of employees in the group, the size of the employer units, and the number of employer units participating in the program. The larger the eligible group and the greater the participation by employer units, the more attractive is the risk to the underwriter, because a wider spread of risks tends to minimize adverse selection that could result from very small employer units where people may join the union and participate in the program to secure benefits. Ordinarily, the problem of participation does not arise from negotiated trusteeships since benefits usually are provided on a noncontributory basis, with all eligible employees insured.

2. *Provisions of the Trust.* The underwriter must review a signed copy of the trust agreement to ensure that the contract is issued to the proper entity. Items such as the eligibility rules, provisions regarding trustees, description of benefits, and provision for audits are all outlined in the trust. This information is of consequence in determining the desirability of the risk.

Most trust agreements follow a fairly standard pattern. The trust is created for the benefit of the employees under the terms of a collective bargaining agreement. The agreement typically requires that the employer pay a certain amount into the trust fund, usually for each hour of covered employment of the union member. The underwriter usually reviews any sections of the collective bargaining agreement that pertain to the insurance matters under consideration.

3. *Funding.* The scale of benefits provided for the members and their families depends on the success of union negotiators in the wage bargaining session. The underwriter may be asked to determine what benefits can be purchased by a fund of a given size. Conversely, an underwriter who reviews a risk where the contribution level already is fixed is concerned with whether or not the contributions are sufficient to purchase the benefits desired.

Because the funds available for the purchase of benefits are predetermined by the collective bargaining agreement, the insurer often is asked to guarantee rates for the entire term of the agreement. Accordingly, the underwriter usually includes additional margins in the rates to cover anticipated inflationary increases in medical care costs as well as the additional risk inherent in a long-term guarantee.

When negotiated trusteeships are set up, the underwriter may participate in the preliminary discussions concerning the plan provisions. When plan changes are under consideration, the underwriter also participates, making suggestions on how to stabilize and improve the program to provide optimum use of the funds available.

4. *Characteristics of the Group.* Many of the factors the underwriter consid-

ers when evaluating the negotiated trusteeship are the same as those applicable to single-employer groups. Certain factors, however, are unique to negotiated trusteeships. These are discussed below.

a. *Eligibility*

Three general methods are used to establish eligibility rules for employees in Taft-Hartley Welfare Fund plans.

- One method of establishing eligibility rules requires that the employee work a given number of days, weeks, or months with a particular employer before becoming insured. This method, comparable to the eligibility provisions in single employer groups, is appropriate where employment is fairly stable, not cyclical or seasonal, and where there is little shifting of employees among employers.

- Other methods, particularly applicable to industries that do not meet the test of employment stability, are based on the accumulation of credited hours of employment. One of these methods determines eligibility by considering the credited hours of work during a previous period (called an accumulation period). For example, a person who has worked 300 hours in the previous calendar quarter could be eligible for benefits for the next calendar quarter.

- Another method, called a reserve bank arrangement, requires all hours worked by an individual to be credited to the member "hour bank." An employee who accumulates a minimum number of hours becomes eligible for benefits. Then, for each month in which the individual is provided coverage, a specific number of hours is withdrawn from the bank. When there are no longer enough hours in the bank to provide for the next month's coverage, the insurance terminates.

The second and third methods are appropriate for industries such as the building trades where employees often work for different employers on different days. Under these unstable employment circumstances, having sufficient reserves in the trust fund to cover the cyclical nature of the employment is an important underwriting consideration. Purchasing lower benefits than the anticipated employee contributions would produce is one way to accomplish this goal. Another method is requiring employees to work for a specific period of time that does not count toward their hour bank to determine the effective date of insurance. Put another way, an underwriter might set a waiting period of up to six months for any person not previously eligible in order to build reserve funds. This initial waiting period facilitates both accumulation of employee data and funds for administrative expenses.

The underwriter evaluates eligibility from many standpoints:

- Who is eligible? Of prime concern is the possible inclusion of individuals under the trust who are not likely to have regular, continued employment.

- Will the eligibility rules and the contribution formula produce adequate funds for the cost of insurance? Here the main concern is the question of the anticipated average number of hours worked by individuals who will be eligible, and allowing flexibility for seasonal or recessional effects.

- What is the length of the accumulation period? This question directly relates to the stability of employment. If there is high turnover or transfers among employers, then a longer accumulation period is desirable to help assure adequacy of funds.

- How are credits earned during periods of disability? Here the underwriter's concern is making provision for continuing coverage for a reasonable period if the employee is disabled and unable to accumulate work credits.

- Are waiver of premium disability claims reported promptly?

- How complex are administrative procedures? Are the eligibility requirements so complex that the detailed recordkeeping required is either difficult or costly to handle?

- Are there self-pay provisions? Self-pay provisions enable an individual to remain insured should coverage terminate due to insufficient credits or hours. A short self-pay provision might be desirable, whereas a self-pay provision of a long duration (a year or more) may allow individuals to select against the plan.

An employee working under permit presents a unique problem. The employee comes either from another geographic area to work in a locale where the current labor need is greater, or may be a new local member working under permit before becoming a permanent union member in good standing. The underwriter determines what agreement exists for such employees in the neighboring areas for two reasons: to provide coverage for those entering the local employment market, and to provide for suspension of coverage for those workers who temporarily are employed elsewhere. This type of labor mobility is most common in the building trades industry.

b. *Administrative Facilities*

A most important underwriting evaluation in a negotiated trusteeship is the analysis of the existing or planned administrative facilities. Premium payment and claim certification are made on the basis of employer reports and the accuracy of the employer-employee data recorded in the fund office. Usually, each employer participating in the fund sends in monthly reports of the work done by employees who are covered under the bargaining agreement. This report, which lists the employee's name, social security number, and the total hours worked during the month, is the basis for determining the particular employer's contribution to the fund.

The fund office performs the following administrative functions:

- receives and keeps the employer's reports,
- maintains the employee data, such as date of birth, beneficiary, etc.,
- keeps records on each employee with respect to eligibility under the plan,
- certifies the eligibility of claimants to the insurance company,
- determines the eligibility of employees for benefits and submits monthly premium statements and statistics to the insurance company,
- keeps claim control records on each claimant,
- issues certificates of insurance for new employees becoming eligible, and
- prepares statistical summaries periodically for the insurance company for the purpose of determining rate adjustments.

The underwriter often calls upon experienced technical specialists within the insurer's group insurance administration department to assess the administrative facilities of the fund and other relevant factors.

TRADE ASSOCIATIONS

In establishing trade association plans, the insurer often sets a minimum employer participation (for example, at least 50 percent of the eligible employer-members of the association and no less than 100 employees) before it will accept the risk without other special underwriting requirements. Sometimes the statute of the state sets minimum requirements as to the number of lives required and the average number of lives per employer unit. When an insurer approves a group on a guaranteed issue basis, the underwriter wants to be certain that employers who are only indirectly involved with the industry and have "associate" or "honorary" membership in it are not admitted to the plan. When minimum participation levels are not required, insurers often include strict preexisting condition clauses in the plan for all participating members. They even require that individual employees submit medical evidence of insurability when an employer unit is below a certain size (such as fewer than ten employees).

As with negotiated trusteeships, the underwriter also is concerned that the trade association program administrator has sufficient staff and experience for a strong, central plan administration.

If the program of the trade association is to be marketed over broad geographic areas, plan design also may create special problems. For example, medical care cost levels vary throughout the country. To avoid adverse selection for a single plan designed for all employers in the trade association, the underwriter includes different area rates that reflect the different cost levels in the plan. The use of a single plan and a single rate would result in overutilization of the plan by those employers in the higher-cost-level areas; those in low-cost areas would tend not to participate in the plan at all.

MULTIPLE-EMPLOYER TRUSTS (METs)

A number of state laws specify that group life insurance and group health insurance can be provided only to groups of ten or more employees. Multiple-employer trusts or association group plans, therefore, are the only way in which many small employers can purchase group insurance. Most states will waive the size requirement if the master contract applies to a group of more than ten insureds (in total) in the multiple-employer trust or association group.

These trusts provide association group coverage to single employers who usually are not members of an association. In effect, the sponsor of a MET (agent, broker, or insurer) creates an association for the express purpose of bringing together a number of small employers who wish to purchase group insurance coverage with some of the same advantages offered to large employers. The MET sponsor designs the plan, establishes the underwriting rules for participating employers, administers the plan, and is responsible for the adequate financing and reserving of the MET. A legal trust holds the master contract and is the entity that handles all financial transactions.

In addition to all the other underwriting factors mentioned, a principal concern for any association or multiple-employer trust plan is one of selection against the plan itself. Employers that are large enough to have their own employer-employee group insurance plan, and who anticipate lower expected claim costs because of their group's favorable characteristics, often contract for a plan of their own directly with an insurer. These employers expect to obtain a more favorable cost and desire to design their own benefit plan. Conversely, employers with less favorable characteristics that may be faced with a rate increase from their current health insurers frequently discontinue their direct group programs to join an association or MET plan. To avoid this situation, the underwriter carefully ascertains that well-defined underwriting standards exist for such groups.

FRANCHISED DEALERS

Although employers in the same industry can join or form a multiple-employer trust, they sometimes secure insurance coverage as franchised dealers. These dealers (hamburger chains and independent gasoline stations, for example) operate under a franchise from a manufacturer or supplier to merchandise the manufacturer's product.

In underwriting this type of risk, two principal factors are considered. The underwriter first determines whether the group insurance statute of a particular state is sufficiently broad in its definition of employees to include the individuals applying for insurance. Many states do permit the writing of group insurance of affiliated corporations that are under common control through contract. Second, the insurance underwriter ascertains that, where policyholders extend benefits to their franchised dealers, the eligibility requirements for participation do not create selection against the insurance program. Eligibility for the group insurance plan generally is based upon the sales volume of the franchised dealer.

PROFESSIONAL ASSOCIATIONS

These are some important factors evaluated in underwriting a professional association group, such as a state medical society.

■ How strong is the reason for belonging to the association other than for potential insurance benefits? If most eligible professionals are not association members, a greater possibility of selection against the insurance program will exist.

■ How strongly will the association endorse the proposed group insurance plan? A strong backing will result in better participation.

■ How good are the experience, market knowledge, and administrative facilities of the agent-administrator? The experience, knowledge, and administrative facilities of the producer generally are considered the most important ingredients in the success of this type of plan.

■ What are the contents of the association by-laws and constitution related to providing insurance benefits for members? Does the association have the authority to undertake such a program?

■ What are the legal impediments to issuing a group insurance policy or individual policies? Does the state in which the association is located permit such coverage? If the association has members in more than one state, do the laws of the states other than the one in which the association is domiciled permit such coverage on its residents under a group contract issued in the domiciled state?

■ What expenses will be incurred in soliciting and administering this type of program? Participation in these plans is often low and the cost of mass-mailing expensive. The underwriter will be certain, therefore, that premium rates have sufficient margin to handle this expense factor.

SOLICITATION

The expense involved and geographic problems make it difficult for an agent to personally enroll the full membership of an association in a group program. Instead, agents generally use a mail solicitation containing full details of the program. The underwriter, especially concerned with the contents of the solicitation material, usually reviews it thoroughly before printing.

The producer often conducts the mail campaign and bears the expenses involved. Unlike employer-employee contributory group insurance plans, which have a high percentage of participants, an insurance solicitation from members of a professional association usually results in only 5 to 20 percent of the members joining. Several reasons may account for this low participation:

- Members of the association often are eligible for similar benefits under other programs;
- Since the member pays the full premium cost of the plan, which may be higher than other alternatives (such as purchasing benefits through plans of other associations), participation is discouraged; or
- People tend to ignore mailing pieces and throw away promotional material.

Usually there is an initial solicitation period, sometimes called the "charter enrollment," which ranges from 60 to 90 days. In order to maintain participation, annual resolicitations are common. The resolicitation is normally the same as the original charter enrollment, with the possible exception that members who have previously been declined are not resolicited.

POTENTIAL FOR ADVERSE SELECTION

Because of low participation in professional association programs, the potential is high for selection against insurance companies. Usually, therefore, insurers require each applicant, as part of enrollment, to submit satisfactory evidence of insurability. A health questionnaire concerning applicants and dependents accomplishes this purpose. The application then is either accepted or declined on the basis of the answers to these questions or on supplemental information the insurer obtains, such as attending physicians' statements. Insurers seldom use medical examinations because they are difficult to arrange, especially when mailings are national in scope. If a member is declined, the insurer returns the premium remitted with the application.

As an additional protection against adverse selection, professional association programs usually limit eligibility to actively employed members. This provision, however, is less effective than with single-employer groups. Often, difficulty exists in defining active employment in certain professions in a way that can be disproved if the validity of a submitted claim is questionable.

The policy often limits or excludes coverage for a time period, usually six months to two years, during which no benefits are payable for preexisting conditions. This permits the underwriter to be somewhat more liberal in accepting the risk, as well as providing additional protection for the insurer against misrepresentation of existing physical conditions.

SPECIAL POLICIES

Some state laws do not permit the issuance of group insurance to professional associations. In these instances professional association members are insured using specially developed individual policies (usually called franchise or wholesale policies). A central administration point is retained to assure persistency. Standards for enrollment, participation, age limits, eligibility, and plan benefits generally are similar to, but not the same as, those used for issuing a regular group policy.

PUBLIC EMPLOYERS

An insurer can issue a group policy to a public employer under the usual employer-employee form of coverage. To insure employees of a municipality, county, or state government, the underwriter determines if governing statutes:

- permit the public employer to contract for group insurance,
- permit the employer to make payroll deductions for the employee's share of the premium cost, and
- appropriate public funds to cover the employer's share of the cost.

Generally, the writing of plans for public employers depends on whether or not a state statute permits them. Also, the political subdivision involved should have its own enabling legislation that permits it to contract for group insurance.

The underwriter also looks into the question of the employer's contribution to the cost of benefits. In some cases there is little or no contribution by the political subdivision, resulting in low participation and adverse selection. There has been a trend in recent years, however, for political subdivisions to pick up more of the cost of benefits, eliminating some of this problem.

Persistency is also a problem in public employer plans. Changes in political party control and in the individuals making the decision regarding group insurance often result in a change of insurer. Likewise, local statutes may require that the plan be submitted periodically for bids, which increases the possibility of a change in insurers for a small difference in gross cost and with no recognition of net costs. The underwriter might require a rate adjustment to shorten the period over which acquisition expenses are amortized if the history of the group shows a number of changes in insurers.

All participants must meet the plan's eligibility requirements. Political patronage may cause appointment of individuals to job functions that require very little of their time. They might be employed full-time elsewhere or be incapable of true full-time employment because of an existing disability.

Also, the underwriter times renewal underwriting action with the budget approval date of the public employer to ensure the necessary funds.

CLUBS AND FRATERNAL ORGANIZATIONS

Except for a few insurers who specialize in writing such groups, most underwriters regard social and fraternal groups, in which membership is not related to occupation or employment, to be ineligible risks. Two reasons explain this decision. First, individuals may join the group primarily for purposes of securing the insurance. A potential participation problem exists in most clubs and fraternal organizations, both in securing participation and maintaining it, because most of their members already have similar programs available to them from their employers. Consequently, insurers usually offer only group life and accidental death and dismemberment insurance to these risks, subject to evidence of insurability.

MASS-MERCHANDISED INSURANCE

Group insurance gives people an opportunity to secure broad coverage at lower cost through the mass purchasing power of a group. One method of securing the advantage of reduced administrative cost inherent in mass purchasing is to offer the group program through organizations that already have billing systems for the collection of monies from their customers. The introduction of computerized billing systems in most large organizations has made it possible for them to act as the administrator of an association plan comparable to a professional association plan. In this category are organizations such as banks and gasoline companies who issue credit cards, retail store customer accounts, and public utilities.

However, because individuals who would be eligible for this type of insurance usually have group insurance benefits through their employer, coverages offered usually are limited to lower-cost specialty types, such as term life insurance, accidental death and dismemberment insurance, or hospital indemnity benefits providing a disability income benefit for each day of hospital confinement. The criteria for writing this type of program is the ability to collect the premium regularly (usually monthly) from the policyholder by adding it to an existing collection system.

Insurers offer term life insurance usually only with evidence of insurability. They usually offer health insurance, because of the low-cost limited benefits provided, relying on restrictive preexisting condition clauses.

SUMMARY

Risk selection is a vital and primary function of any insurer. The insurance underwriter, using various methods and informational sources, performs this essential task. The underwriting of group business, whether for single employers or other types of cohesive groups, requires investigative and analytical skills, careful attention to detail, and a thorough knowledge of the insurer's business philosophy.

KEY TERMS

Acceptable Group
Adverse Selection
Census Data
Contributory Plan
Coordination of Benefits (COB)
Credibility
Duplicate Coverage
Eligibility
Eligible Group
Evidence of Insurability
Experience
Insurer's Philosophy
Key Employees
Late Entrants
Loss Ratio
Mass-Merchandised Insurance
Medical Underwriting
Minimum Participation
No Loss-No Gain
Noncontributory Plan
Overinsurance
Participation
Permanency
Persistency
Plan Design
Preexisting Condition
Previous Coverage
Reasonable Benefits
Request for Proposal
Resolicitation
Risk
Secondary Health Condition
Single-Employer Group
Solicitation Period
Spread of Risk
Substandard Risk
Transferred Risk
Turnover
Underwriter
Underwriting
Uninsurable
Waiting Period
Workers' Compensation Insurance

VI

SPECIAL UNDERWRITING SITUATIONS

INTRODUCTION

In addition to basic risk selection, a group underwriter deals with the variables of an insured group. Specific coverages and plan changes require different approaches. In special situations, individual members of a group are underwritten. Insurers themselves sometimes reinsure with other insurance companies.

UNDERWRITING SPECIFIC COVERAGES

The basic benefit structure of life insurance, disability income, and medical care expense insurance offers almost unlimited variation and flexibility in group contract design. Although all group insurance programs generally have a similar framework, many differences exist, and often unique provisions are involved in the details of various group contracts, especially on larger groups. These variations arise because insurers commonly tailor a plan to a prospective policyholder's or a producer's specifications, provided the adjustments are within the limits of sound underwriting principles and the administrative and claim capabilities of the insurer. In addition, the underwriter often initiates benefit variations to meet a specific purpose.

In underwriting a specific type of coverage, the underwriter has three principal concerns that are applicable to all group coverages:

- adverse selection potential,
- benefit levels, usually with regard to maximum amounts, and

- appropriateness of certain benefits for a given group and any special benefit provisions needed because of the nature of the group.

For nonstandard types of coverage, however, the underwriter additionally must consider the more fundamental items of risk selection, such as:

- insurability for the form of coverage,

- the best interests of the employer, individuals to be insured, and the providers of the services involved, and

- the possible creation of administrative problems.

Also, the underwriter analyzes the nature and level of benefits to be provided in relation to the financial status of the group and to the economic conditions in the geographic area where the group is located. The type of benefit or benefit level appropriate for a high cost-of-living area or for a well-paid group of employees could result in an unsatisfactory underwriting situation for a dissimilar group. A reasonable benefit structure is important to keep the cost of the group plan attractive to the purchaser and to avoid overinsurance, which encourages uneconomical use of plan benefits.

The industry of a particular group also may affect the type of coverage and the level of benefits. For example, the industry of the prospective group policyholder frequently determines the inclusion or omission of accidental death and dismemberment coverage for occupational protection—24-hour coverage—or for non-occupational protection only.

MEDICAL CARE EXPENSE BENEFITS

Insurers underwrite these benefits—basic, major medical, dental, and vision care—in a number of ways.

BASIC BENEFITS

In establishing the level of benefits for basic medical care expense benefits, the underwriter's principal concern is adherence to the insurer's philosophy. Most insurers require the employee to assume some portion of the cost of medical care (deductibles, coinsurance) to discourage overutilization. Quite commonly, even those insurers that permit full or 100 percent benefit programs for their larger groups often insist on scheduled benefits in their program for smaller groups.

When hospital benefits are written as a basic benefit, policyholders usually have greater demand for full protection; therefore, insurers will provide service-type, semi-private room and board benefits. To provide full semi-private coverage, the underwriter must determine the level of hospital charges in the geographic area where the plan will operate. Various organizations, such as the American Hospital Association, publish statistical information by geographic cost for reference purposes. With regard to Managed Care Plans, the underwriter must understand the agreed-upon contractual arrangement with hospitals, and must know if those arrangements include Per Diem, DRGs, discount off charges, etc.

Occasionally, the underwriter encounters a group where the loss experience shows a high incidence of small claims. This situation indicates the overutilization of benefits and can result from many causes, including:

- a plan design that provides miscellaneous hospital charges for outpatient services within 24 to 72 hours of an accidental injury;
- the income level of the employees to be insured. Employees with high incomes may seek more frequent treatment; those with low incomes may utilize a general hospital facility instead of a personal physician; or
- the location of the employees to be insured. In rural areas physicians may provide general treatment through clinics that would qualify as hospitals under most group insurance contracts.

Where a high incidence of small claims exists, the underwriter may request inclusion of a deductible in the basic hospital benefit plan to reduce the overutilization of benefits. Another way of handling the problem is to take into account the overutilization in setting the group's rates.

Requests for service-type benefits are not limited to hospital expense benefits; insurers also write plans covering the full, usual, and customary charges for surgery and in-hospital physician's visits. The underwriter, when requested to provide these benefits, determines the utilization level that will be prevalent based on the employees' incomes and the local charges made by physicians, establishing a rate which incorporates these factors plus trends for future inflation and utilization.

MAJOR MEDICAL EXPENSE BENEFITS

The general underwriting considerations used for basic medical care expense insurance also apply to major medical coverage. However, major medical coverage is more sensitively tuned to geographic cost considerations because the coverage involves little use of limits on covered charges for specific types of services. The basic design differences in major medical plans, whether supplemental or comprehensive, are the standard use of deductible amounts, coinsurance provisions, lack of internally designed amounts, and a single larger overall maximum benefit. These variables differ according to the desires of the policyholder, although the choices available usually are more limited for smaller groups.

Major medical plans broadly define what constitutes a covered medical expense and a high benefit maximum—causing the underwriter to be concerned with the effect that an extensive, existing health condition can have on the experience of a plan. It is impractical in most situations to try to analyze the individual health conditions of all employees and dependents. An underwriter is likely, therefore, to apply a preexisting condition limitation where permitted by state law and where the size of the group does not produce sufficient large premiums to spread the risk of existing conditions. A prospective group that is a limited portion of a larger group, such as officers or supervisory employees, could produce greater than normal adverse selection, especially if major medical coverage is being considered. The underwriter in this situation takes a more conservative approach in reviewing the group and might decline to write the limited portion of employees unless there is minimum number of lives to provide a spread of risk.

Rapidly rising medical care costs have resulted in increasing policyholder interest in cost containment. Policyholders are finding full (100 percent) benefit programs too expensive unless employees make significant contributions to the cost of coverage for themselves and their dependents. More policyholders are revising plans to introduce increasing deductibles and coinsurance so that their employees pay a share of their medical care bills. Increased emphasis on plan design to encourage second surgical opinions, outpatient diagnostic testing, outpatient surgery, wellness, and precertification of hospital confinements are all desired features of today's medical care expense plans.

Contracting with providers helps reduce the cost of each service. Medical management and utilization review help control the use of services. These features are part of most Managed Care plans.

DENTAL EXPENSE BENEFITS

Whether written alone or integrated with a major medical comprehensive plan, dental coverage requires special underwriting considerations for several reasons:

- Dental treatment offers broader options than medical care and treatment, allowing the patient to choose in such areas as fixed versus removable bridgework or gold versus non-gold inlays. Alternative ways of handling a specific condition are also available and offer a broad range in cost;
- The range of charges by dentists has a much larger spread than charges for medical care and treatment by medical doctors;
- Many dental charges can be deferred, giving the insured person the opportunity to select against the plan's provisions; and
- Many dental expenses, such as capping or some orthodontic treatment, are partially or wholly cosmetic, and thus are elective in nature.

Because dental insurance is not as widespread as medical care expense insurance, a particular group may not have prior experience on which to base rates. When an employer introduces a new dental program, employees who have been lax in proper dental maintenance often have accumulated, and seek correction of, major problems. This possible extraordinarily high utilization of the plan in its early years concerns the underwriter. The situation may be even worse when a policyholder announces a new dental plan many months before the effective date and employees postpone all but emergency care until that date.

To help offset these factors, the underwriter might request that special limitations be put into a new program such as:

- a reduced annual maximum to limit the insurer's liability and simultaneously encourage less costly courses of treatment,
- a lower coinsurance percentage for those types of expenses that are either optional (such as gold mate-

rial) or that are not a part of normal annual maintenance costs,

- incentive coinsurance, which provides a lower coinsurance factor (such as 60 percent in the first year), with subsequent increasing percentages each year to encourage spreading of claims,

- an advance approval requirement, often called a pretreatment plan, whereby the employee is required to submit the proposed treatment and its cost for prior approval by the insurance company if anticipated costs exceed a certain amount, such as $200,

- the inclusion of a provision basing the benefit on the least costly alternative treatment as determined by the insurer, based on a review of the pretreatment plan,

- a longer eligibility period before the employee can be insured for dental benefits, or

- a limited benefit for late entrants.

Additionally, as stated above, a substantial period of employees' advance knowledge of the effective date of a dental plan encourages deferral of current needed dental care until the plan will cover them. This situation will require an additional premium to reflect the higher claim cost.

Special consideration also will be required when the business has employees who are in direct contact with the public. Risks involving salespersons, teachers, and those in the entertainment industry, for example, tend toward greater utilization of a dental care plan, especially in the elective areas, where cosmetic dental work results in higher dental expenses than normally might be anticipated.

VISION CARE EXPENSE BENEFITS

Because insurers generally provide most vision care benefits on a scheduled basis (paying a specific allowance for each expense), adding vision care coverage to a group plan currently in effect usually presents no major underwriting problems. To a limited degree, however, underwriters expect a higher utilization level by members in certain groups. Members of groups with a large number of employees in personal contact with the general public, such as salespersons or teachers, often are concerned with the aesthetic effects of their eyeglasses and might lean toward maximum utilization for replacement of frames.

SHORT-TERM DISABILITY INCOME INSURANCE

In underwriting this coverage the underwriter realizes that short-term disability income provides partial income replacement for a short period of time, for example, up to 52 weeks of an employee's total disability. The insurer's underwriting rules usually stipulate that under no circumstances will benefits exceed a specific percentage of salary, usually 66⅔ percent. Two-thirds of the insured's salary may seem to be a low percentage, but the percentage is applied to gross, not net, earnings. The benefit level actually provides the insured with more than two-thirds of take-home pay.

Insurers carefully control benefits in relation to earnings to prevent unjustified claims and increased cost of claims because of malingering. In keeping with this concept, underwriters establish group short-term income benefits on several common bases including earning schedules, occupational schedules, and maximum amounts of attainable income.

The group underwriting standards of each insurance company usually stipulate the maximum amount of weekly indemnity that a group plan can provide. Insurers base this amount on the number of employees, the premium produced, or the total volume of short-term income benefits in force on the effective date of the program. Often, insurers permit higher weekly maximum benefits for 13-week plans than for 52-week plans for a specific group, to reflect the potential for larger claims in the longer benefit period.

In analyzing the risk, the possibility of selection against the insurer is the primary underwriting concern, even though the actual plan of benefits falls within the insurer's standard rules. In this regard the underwriter asks the following questions:

- Does the number of employees tend to fluctuate?

- Are there any seasonal employees, or do working hours vary so that benefits might at some point reflect a continuation of income higher than the take-home pay if the individual continued to work the shorter hours?

Additionally, the underwriter checks on the distribution of insured salaries within the group. If the executives receive a substantially higher income than the majority of employees, the underwriter may recommend limiting the maximum benefit to a level that will produce a reasonable disability income only for the lower-salaried employees in order to produce a better spread of risk.

FEDERAL LEGISLATION AFFECTING BENEFITS

The federal income tax withholding and Federal Insurance Contribution Act (FICA) tax may affect short-term disability income benefits received by the employee depending on who pays the premium. Benefit plans paid for by the employer may be subject to federal income tax.

The employee may elect to have the insurer reduce the benefit payments received by withholding a portion of the benefit. The employee, though, must make this request in writing.

The voluntary income tax withholding is a requirement of Public Law 96-601, effective May 1, 1981. A second law, Public Law 97-123, effective January 1, 1982, requires insurers to withhold FICA tax on short-term disability plans that are paid for by the employer. If the employee pays for the plan, the benefits are excluded from FICA tax. The insurer is responsible for remitting the employee's share of the FICA tax to the federal government.

BENEFIT PERIOD

Most short-term disability income plans have a maximum benefit period of 26 weeks. Group contracts providing a benefit period in excess of 52 weeks involve different underwriting considerations that most insurers treat as a separate line of business—long-term disability income insurance. Because of the effect of Social Security disability benefits, which can provide a substantial income to an individual who has been disabled for five months, the underwriter of a short-term plan often uses an offset provision if more than 26 weeks is requested. This offset provision reduces the disability benefit by all or part of the amounts received from Social Security. Since Social Security's approval rates and policies may change from time to time, the underwriter needs to exercise caution in rate setting. It is difficult to anticipate what effect, if any, Social Security will have on plans offering between 26 and 52 weeks of coverage.

BENEFIT WAITING PERIOD

Insured group members often must wait before they are eligible for benefits. Although often not used for accident-caused disabilities, insurers apply a waiting period of at least three days, and usually seven days, to disabilities resulting from sickness since they occur more frequently or are likely to involve minor conditions. The incidence of accident varies with age. For example, the underwriter may decline to write a plan with first-day accident coverage on a group with a large number of older people, since the incidence of accidents increases as a person gets older.

AGE OF GROUP MEMBERS

Insurers adjust short-term disability rates according to the ages of persons insured. The underwriter, however, may require benefit restrictions for a group composed of an unusual number of older people, since they are higher risks for disability income coverage.

EMPLOYMENT CONDITIONS

Since short-term disability income insurance replaces part of lost income, the group underwriter's concern in setting the benefit level is that a particular risk presents both stable employment practices and predictable income. When all or part of the risk shows a degree of temporary or seasonal employment, or where employees are subject to unpredictable earning levels, the underwriter may have to either make adjustments in the plan or decline the risk entirely. For example, the income of commission salespersons may fluctuate materially. If insurers include these persons in the program and base their benefits on most recent income, adverse selection against the program might result. Not only would malingering be a problem, but insureds might defer even legitimate claims (for example, elective surgery for a hernia) until they are entitled to the maximum benefit during a period when sales income would be at its highest. In such situations insurers often use special definitions of earnings—for instance, basing the benefit on the prior year's earnings reported for federal tax purposes.

OCCUPATIONAL COVERAGE

Insurers ordinarily write short-term disability income insurance on a non-occupational basis since most groups provide occupational coverage through workers' compensation insurance. Employers do, however, occasionally request occupational coverage (frequently called 24-hour coverage). For a group not eligible for workers' compensation coverage, or for a group wanting disability income coverage, regardless of cause, which exceeds the maximum workers' compensation benefit, the group policy usually stipulates the regular benefit provided for all disabilities and indicates that it will be reduced by any workers' compensation payment. In such cases the underwriter gives special consideration to any employment hazard that might affect the experience under the plan. For example, except for clerical operations, insurers seldom provide accident coverage beginning the first day, because the plan would be subject to a large number of claims resulting from minor work-related accidents lasting only one or two days.

LONG-TERM DISABILITY INCOME INSURANCE

The underwriting of long-term income insurance is more involved and applies different yardsticks than short-term disability income insurance, principally because of the higher amount at risk, the relatively small premium, and low incidence of claims. It is extremely desirable that a group underwritten for long-term disability income benefits be expected to both remain in force for some time and have a stable operation.

The prospective group must be one whose eligible employees will experience very stable employment. Long eligibility waiting periods (up to one year) often are used to restrict coverage to the more permanent employees. In addition, these plans quite often limit eligibility only to certain classes of employees, excluding those (such as hourly paid employees) that do not have the stability desired.

Only the more desirable groups are insured, and employee eligibility is restricted to the more permanent (and presumably more healthy) employees.

BENEFIT LEVELS

The relation between benefit amounts and employee earnings is an extremely important underwriting consideration. This factor is especially significant in the long-term disability income area because of the extent of the insurer's risk and the possibility of overinsurance. For example, benefit durations of up to normal retirement for illness or injury and monthly indemnities of up to $3,000 are typical long-term disability provisions that indicate the substantial risk insured under this coverage.

Although insurers recognize the principle of conservative monthly indemnity benefits in relation to an individual's earnings, they differ significantly in the manner in which they implement this concept. Some insurers may require a relation between benefits and earnings as low as 50 percent, although 60 percent or 66⅔ percent are probably more typical. Insurers sometimes allow a higher relation but require application of a lower percentage to the higher amounts of monthly benefits. This procedure recognizes the fact that, as an individual's income increases, net take-home pay becomes a smaller proportion of gross earnings because of the effect of the graduated income tax. The insurance company's objective is to achieve a reasonable difference, such as 20 percent to 25 percent, between long-term disability income benefits and net earnings.

As part of this control, group policies usually provide that the disability income benefit otherwise payable will be reduced (offset) by any amounts received from other sources, such as Social Security Disability Insurance (SSDI). Since long-term disability income benefits are almost always written as 24-hour coverage, it is standard procedure to integrate them with any workers' compensation benefits that may be payable.

Insurers usually include a minimum monthly benefit, such as $50, which is not subject to the reduction by other insurance. This benefit guarantees that an employee who is paying for the insurance will not have all the benefits eliminated because of the above offsets. This type of provision is compulsory in some states.

FEDERAL LEGISLATION AFFECTING BENEFITS

Long-term disability income benefits received by the employee are affected by federal income tax withholding and FICA tax to the same extent as short-term disability benefits. Public Law 97-123, referred to in the prior discussion of short-term benefits, requires insurers to withhold FICA tax on long-term disability plans with a disability qualification period of less than six months. This stipulation specifically involves plans paid for by the employer. If the employee pays for the plans, the benefits are excluded from FICA tax. The insurer's responsibility is to remit the employee's share of the FICA tax to the federal government.

OTHER FACTORS

As with short-term disability income insurance, insurers avoid groups with many individuals in the age 50-and-over category, since benefits usually are payable to normal retirement and both the incidence and average length of disability is much greater in this age group. Similarly, insurers normally do not underwrite groups with low salaries, since not only will Social Security provide adequate disability income benefits but also the payment of low salaries indicates a less stable, and possibly an unhealthy, risk.

LIFE INSURANCE

Group life insurance does not present as many rating problems to the underwriter as does health insurance for the same group. Except for substantially large policyholders, past experience is usually no indication of future mortality statistics. In fact, the claims experience of any insurer would show that the majority of smaller groups have no death claims in any one year.

INDUSTRY ADJUSTMENTS

A group life insurance rate table allows some industry adjustments to reflect the better or poorer mortality experience of specific groups. For example, a higher rate might apply to police groups; a lower rate would apply to teacher groups. Underwriters are particularly concerned with severely hazardous occupational groups, such as students at a parachute jumping school, that may not be specifically listed in the rate table but for which special rates may have to be developed.

BENEFIT SCHEDULES

Insurers prefer schedules of benefits that provide amounts of insurance that are proportionate to earnings. Schedules that provide small amounts for the majority of employees while giving substantial coverage to a limited group (company officers, for example), often are unacceptable since they contain substantial elements of adverse selection and may have regulative ramifications. To control this possibility, insurers use a mathematical relationship to determine the maximum benefit to be issued on any one life without medical evidence of insurability.

The underwriting rules of a particular insurer might limit the maximum benefit on any one life to not more than two-and-one-half or three times the average amount of insurance in the plan or to 10 percent of the total volume in the group. For example, if the requested schedule of insurance on a group of 20 employees would produce a total volume of $200,000 ($10,000 average per employee), the following maximum benefits might be applicable:

- If the insurer's rule is two-and-one-half times the average, the maximum benefit would be $25,000;
- If the insurer's rule is three times the average, the maximum benefit would be $30,000; and
- If the insurer's rule is 10 percent of the total volume, the maximum benefit would be $20,000.

The insurer could provide amounts exceeding these limits if evidence of insurability for the applicant is acceptable.

The Tax Equity and Fiscal Responsibility Act of 1982 (TEFRA) impacts on life schedules by provisions designed to curb the writing of discriminatory group life plans. A group term life policy, to be nondiscriminatory, must not discriminate in favor of key employees for determining eligibility to participate, or in the type and amount of benefits available under the plan.

SUPERIMPOSED RISKS

Disability income and medical care expense coverages limit benefits if the employee has other coverage. The group life insurance contract, on the other hand, does not prohibit or restrict the employer from purchasing coverage from more than one insurer. However, "pyramiding" coverage—simultaneously purchasing a number of group life plans from different insurers—is a method a group could use to secure a large amount of coverage on an ill executive.

To protect against such occurrences, the insurance application contains questions regarding the existence of, or the concurrent application for, other coverages. The prudent underwriter further investigates groups with other life insurance plans already in force.

MINIMUM PARTICIPATION

The statutes of many states require that group life insurance plans have a minimum participation of 75 percent of the eligible employees so that, under usual circumstances, a sufficiently large number of healthy individuals participate. This 75 percent requirement is also a standard underwriting rule of most insurers for both group life and group health insurance. Occasionally, where permitted by law, insurers will reduce the 75 percent requirement to a lower figure, such as 60 percent, if the particular risk includes certain favorable factors. This reduction might be done for better risks, such as schoolteachers, or for supplemental life plans where the insurer already insures the employer for a basic noncontributory group life insurance plan.

Where initial enrollment is below these minimums, insurers normally offer coverage subject to evidence of insurability.

VOLUNTARY LIFE INSURANCE

Voluntary life, an optional coverage, is similar to regular group term life insurance, but it has a greater possibility of adverse selection for the following reasons:

- The individual usually has a choice of selecting from various amounts in increments of $10,000 up to a specific maximum, such as $100,000. Persons in the more hazardous occupations or those in poor health will select the larger amounts; and
- The participation requirements usually are lower than the 75 percent typically required in group insurance plans.

Because of the inherent adverse selection, insurers require each enrollee to complete a personal health statement, with coverage contingent on its approval. Also, most insurers of this coverage have reinsurance treaties to protect their business by spreading large amounts of coverage over several insurers.

ACCIDENTAL DEATH AND DISMEMBERMENT INSURANCE

Insurers must consider two principal factors in underwriting group accidental death and dismemberment insurance: the benefit amounts and occupational hazards. Under normal circumstances, the underwriter is not concerned with an AD&D plan that is part of a group life insurance program, since this type of program usually does not involve individual selection of amounts of insurance. However, voluntary and business forms of accidental death and dismemberment insurance do have possibilities for selection against the insurer and, therefore, require the underwriter's attention.

AMOUNTS OF INSURANCE

In the normal form of group accidental death and dismemberment insurance, the amount of benefit usually matches the group life insurance amount. An insurer may provide a benefit of two or three times the group life insurance amount and, in certain instances, a higher benefit for certain limited types of accidents, such as those occurring on a common conveyance—a bus, train, or airplane. In these circumstances, the group life insurance underwriting requirements often dictate the amount of accidental death and dismemberment insurance provided. However, in setting the maximum group life insurance amount, most insurers consider both the potential hazard of accidental death and the maximum accidental death benefit they are willing to offer. Also, group life coverage often may continue at reduced amounts for retirees, but insurers usually write group accidental death and dismemberment coverage on active employees only.

OCCUPATIONAL HAZARDS

Certain types of industries, such as high steel construction, present an additional occupational hazard. To cover these hazards, the insurer's rate manual usually contains special "industry" rates that are higher than those normally charged. Additionally, the manual includes certain types of occupations that will not be accepted for 24-hour accidental death and dismemberment coverage.

Risks, as presented to the group insurance underwriter, however, often are not clear-cut. Certain situations require underwriting judgment to determine the degree of occupational risk and the amount that the underwriter is willing to accept. Factors influencing this judgment include:

- The amount of common business travel. The underwriter would be concerned if the business of the policyholder requires a large number of employees to travel simultaneously on the same conveyance, thus presenting the high hazard of a major common disaster;
- The testing or handling of hazardous materials. The primary concern is the potential for a serious disaster resulting in multiple accidental deaths;
- The proportionate exposure, if a major portion of the employees in the group is involved in a hazardous occupation; and
- The proportion of older persons in the group exposed to the occupational hazards. Older persons, often having slower reflexes, are involved in substantially more accidents involving machinery and other mechanical equipment.

VOLUNTARY AD&D

As with basic accidental death and dismemberment (AD&D) insurance, this optional coverage offers a greater possibility of adverse selection for the following reasons:

- The insured usually has a choice in selecting the amount of insurance. The choices are high amounts, quite often in excess of $100,000. The ability to select can produce, in any group, very large claims when compared with the premium involved. Employees in the more hazardous occupations or who are more prone to accidents will select the larger amounts.

- There usually are lower participation requirements than the 75 percent required for the normal group insurance plan. Generally, since this plan covers accidents only, the effect of adverse selection resulting from poor prior medical conditions is not as significant. However, individuals who participate in these voluntary plans often have a higher incidence of claims.

BUSINESS TRIP AD&D

In underwriting this form of accidental death and dismemberment insurance the underwriter looks for excessive exposures, like substantially large amounts of travel, or types of risks that have large numbers of employees traveling together, such as company conventions or sports teams.

RENEWAL UNDERWRITING

Effective renewal underwriting is essential to ongoing satisfactory results. At each renewal the underwriter conducts a thorough review to make certain that the group renew on a basis satisfactory to the insurer. It is necessary both to determine if an existing group continues to fall within the parameters set by the insurer for acceptable groups and to establish a renewal rate level based on an accurate projection of anticipated claims and expenses.

The same factors that were significant in accepting a group initially are also important at each renewal. Major changes in the plan of benefits, employee characteristics, participation levels, methods of funding, and managed care arrangements are examples of changes that require close scrutiny by the underwriter. Changes in group size and employee mix resulting from the downsizing of a company, severe economic conditions, or the buying and selling of large operations also must be considered.

AMENDMENT UNDERWRITING

Underwriting of a group plan is a continuing process. After issue, a group policyholder may alter benefits and participant classes.

BENEFIT CHANGES

Changes in the benefits provided under a group plan occur frequently. These changes may or may not coincide with renewal rate action. When underwriters receive a request for a plan change, they usually review simultaneously the group's claim experience to determine if a rate change is required for the existing benefits and the cost of the requested plan change. In recent years, employers have increased their plan deductible and coinsurance substantially in an effort to stabilize plan costs and to reduce the amount of rate increase needed at renewal.

Also, plans undergo changes in benefits as legislation and/or regulation dictate.

NEW CLASS ADDITIONS

Policyholders often wish to extend coverage under the existing plan of benefits to a class of employees not previously eligible. Benefits might be extended to hourly paid employees previously covered by another insurer or to employees at another location or at a newly acquired subsidiary. If the new class or unit added represents only a small portion of the total group, the underwriter probably will include them automatically under the existing rate structure, assuming that the addition will not cause any significant change in the statistical composition of the group. However, should the additional employees constitute a substantial portion of the overall risk, the underwriter may wish to reexamine the following factors:

- *Administrative facilities:* If the unit is at a different location than the remainder of the group;
- *Sex, age, and salary content:* To determine how the overall risk would be changed;
- *Industry:* To make certain that no additional occupational hazards are being incorporated and that employee turnover is not excessive;
- *Geographic location:* To reconsider medical care costs, at least as they pertain to the additions;
- *Plan of insurance desired:* To develop new rates if it is not the same as the inforce plan; and
- *Previous coverage:* To examine if the unit previously was insured to determine the effect the unit would have on the overall case experience. (The underwriter uses the procedure described in the section in the prior chapter headed "Previous Coverage and Experience.")

UNDERWRITING OF INDIVIDUALS

There are situations in which the insurer will have to underwrite individuals in the group to determine if they are insurable and can be covered under the group program. This underwriting can involve statements of health, medical examinations, and attending physician statements—unlike most group insurance that does not require individuals to furnish evidence of insurability. Also, the rates in a group plan anticipate that a certain number of individuals will have existing medical conditions. Certain circumstances, however, might require medical evidence of insurability of individuals because they do not fall within the scope of this assumption.

LATE ENTRANTS: MEDICAL PLANS

In a contributory medical plan, employees who chose not to participate when first eligible may later decide to join because they expect to have a claim. To prevent this adverse selection, the insurer may require evidence of insurability for each employee and each dependent who is a late entrant, usually in the form of a statement of health. This statement gives information the insurer judges as necessary to underwrite the risk, including the medical history of the employee and dependents, and is the determining factor for the employee's inclusion or exclusion from the plan. In addition to completing the statement of health, insurers may require the late entrants to take a medical examination and to submit further details of prior treatment from their personal physicians, all at their own expense. These provisions also apply to employees who withdraw from the plan but remain employed, and subsequently request reinstatement of coverage. Insurers do not wish to require and review evidence of insurability on a large number of individuals within a group. Such a procedure:

- creates a poor image of the insurance company, especially if applicants are declined,
- leads to poor personnel relationships for the policyholder,
- increases administrative cost and handling of the case, and,
- to a certain extent, defeats the purpose of the group plan.

An insurer that it is underwriting a substantial number of late entrants from a particular policyholder may ask the policyholder to consider a different system, such as enrolling new employees automatically when hired.

LATE ENTRANTS: DENTAL PLANS

Underwriters encounter a special problem not found in medical care plans with late entrants in dental care plans. Dental care and treatment, often elective, can be deferred by the patient for a substantial period of time. The usual form of medical evidence of insurability is not appropriate for dental care plans, since dental conditions do not represent a "preexisting condition" in the usual medical-care sense. An applicant can easily answer "no" to a series of medical history questions and contract for substantial dental treatment shortly thereafter without having made a material misrepresentation.

Insurers use different methods to help protect against this type of selection. The dental plan may include a provision that limits benefits for some period, such as the first 12 months. Under that arrangement, the plan provides coverage during the period only for a checkup, cleaning, and x-rays, but still requires the employee to make a full contribution to the plan. The insurer also may establish special enrollment requirements whereby late entrants can come into the plan only at specific intervals after waiting a substantial period of time following application. Finally, the insurer may refuse to admit late entrants into the plan until after they actually visit a dentist for a general check-up and submit a treatment plan from the dentist outlining the dental work needed. In this case, the insurer may refuse coverage until all work is completed.

REINSTATEMENT OF MAJOR MEDICAL/ COMPREHENSIVE MAXIMUMS

Many major medical contracts have provisions for reinstating an employee's overall maximum benefit upon submission of evidence of insurability satisfactory to the insurance company. In these cases the individual completes a form comparable to the one used by late entrants. This information, together with the employee's prior claim file and medical examination if required, enables the underwriter to determine if the maximum benefit can be reinstated. Some plans also provide an automatic annual reinstatement of a portion of the maximum, such as $2,000 or $5,000, without evidence of insurability.

SMALL GROUPS

For small groups, the possibility of adverse selection by the employer against the insurer is high, particularly for groups under a certain size (usually ten employees). Most insurers hold that even the most restrictive of contractual provisions on preexisting conditions will not protect them against situations where an employer purchases a program to provide protection for a specific employee with a major physical disorder. In such a case, the insurance company may require a statement of health from the employee and each dependent and have this evidence of insurability reviewed by a person trained in medical underwriting. It may also request medical examinations and physician's statements.

The handling of a risk in which an individual is found to be uninsurable differs among insurers according to their underwriting philosophies and statutory limitations. Some insurers decline the entire group if even one of the employees is not insurable. However, some states mandate that when an insurer declines any employee or dependent who was insured by the previous insurer, that insurer must decline the entire group. Other insurers have the uninsurable individual waive coverage and then cover those in the group who are insurable. In those states requiring no loss of coverage when an insurer is changed, the insurer may not use this option.

EXCESS AMOUNTS

Insurers usually establish maximum liabilities for "guaranteed issue" benefits for certain types of coverage. These limits often are based on the size of the group insured, but sometimes are specific dollar amounts. For example, a group of 25 employees might have a group life guaranteed issue amount of $50,000 under a schedule of benefits that provides "one times salary." This would be the maximum nonmedical benefit for anyone making $50,000 or more a year.

To meet the needs of a buyer, an insurer will permit individuals in a group to become insured for higher amounts—that is, amounts in excess of guaranteed issue benefits—if they submit evidence of insurability. These requirements are most prevalent for group life and long-term disability income insurance. The degree of medical evidence required is related to the risk involved. Sometimes as little as a three-question health statement is used; at other times a full medical examination may be required.

RESOLICITATION

When a large number of employees within an eligible group are uninsured, the insurer may wish to resolicit all the employees to bring participation up to required underwriting standards. The insurer may be willing to waive the requirement for evidence of insurability provided a specific number or percentage of the eligible, but uninsured, employees enroll. Additionally, the insurer must review the plan to determine what caused the participation to drop, so that it can correct the situation. These resolicitations, often called "open enrollments," follow certain procedures:

- A short period of time, such as two weeks, is permitted for resoliciting the group, in order to exert pressure on the policyholder to complete the project; and

- An insurer requires a minimum number of additions during the enrollment period in order to waive the evidence of insurability requirement. Normally, this number is 50 percent of currently eligible, but uninsured, employees. The insurer requires more than 50 percent if it would take that much to bring the group up to the usual 75 percent minimum participation level.

REINSURANCE

Reinsurance is the method used by an insurer to reduce its liability by transferring part of the coverage for a policyholder or a block of business to another insurer. It allows an underwriter to assume more liability. Smaller insurers also use reinsurance to secure the assistance and advice of another insurer in underwriting a group and in setting rates. The insurance company issuing the policy to a group is called the ceding company; the insurer that agrees to accept a part of the risk is called the reinsurer.

In group insurance the two principal reinsurance methods used are quota share and excess risk.

QUOTA SHARE

Under this method, sometimes called coinsurance, the reinsurer assumes a certain percentage of the entire risk. The ceding company pays that percentage of the premium to the reinsurer, less some allowance for commissions, taxes, and other expenses. The reinsurer then pays the same percentage of the claims to the ceding company. If an experience refund is earned by the policyholder, the reinsurer reimburses the ceding company for its percentage of the refund.

EXCESS RISK

Under this method, the ceding company determines the maximum amount of insurance (called the retention limit) it wants to take on any one person, and reinsures all or most of the excess. Following are some examples of this method:

EXAMPLE A

A group life insurance plan insures all employees for one year's salary to a maximum of $100,000. If the ceding company's retention limit is $40,000, all insurance over $40,000 on any one employee is reinsured.

EXAMPLE B

An accidental death and dismemberment plan provides $25,000 of insurance on each employee. To protect itself against a single accident resulting in multiple deaths, the ceding company may purchase reinsurance to cover all claims that exceed a combined total of $100,000 if they result from the same accident.

EXAMPLE C

A long-term disability plan pays a benefit of $2,000 a month to age 65. The ceding company may purchase reinsurance that will pay 100 percent of any benefits payable after two years. In this case, the ceding company will pay the first $48,000 (24 months at $2,000 a month) and the reinsurance 100 percent of anything over this amount.

Reinsurance is a contract between two insurers; a group policyholder is not involved in the arrangement. Failure of the reinsurer to pay its portion of a claim does not relieve the ceding company of its obligation to pay the benefits under the policy as written.

SUMMARY

It is evident from this chapter that, in addition to basic risk selection, the underwriter handles many disparate situations unique to specific policies and policyholders. Group underwriting is an ongoing, detailed, and challenging process.

KEY TERMS

Amendment Underwriting
Benefit Levels
Ceding Company
Contributory Plan
Discriminatory
Eligibility Period
Eligible Employee
Employment Conditions
Enrollment
Exposure
FICA
Guaranteed Issue Amounts
Incidence of Claims
Insurability
Insurance Application
Key Employees
Malingering
Medical History
Nondiscriminatory
Open Enrollment
Overutilization
Public Law 97-123
Pyramiding
Reinsurance
Reinsurer
Renewal Underwriting
Retention Limit
TEFRA
Treatment Plan
Voluntary Coverages
Waiting Period

VII

Pricing

INTRODUCTION

Each group insurance coverage has a price, called a premium rate. That rate, multiplied by the number of people insured for a particular coverage (or by the volume of insurance in effect for coverages such as life, and accidental death and dismemberment insurance) produces premium for the coverage. The total premium to be paid by the group policyholder is simply a matter of totaling the premium for each coverage in effect. Premiums usually are paid monthly but may be paid less frequently, such as semi-annually or annually.

The insurer's actuaries establish the bases for determining premium rates. An actuary is an expert in the technical aspects of insurance, particularly skilled in mathematics and in the use of statistical data. Among the actuary's primary responsibilities are the development of manual premium rates and experience refund formulas.

THE OBJECTIVE OF PRICING

The insurer's pricing objective is to write business at profitable rates. To achieve this objective, the insurer seeks an appropriate balance in establishing the rates charged its policyholders. Therefore, group insurance premium rates take into account three elements: adequacy, competitiveness, and equity. These elements allow insurers to serve policyholders fairly and to avoid impaired financial results because of inadequate premium rates or impaired sales results because of higher than adequate premium rates.

Unwarranted optimism that charges policyholders inadequate rates will lead to financial losses; undue conservatism can encourage potentially profitable policyholders to seek insurance elsewhere and also can lead to adverse financial results. Thus knowledge, experience, and sound judgment are the basic ingredients to effectively manage the pricing of an insurer's group insurance portfolio.

ADEQUACY

To maintain a secure financial position, insurers develop premium rates that cover all costs of doing business, including anticipated claims and all administrative expenses. The premium rate also provides for possible higher than anticipated claims and for the insurer's surplus (profit) objective.

Adequacy of premium rates is fundamental to the success and solvency of any group insurance operation. Because of their concern with insurer solvency, some states require group insurance rate schedules for policies issued in their states to be filed with their insurance departments.

However, even without specific state laws, the insurer's desire to obtain satisfactory financial results is sufficient reason to charge rates that fulfill the objective of adequacy.

COMPETITIVENESS

Keen competition in the group insurance field makes it imperative that an insurer offer competitive products to acquire and retain policyholders. A prospective policyholder evaluates an insurer by quality of its products and services in relation to its prices. An insurer demonstrates quality of service in many ways, such as assistance and flexibility in plan design and administration, efficiency in claims handling, cost control activities, and communications with the policyholder's insured employees.

Therefore, when establishing rates, an insurer recognizes that excessive rates for the level of benefits and services provided will significantly reduce the probability of obtaining new policyholders and retaining existing ones.

EQUITY

To be equitable, a premium rate structure charges each policyholder a rate reflecting the expected cost of providing its insurance coverage. This is important in the complex insurance business that so directly affects the public interest. Clearly, the insurer's interest leads it to avoid losing opportunities for sound business by overpricing its product for certain segments of the market. Insurers also need to avoid attracting unsound business by underpricing for other market segments. The closer the insurer's premium rates reflect the expected cost of each policyholder's coverage, the more favorable will be the combination of its sales and financial results.

Practically every state has laws against unfair discrimination in insurance transactions. Moreover, sound judgment suggests that equity, even if not indicated by ethical principles or required by law, would be necessary for practical business reasons.

BASIC COMPONENTS OF THE PREMIUM RATE

The basic components of the group insurance premium rate can be expressed as follows:

Premium = Claims + Margin + Expenses + Profit.

EXPECTED CLAIMS

The main component of a group insurance premium rate is the portion that provides the insurer with sufficient funds to meet those claims the group is expected to incur during the rating period. The typical starting point for the development of this component is a study of past claims experience, usually based on:

- the past experience of the insurer's group insurance business,
- data from intercompany studies such as those published periodically in the *TRANSACTIONS* of the Society of Actuaries, or
- the past experience of the group itself.

However determined, the insurer projects the group's past experience to the period to which the rates will apply. It takes into account any anticipated changes—inflation or considerable change in the average age of the group, for example—in the characteristics of the risk and the environment that may affect claims costs for a particular coverage.

MARGIN FOR HIGHER THAN ANTICIPATED CLAIMS

The estimate of future expected claims obtained from analysis of past claims experience and other influences may be reliable, but will not be exactly correct. Therefore, the insurer usually includes a protective financial margin in the premium rate in case higher than anticipated claims result. Any amount remaining in this margin between actual and expected claims may be returned to the policyholder as an experience refund.

EXPECTED EXPENSES

The insurer includes a sufficient amount in the premium rate to meet its anticipated expenses. Typically, the expense formula considers the economies of increasing group size, that is, premiums and number insured. The expense charge becomes a smaller percentage of premium as the size of the group increases. The expense charge also varies according to the types and number of coverages and services provided under the plan.

CONTRIBUTION TO SURPLUS

This element of the premium rate provides for the establishment and maintenance of the insurer's general surplus funds and, in the case of a stock company, for satisfactory profits for its stockholders. The insurer's surplus of assets over liabilities assures policyholders that their claims will be honored even if there should be periods when an insurer's current costs exceed current income.

FACTORS THAT INFLUENCE RATES

The type and level of benefits are, of course, the primary determinants of the level of group insurance rates. However, even where benefits are nearly identical, the frequency and severity of claims will cause the claim levels to vary from one group to another, and from one period in time to another. Eight common factors that influence this are discussed below.

OVERALL PLAN DESIGN

In a medical benefits program the existence or absence of specific benefit provisions can often have a dramatic impact on employee utilization of medical services. The use of methods such as coinsurance, deductibles, and second surgical opinions will all influence the claim level of the plan. In addition, the existence or absence of other choices for employees—HMOs, PPOs, alternative medical indemnity plans, medical spending accounts—will significantly impact overall claim levels.

Plans under which an employee pays 20 percent coinsurance will have overall plan costs that are *more* than 20 percent less than a plan without such a feature, since the 20 percent cost borne by the employee can reduce overutilization. Similarly, deductibles can lessen employees' seeking treatment for minor illnesses since they will pay initial costs themselves.

When employees choose between a traditional indemnity insurance plan or an HMO, they tend to choose the plan that is most advantageous to themselves. Young, single employees, for example, without established ties to a particular physician often are attracted to HMOs by the low out-of-pocket costs and the preventive care. On the other hand, employees and their family members who have existing relationships with specific physicians and hospitals often will not join an HMO if it requires them to change physicians. These people are likely to be the older, less healthy persons; therefore, the average group of people remaining in the indemnity program will be older, less healthy, and more costly.

Today's rapidly changing health care environment has resulted in development of a myriad of different managed care arrangements that often blend aspects of traditional indemnity insurance with HMOs and PPOs. Pricing must consider the effect of the employee choices described above. In addition, the prices also must include the economic effects of the degree to which providers of the medical care have been brought into the managed care program. To price any of these arrangements, the insurer asks certain difficult and challenging questions.

■ Are the physicians at risk for any of the claim costs?

■ Must the employees and dependents choose a primary care physician who is committed to managing their claims?

■ To what extent have the providers agreed to "hold the line" on price increases?

■ How extensive is the provider network—that is, will most care be delivered by those providers?

These questions overlay the more traditional, and still important, factors that are described below.

AGE

Age affects both life and health coverages. Life insurance loss experience reflects the fact that the rate of mortality steadily increases from ages in the mid-twenties. Similarly, health insurance experience reflects differences in claim frequency and, for most coverages, in claim severity, among different age groups. A 50-year-old person is more likely to experience a long illness than a 30-year-old one. In the case of maternity coverages the reverse is true; maternity claim frequency decreases as women advance beyond age 30.

The age factor will have increasing impact as the U.S. population grows older.

SEX

With some exceptions such as supplemental accident expense benefits, health care coverages (exclusive of the impact of maternity claims) generally show higher claims costs for women than for men. Various studies have shown that women become disabled more often, require hospitalization more frequently, and have more surgery, medical treatment, and dental services than men, particularly at ages under 65. The expected employee health insurance claim costs of an all male group, therefore, would be considerably less than for a comparable group in which the proportion of women was, for example, 75 percent of the total.

On the other hand, throughout the range of ages typically covered by a group insurance plan, women live longer; therefore, the cost of life insurance is lower for women than for men.

Legislation to disregard sex in rating (unisex rating) has been proposed as a consideration in determining premiums. The possibility of retroactive enactment or the setting of an effective date that would not give adequate preparation time for compliance concerns insurers. Because sex currently is a key factor in the rate determination process, such legislation would have an impact on the method of calculating group insurance rates.

INCOME

Medical care claim costs tend to be higher for persons with higher incomes. Physicians' charges sometimes are influenced by a patient's ability to pay; also, persons in higher income brackets often seek more frequent or extensive medical care. Since people in higher income brackets generally utilize dental care more frequently than others, dental claim costs also are higher for such individuals.

A trend, however, indicates the leveling of medical care charges among persons in different earning brackets. Two factors—general availability of medical care expense insurance and federal programs, such as Medicare, that reimburse providers of medical care without consideration of the income of the patient—have contributed to this leveling. As dental care insurance becomes more widely available, a similar leveling of charges may occur.

OCCUPATION

Many insurers recognize significant variations in mortality by industry through discounts or loadings to their standard life insurance rates. Similarly, for certain industries where the morbidity rate is greater than average, insurers may require an increased health insurance premium rate.

The hazard to an employee's health is greater in occupations that require lifting, carrying, or handling heavy objects or that involve exposure to dust, poisons, dampness, or repeated changes in air pressure or temperature. Work sites where such extra health hazards exist include tanneries, furriers, logging operations, and underground mines. The mental requirements, too, of certain occupations present an additional hazard for disability income coverages even when no particular physical hazard is present. There are also occupations—airline pilots or surgeons, for instance—where minor impairments, though not disabling to most individuals, could prevent the performance of normal work duties.

GEOGRAPHIC LOCATION

Medical care expense claim charges vary widely by geographic location. For example, large cities on the West Coast have a different pattern and a much higher level of charges for health care than do most cities in the southeastern part of the United States. These variations in claim costs result from differences in the cost of living, in the availability and organization of health care facilities, and in the general attitude of insured individuals, employers, and physicians toward the use of hospitals and medical care facilities.

LENGTH OF THE PREMIUM RATE GUARANTEE

The length of a premium rate guarantee period offered by the insurer will also affect rates. This is particularly true for coverages such as medical and dental care expense benefits, where cost trends show increases. For these coverages the renewal rate guarantee period is becoming shorter. A one-year guarantee was routinely offered in past years, but the trend is toward a guarantee of six months or less, particularly for smaller groups.

TRENDS IN MEDICAL CARE CLAIM COSTS

A consistent upward trend in medical care claim costs experienced by both insured and self-insured plans has been caused by:

- a sharp rise in medical care charges,
- changes in population demographics,
- increasing utilization of medical care services,
- improved medical care treatments, including advanced testing techniques, life-sustaining equipment, open heart surgery, and organ transplants, and
- cost shifting by providers to cover revenue shortfalls that result from discount arrangements, public programs, and indigent patients.

In addition, the escalating frequency of malpractice suits and the cost of malpractice insurance has influenced hospitals' and doctors' charges, and, in many cases, has encouraged the use of more extensive and expensive testing and treatment procedures.

The economic environment, too, affects health care costs. Medical care claim costs tend to rise during economic recessions because insureds use more elective services in anticipation of possible layoffs and stress-related illnesses increase during these periods.

PREMIUM RATING CLASSES

A key step in the development of a premium rate for group insurance coverage is the establishment of rating classes—distinguished by the degree to which the insurer uses the policyholder's own past claim experience. A particular group is assigned to one of three classes: manually rated groups, fully experience-rated groups, and blended manual/experience-rated groups.

The degree to which an insurer uses a policyholder's own past claims experience depends on underwriting judgment about the reliability of the past experience as a basis for predicting the future claims result. In making this judgment, the insurance actuary uses the mathematical principle of large numbers: the more frequent a contingent event, the greater likelihood that statistical fluctuations will be minimized and that the observed result will represent the true probability of the event.

Flipping a coin illustrates this principle. The true chance of obtaining "heads" is 50 percent. If one flipped the coin only ten times, it is not likely that five "heads" will come up. But if 10,000 flips are tried, the probability of 50 percent being "heads" will be infinitely greater and the result much more reliable. Similarly, an accurate prediction of total claims expected is virtually impossible for a group of 10 employees, but the probability of an accurate prediction for a group of 10,000 employees is considerably greater.

MANUALLY RATED GROUPS

The insurer places in this class those groups that will have premium rates developed independent of their own past claims experience. The premium rates for the coverages for these groups will be the insurer's current manual premium rates—the rates in its manual that reflect the expected claims experience of an "average" group. Groups whose past claims experience are not likely to be a reliable guide to future claims results are generally those in which either a few individuals have been insured under the plan or where, even for larger groups, few individuals might be expected to have a claim.

The manual rate for certain coverages, however, may be adjusted for past experience. For policyholders with, for example, 100 lives, an insurer may decide to take into account, to some degree, the group's past claim experience in developing the premium for coverages with frequent claims such as medical care expense insurance and short-term disability income insurance. On the other hand, the premiums paid for coverages with infrequent claims, such as life insurance, accidental death and dismemberment, and long-term disability income insurance, may be the insurer's manual rates for groups with several hundred or even several thousand lives.

In theory, an insurer could use the manual rate schedule to determine premium rates for all groups, even those with many thousands of lives. However, because the underlying experience of many groups is notably superior to the average and that of others is distinctly inferior, an insurer limits its use of manual rates to what the competitive marketplace does with similar groups.

For example, the insurer that attempts to use manual or average rates for all groups of less than 500 lives usually will encounter certain problems. Many of its groups between 100 and 500 lives with better-than-average experience will seek insurance from an insurer that recognizes such experience in setting rates while those groups with worse-than-average experience will remain. When this occurs, the average experience of the remaining groups usually will worsen, resulting in increased manual premium rates. This action, in turn, will encourage the best of the remaining groups to seek a new insurer, and a new sequence of premium rate increases and policyholder terminations will result. Clearly this phenomenon must be avoided if the insurer is to develop a sound portfolio of group insurance business.

Insurers also must consider whether to establish a single manual rate level that covers a reasonable range of anticipated experience or develop select and substandard rate classifications for groups that vary from the norm. Typically, insurers base such select or substandard rate classifications on objective standards related to risk characteristics of the group, such as occupation and type of industry. These standards are largely independent of the group's prior experience.

FULLY EXPERIENCE-RATED GROUPS

For this class, the insurer determines the point at which the claims component of a group's premium will be based exclusively on its own past claims experience. Key to this determination, which will vary from coverage to coverage, will be the insurer's opinion as to the point at which past claims experience becomes a satisfactorily reliable basis on which to predict future claims results. The point chosen will be that at which (1) the insurer believes that possible distortions in past claims resulting from chance fluctuations will be small, and (2) the use of past results will enable the insurer to satisfactorily predict future claims.

The likelihood of chance fluctuations in total claims decreases as both the frequency of claim per individual and the number of individuals covered under a plan increase. Thus, because of the lower likelihood of chance fluctuations, full experience rating will be used at a significantly lower number of insured employees (such as 500 employees) for a coverage such as medical care that has a high frequency of claims, as compared with life insurance coverage (such as 10,000 life years: 1,000 employees insured for 10 years, 500 employees insured for 20 years, etc.) for which claims are infrequent.

BLENDED MANUAL/EXPERIENCE-RATED GROUPS

The third premium rating class lies between the extremes of manually rated and fully experience-rated groups. Even before the point at which full experience rating is deemed appropriate, it is natural for insurers to assume that including a degree of past claims experience in the calculation process would improve the estimate of a group's future claim results. Most insurers assign a credibility percentage to actual past experience and blend it with the manual or average expected claims level. In determining actual rates for a group, the closer its size to the manually rated class the less the credibility that will be assigned to its actual experience and the greater the reliance on the manual rate. Conversely, the closer a group is in size to the fully experience rated class, the greater will be the reliance placed on its actual experience in determining the premium for the group.

For example, if 20 percent credibility is assigned to the group's experience, 20 percent of the expected claims cost will be based on its actual experience while 80 percent will be based on the average or manual cost. Similarly, a group with 90 percent credibility would have 90 percent of its expected claims cost based on its own claims experience, while only 10 percent would be based on the manual cost. The following illustrates this last example:

Method	*Expected Claims Cost*
Fully Experience Rated	\$60
Manually Rated	\$70
Blended @ 90% Credibility	\$61= (.90×\$60)+(.10×\$70)

DEVELOPMENT OF MANUAL PREMIUM RATES

An insurer customarily prepares a manual of premium rates for each coverage, composed of many factors that combine to fund benefit payments and expenses adequately. To provide flexibility in designing group benefit plans, there are provisions in the rate structure for adjusting the standard schedule of manual premium rates for many variations in requirements and policyholders' wants and needs.

NET PREMIUM RATE

The starting point in the development of manual premium rates is the determination of the expected claims cost of each coverage, referred to as the net premium rate. This rate represents the portion of the total premium rate available for claim payments; it contains no provision for expenses or other considerations. The net premium rate represents the anticipated cost of the benefits—the product of the probability of claim (frequency) and the expected amount of claim (severity).

EXPECTED CLAIMS

The expected claim frequency is the ratio of the expected number of claims occurring during the period for which the premium is being developed to the number of individuals to be insured. For example, if it is expected that 20 out of every 100 insured individuals would have a claim during the period, the probability of claim would be .20 (20 divided by 100).

Where the benefit is a fixed sum, as in life insurance, the expected claim is the stated amount of insurance. For most group health care benefits the expected claim is a variable that depends on such factors as the expected length of disability, the expected duration of hospital confinement, or the expected amount of reimbursable expense.

As a simplified illustration of the computation of a net premium rate, assume a group has a short-term disability income policy providing a $10 weekly disability benefit, starting with the eighth day of disability. The probability of claims (frequency) would be the proportion of insured individuals who have a disability of at least eight days in a month. For example, suppose that 2 out of every 100 individuals become disabled during a month. The claim frequency would be .02 (2 divided by 100). If the average period for which disability benefits are payable is five weeks, the average amount of claim for a benefit of $10 per week (the benefit payable for five weeks) would be $50, the expected amount of claim. The net monthly premium rate, therefore, would be:

> Claim Frequency × Expected Amount of Claim
>
> .02 × $50 =
> $1.00 per $10 weekly benefit

CONVERSION OF NET TO MANUAL PREMIUM RATE

Net premium rates are then converted to manual premium rates by adding factors for expenses, contribution to surplus or profit, and higher than anticipated claims.

Finding an equitable, yet simple, basis of increasing the net premium to arrive at the manual premiums is difficult. For example, the amounts of certain expenses, such as commissions and state premium taxes, are related to the size of the premium. Other expenses, such as those associated with processing the application, setting up the necessary policy records and issuing the master contract, are essentially the same from one group to another. Still other expenses depend on the number of lives involved, such as the expenses of printing announcement booklets and certificates and establishing and maintaining records of the persons insured. Claim settlement expenses tend to vary by the number of claims and type of coverage. Furthermore, the theoretical provision for such items as contribution to surplus and higher than anticipated claims experience usually is smaller (as a percentage of premium) for large groups than for small groups.

The formula developed to provide for these charges usually attempts to recognize this complex pattern of expenses in as reasonable and practical a way as possible. For example, for a particular coverage the addition to the net premium rate to obtain a manual premium rate often is made in the form of a percentage or a percentage plus a constant, and an adjustment is made to the final rate that reflects the size of the group. Such an approach usually provides satisfactory results when the rates are applied to standard plans of modest size.

THE RATE MANUAL

Two approaches are used to develop the rate manual that the insurer will use for the calculation of manual rates for specific groups. One is to develop a separate rate for each category for which the insurer believes there will be different claims costs. This method is commonly used for life insurance, with rates developed for each age for males and females separately.

The other approach is to establish a single standard rate and to adjust it to reflect the specific characteristics of a group, such as age, sex, and income, that are expected to affect the cost of claims for the coverage. Sometimes the two approaches are combined, such as when a percentage rate adjustment is applied to the life insurance rate calculation to provide discounts reflecting expected favorable claims experience from certain occupations.

The chart on page 159 shows the various factors affecting claims costs, which generally affect manual rates for various group insurance coverages.

To reflect the different proportion of the premium needed for expenses (and often the desired margin for contribution to surplus and higher than anticipated claims experience), manual premium rates usually are adjusted by a percentage reduction or increase that depends on the size of the premium before the adjustment. The premium used in the table of loadings and discounts usually is the total premium for all of a group's coverages. Some insurance companies also use the number of employees in determining the adjustment.

Most insurers design the table so that there is no percentage increase or decrease (that is, the manual rates need no size adjustment) for certain size cases. For smaller cases the table may apply percentage increases, and for larger cases the percentage reductions increase as the premium gets larger. The chart on the following page illustrates this concept.

SOURCES OF RATE-SETTING DATA

A number of data sources are available to the insurer for assistance in establishing manual rates. Large insurers often rely heavily on their own studies of claims experience. Other insurers, whose experience may not be broad enough to allow a statistically valid analysis, usually turn to various intercompany claim experience studies conducted under the auspices of the Society of Actuaries. Some insurers also may choose to employ a consulting actuary to obtain advice on premium rates and related matters.

INTERCOMPANY STUDIES

Experience data contributed by a number of the large writers of group insurance are collected regularly by the Committee on Group Life and Health Insurance Experience of the Society of Actuaries. The composite experience, and a discussion of the results, are published in the "Annual Reports" volumes of the *TRANSACTIONS* of the Society of Actuaries. These reports provide experience periodically on group life insurance, short-term and long-term disability income insurance, basic hospital-surgical insurance, and major medical expense insurance.

The time period required to collect and publish the experience data often limits their value for establishing current health insurance rate levels. Even in such cases, though, these studies provide a useful record of past results that can serve as a base in the rate-making process and, when compared from year to year, will indicate trends in experience results.

INTRACOMPANY STUDIES

Many of the larger insurers make periodic analyses of their own group insurance experience. They accumu-

	Age	*Sex*	*Income*	*Industry Occupation*	*Geographic Area*	*Cost Trend*
Life Insurance	Yes	Yes	—	Yes	*	—
AD&D	Yes	Yes	—	Yes	—	—
Disability Income	Yes	Yes	Yes	**	—	—
Hospital and Surgical Expenses	Yes	Yes	Yes†	**	Yes	Yes
Major Medical	Yes	Yes	Yes†	**	Yes	Yes
Dental	Yes	Yes	Yes†	**	Yes	Yes

*While not common in the United States, a number of companies adjust rates by geographic area for life insurance coverage sold in Canada.

**Some insurers make rate adjustments for selected categories of groups for which significantly different than standard experience is expected. Other insurers make no adjustments, but may choose not to write groups for which significantly higher than standard claims experience is expected.

†Many insurers no longer use this factor in the manual rate computation as an influence on claim costs.

ADJUSTMENT FOR CASE SIZE

Table of Volume Loadings and Discounts

Monthly Premium Volume Before Adjustment for Case Size — *At Least*	*But Under*	*Percentage Premium Adjustment*
	$ 200	1.25%
$ 200	225	1.23
225	250	1.21
250	275	1.19
275	300	1.17
300	325	1.15
325	350	1.13
350	375	1.11
375	400	1.09
400	425	1.08
425	450	1.07
450	475	1.06
475	500	1.05
500	550	1.04
550	600	1.03
600	700	1.02
700	800	1.01
800	1,000	1.00
1,000	1,100	.99
1,100	1,200	.98
1,200	1,300	.97
1,300	1,400	.96
1,400	1,600	.95
1,600	1,800	.94
1,800	2,000	.93
2,000	2,500	.92
2,500	3,000	.91
3,000	4,000	.90
4,000	5,000	.89
5,000	7,500	.88
7,500	10,000	.87
10,000 & over		Refer to Home Office

late this information as a by-product of the claims payment process. One large life insurance company, for instance, publishes a quarterly *Statistical Bulletin* that gives useful information on accidental deaths. Periodically, it also makes studies of hospitalization among its own employees. Intracompany studies are, of course, more up-to-date than the intercompany studies and have the additional advantages of reflecting the insurer's own product, underwriting philosophy, sales methods, and administrative and claim procedures. Some of these intracompany studies also appear from time to time in the *TRANSACTIONS* of the Society of Actuaries.

SPECIAL STUDIES

Members of the the Society of Actuaries have made special studies that examine in greater detail the many independent variables that may affect group mortality and morbidity experience. These studies have been published in the *TRANSACTIONS* of the Society of Actuaries and are of considerable value in rate-making.

Special studies have been made in such areas as short-term disability income, hospital, surgical, and major medical expense insurance. In certain areas, information gained from the experience of individual health insurance products also may be of assistance in the development of group health insurance rates.

OTHER SOURCE MATERIALS

A wide variety of other source materials is available. By way of illustration, the National Safety Council publishes annually a booklet entitled "Accident Facts" that is especially useful in studying accidental death rates and the relative incidence of on-the-job injuries. Each year the Health Insurance Association of America releases a survey of hospital charges by geographic location and type of accommodations.

Many special reports have been published by the various agencies of the Department of Health and Human Services—the Social Security Administration in particular. These reports include statistics on illness; accidental injuries; disability; use of hospital, medical, and dental services; and other health topics.

MANUAL RATE DEVELOPMENT FOR SPECIFIC COVERAGES

In developing rates for their rate manuals, insurers consider certain factors for various types of benefits.

HOSPITAL AND SURGICAL EXPENSE BENEFITS

Manual rates for hospital expense coverages usually have two components: a rate for the daily room and board benefit and a rate for the ancillary services and supplies.

Hospital charges differ substantially by geographic area, particularly between urban and rural areas. Also, age distribution and the proportion of men to women influence initial premium rates for employee hospital expense insurance. Few industry classifications have experience sufficiently below average to make it necessary to apply occupational loadings to hospital rates.

The factors affecting manual rates for surgical expense insurance basically are the same as those for hospital expense insurance.

PREGNANCY EXPENSE BENEFITS

Pregnancy benefits selected by policyholders before 1978 traditionally were different from those chosen for other conditions requiring medical care; therefore, insurers commonly developed separate pregnancy expense benefit rates. With the enactment of the federal law in 1978 requiring employers to provide the same benefit for pregnancy as for any other conditions, it is now common to include these benefit costs with the disability income and medical care expense rates charged the group.

Naturally, the effect of this benefit on the employee rate rises as the female content of the group increases. Too, dependent rates for medical care expense may increase as the number of married female employees insuring their dependents increases, to recognize that a smaller proportion of the dependents covered are women.

Age rating of the pregnancy benefit is common practice, for there will be more pregnancy claims in a group that insures a large number of women at younger ages than in a group insuring a large number of women over age 40.

MAJOR MEDICAL EXPENSE BENEFITS

The calculation of premium rates for major medical insurance requires adjustments for a number of factors that have been found to affect its cost. These factors include items relating to specific policyholders and employees such as age, income, geographic area, sex, and occupational hazards. Variations of the specific benefits of the particular plan—such as the type of deductible (per cause or all cause), the deductible amount, the deductible accumulation period, coinsurance, type and amount of the overall maximum benefit, out-of-pocket limitations, mental illness restrictions, and other internal limits on benefits—require further adjustments.

For supplementary major medical insurance, the rate calculation also must take into account the underlying basic plan of benefits that will pay before any benefits are paid under the major medical plan. This procedure applies regardless of what insurer provides the basic plan coverages.

Rate calculations for Managed Care plans must take varying copayments, provider contracting, and Medical Management, such as utilization review of the services, prospective payments, and other factors, into consideration.

DENTAL EXPENSE BENEFITS

In general, insurers compute dental expense rates in a manner similar to computation of premium rates for other health care expense coverages, including adjustments for age, income, geographic area, sex, and occupation. However, recognition is given to specific characteristics of dental claim costs, such as the need for bridgework increasing with age. Also, some occupations with lower than average medical care costs have an average dental care cost that is higher than average. This result occurs for people in those occupations where contact with the public makes personal appearance important.

Some insurers have introduced other adjustments, such as decreasing premium rates for plans that had a previous dental insurance program. This step is based on the assumption that the existence of a prior plan indicates a lower proportion of needed dental care than is needed for a group without such a plan. If no prior dental program has existed, some insurers adjust initial rates according to how long prospective participants have been aware of its potential introduction. This adjustment recognizes that participants will tend to postpone needed dental treatment until after the plan takes effect.

Finally, because dental coverage is mostly elective and the potential for selection against the plan is greater than for most coverages, some insurers also apply loading on plans that are written on a contributory basis.

SHORT-TERM DISABILITY INCOME INSURANCE

Manual rates for short-term disability income plans vary according to:

- the benefit waiting period,
- the maximum benefit period per disability,
- whether the coverage is on a nonoccupational or a 24-hour basis,
- the group's average age, and
- the proportion of benefits provided to female insureds.

Insurers also may adjust rates for occupational hazards if coverage is written on a 24-hour basis. Determination of rates for unusual occupational hazards usually is based on industry classification. The claims experience of some classifications, however, is sufficiently worse than average (substandard) to require a substantial increase in the premium rate. For non-occupational coverage, insurers seldom require an extra premium charge for substandard industry experience.

Policies issued to comply with compulsory state disability plans, such as those in New Jersey, New York, and California, have basically the same premium rate schedules as those for other short-term disability income policies. These rates include a sufficient margin to cover the assessments levied on insurers for certain expenses and for benefits to the disabled unemployed under the state disability plans.

LONG-TERM DISABILITY INCOME INSURANCE

Rating variables for long-term disability income insurance are similar to those for short-term disability income insurance. Rates usually are expressed in terms of $100 of monthly benefit or covered payroll and are shown in rate manuals by sex or age, either by individual ages or by five-year age brackets. In addition, in view of the long-term nature of the benefit and the desire to avoid overinsurance, insurers usually integrate benefit payments with Social Security and similar disability benefits for which the employee is eligible. As a result, rate credits reflecting income benefits from other sources are developed in the course of calculating the manual rate.

Because of the sensitivity of disability claims experience to general economic conditions, insurers generally review long-term disability income coverage rates whenever economic conditions change or are expected to change.

GROUP TERM LIFE INSURANCE

Insurers develop group term life rates from published mortality tables with adjustments by their insurer's actuaries that reflect company experience and objectives. The rates may show separate rates for men and women or use a combined rate table approach (unisex table on page 164).

The insurer determines each policyholder's monthly premium by multiplying the total amount of insurance (in thousands) at each age by the tabular monthly premium rate per $1,000 of insurance for each age and accumulating the results. Premium adjustments may then be made to the accumulated results to reflect such factors as a preferred industry discount or industry loading for hazardous occupations, a constant expense loading, and a size discount based on the amount of monthly premium. Next, the premium is divided by the total volume of insurance (in thousands) to produce an average monthly premium rate per $1,000 of insurance for the employer's group case. Finally, the employer's monthly premium is obtained by multiplying the total monthly volume of insurance (in thousands) by the average monthly premium rate. The example on page 164 illustrates a way of calculating a group term life insurance premium.

ACCIDENTAL DEATH AND DISMEMBERMENT INSURANCE

Important sources of information on group accidental death claims are the reports on the intercompany studies conducted by the Committee on Group Life and Health Insurance of the Society of Actuaries. The data in these reports, classified according to the industry of the employer, serve as a guide in establishing and reviewing the industry classifications used in the rating of AD&D issued on a 24-hour basis.

Adjustments may be made according to whether the coverage applies to employees or dependents. The rates depend on whether the coverage is to be nonoccupational or on a 24-hour basis. Several categories of risk classes, based on the degree of accident hazard in the particular industry, typically are used in the rating of 24-hour coverage. The rate for nonoccupational coverage may be independent of the industry factor.

EXPERIENCE-RATED PREMIUMS

Experience-rated premiums reflect the claims and expenses expected for

	(1) Volume of Insurance		×	(2) Monthly Rate Per $1,000		=	(3) Monthly Premium	
Age	*Male*	*Female*		*Male*	*Female*		*Male*	*Female*
20	$ 300,000	$ 400,000		$0.12	$0.07		$ 36.00	$ 28.00
30	1,200,000	1,100,000		0.14	0.08		168.00	88.00
40	800,000	600,000		0.30	0.18		240.00	108.00
50	400,000	200,000		0.84	0.59		336.00	118.00
60	60,000	30,000		2.13	1.70		127.80	51.00
	$2,760,000	$2,330,000				Total	$907.80	$393.00

Male + Female monthly premium	$1,300.80
Monthly premium after 10% industry loading ($1,300.80 × $1.10)	1,430.88
Monthly premium after $10 constant expense loading	10.00
	$1,440.88
Monthly premium after size discount ($1,440.88 × .95)	$1,368.84
Monthly premium rate—per $1000 (1,368 divided by 5,090*)	0.27
Final monthly premium (5,090 × .27)	$1,374.30

*Total volume of insurance is $5,090,000 ($2,760,000 + $2,330,000)

The monthly premium rate per $1,000 ($0.27 in this example) remains in effect during the rating period, and each month that rate is multiplied by that month's volume of life insurance to determine the monthly premium payable.

a policyholder's specific plan of benefits. Most insurers use past claims experience to develop premium rates only for groups that satisfy certain size requirements, as explained earlier in the chapter. These requirements vary from coverage to coverage and from insurer to insurer.

Typically, for groups that meet the minimum size requirement, the degree to which the group's premium rates are based upon past claims experience, rather than on manual rates, gradually increases until the full experience rating point is reached. At that point the manual is ignored completely and a group's premium is based exclusively on the expected claims of the specific group as developed by an actuarial formula related to the group's own experience.

In some respects the calculation process for experience-rated coverages is simpler than for manual-rated coverages, since the many risk characteristics of the group affecting claims costs already are reflected, in the aggregate, in the actual claims experience of the group. The aggregate effect of such factors as age, sex, and income composition of the group is reflected in the claims experience, and specific adjustment for them is required only to the extent that they are expected to change.

REASONS FOR THEIR USE

The process of determining experience-rated premiums was conceived and developed by insurance companies, but an increasing number of other types of organizations, such as Blue Cross and Blue Shield, now are using the technique in some form. Insurers use experience rating if they expect it will improve their ability to provide for the expected claims and expenses of the policyholder, since:

- It achieves greater equity among policyholders, because it adjusts the cost of insurance in a manner more commensurate with the expected cost of each policyholder than is possible through the exclusive use of manual rates.
- The competitive environment demands that each insurer make every effort to retain groups with favorable experience. Unless an insurer can provide coverage to such groups at a reasonable cost, it runs the risk of losing such policyholders to another insurer that more closely reflects the expected costs of their programs in its rates.

DEVELOPMENT OF EXPERIENCE-RATED PREMIUMS

As explained earlier, insurers base rates for certain group coverages on all or part of a policyholder's past claims experience. An expected claim cost must be ascertained.

CHOICE OF AN EXPERIENCE PERIOD

The starting point in ascertaining the claims element of the premium rate is determining of the actual claims experience for a stipulated period of time. For example, selecting the most recent 12 months for which claims experience is available eliminates the potential bias from the normal seasonal variations in claims for certain health insurance coverages, such as short-term disability income and medical care coverages. The choice of the most recent 12 months would assure that each portion of the year received equal weight in the experience. It would also permit the insurer to use its most recent experience, thereby more accurately reflecting any changes in the nature of the risk being insured.

On the other hand, the insurer may believe that the nature of the risk has remained constant over time and that greater accuracy would be obtained by combining several years of experience. The impact of any chance fluctuations in the recent experience would be lessened by the use of a larger experience base. If this procedure were followed, the insurer might decide to assign proportionately higher weight to recent experience and lower weight to older experience. The combining of several years of experience is often used for life insurance coverages. In reviewing the claim experience of policy holders with more than one option available to the employees, the risk of each option must be understood and evaluated. Even more than one year's experience may be biased due to antiselection against one of the options.

VALUE OF INCURRED CLAIMS FOR THE EXPERIENCE PERIOD

After choosing an experience period, the insurer determines the value of the policyholder's actual incurred claims during the experience period. (Incurred claims for a particular period are those claims which the insurer is obliged to pay because the insurance was in force during the period.) The value of incurred claims usually is not directly available, since some claims incurred in a recent period often take months or, in some cases, years before final payments can be made. Therefore, insurers usually need to estimate the value of claims that were incurred during the experience period but which will not be paid until some time in the future.

In addition, a portion of the claims paid during the experience period may have been incurred prior to the period. These claims must be eliminated from consideration in order to determine the proper value of claims incurred during the experience period. To obtain the true incurred claims for the experience period, the claims paid during the period will be modified as follows:

Incurred Claims	=	Claims paid during the period
MINUS (−)		Claims paid during the period but incurred during prior periods
PLUS (+)		Estimated value of claims incurred during the period and to be paid in future periods

An insurer generally estimates the value of claims that have been incurred during a period but which will be paid after the close of that period—basing these estimates on its past experience of the proportion of incurred claims that are paid after the close of comparable experience periods for the type of coverage in question. For example, an insurer's experience might indicate that an amount equal to 25 percent of incurred claims for the period will be paid after the close of the period.

Estimates of the value of such claims and, hence, the actual value of claims incurred during the period vary in accuracy. Generally, they are more accurate for the larger group accounts whose level of claims paid after the close of the period is sufficient to warrant credibility.

ANTICIPATED AMOUNT OF CLAIMS FOR THE PROSPECTIVE RATE

Having obtained the incurred claims result for the experience period, the insurer next considers the projection or estimation of the anticipated amount of claims for the prospective rate period. The projection will normally take into account changes in the basic risk characteristics, such as age and income of the group since the beginning of the experience period. It also will consider changing economic and medical factors.

Insurers consider in their rate projections the general business environment that might affect the level of claims. For instance, a change in the general economic conditions in the policyholder's locality might suggest modification of past disability income experience to arrive at an estimated disability income claims level for the future period, since claims experience under this coverage is likely to be influenced by such a factor.

The cost of medical care coverage, too, in recent years has been impacted by dramatic changes and developments in the cost of medical care services, in the utilization of medical care services and facilities, and in medical technology. The involvement with alternative delivery systems and acceleration of cost shifting have also had a significant effect.

Since medical care coverage normally is offered on a reimbursement basis, the cost of a particular claim cannot be determined in advance. The level of benefits ultimately paid out also will be quite sensitive to the effects of price inflation—with the costs of medical services rising in recent years at a rate far in excess of that of the general economy. Hospital costs, doctors' charges, and the cost of medicines, however, have risen at varying rates. As a result, for broad coverages such as major medical, insurers often assign weights to the various elements of coverage to project the aggregate effect of price inflation. Also, patterns of utilization have been changing, for the most part resulting in increased utilization of available services. These patterns also require evaluation.

The insurer also anticipates the effect of changes in medical technology and practice upon its future claims costs. Certain formerly common procedures, such as tonsillectomy, have fallen into disfavor. However, modern advances, such as intensive and coronary care units and new heart and kidney procedures, have significantly affected the cost of medical care expense insurance. New technology may lead to better and cheaper ways of providing certain aspects of medical care, but the indicators are that, for the foreseeable future, new and better procedures will lead to still higher costs. Whatever direction costs take, the effect of changing medical technology will be a factor in the setting of related premium rates.

All the factors described previously are considered in the context of the benefits offered a group. The following examples demonstrate the wide variation in the insurer's claims cost, under similar conditions, that can be traced to variations in benefit design. Both instances assume a 10 percent annual rate of increase in the cost of medical care services and a 3 percent annual rate of increase in utilization, as well as no change in the medical technology for treating the condition.

The first example is a plan that reimburses the individual for the amount of room and board charges during each day of hospitalization, subject to a maximum daily benefit of $100. The hospital in the locality in question has been charging $100 per day. In this example, an increase in the hospital charge of 10 percent to $110 would have no effect on the insurer's claims cost due to the policy limitation. The only anticipated increase in claims cost would arise from increased utilization. Under these assumptions the insurer's claims cost would rise by 3 percent.

The second example concerns a major medical plan with a $100 surgical deductible. It will be assumed that the average surgeon's charge for a particular procedure was $200. If this average charge and the amount eligible for reimbursement rises 10 percent to $220, and 3 percent more people have this operation, the insurer's claims increase would be as illustrated in the chart below.

Accordingly, under identical assumptions with respect to outside influences, the insurer's claim costs can be greatly affected by the design of the benefit plan. In the first example the increase was 3 percent; in the second it was nearly 24 percent.

In summary, the development of expected claims is basically a two-step procedure. It is based first on the determination of actual claims for a past experience period, and then on the insurer's estimate of the degree to which anticipated changes in the characteristics of the risk and the environment will affect claim costs un-

NEW COST

Increase in the Insurer's Claim Cost = Prior Cost

$$\text{Increase} = \frac{(\text{Insurer's New Benefit Payment}) \times (\text{Number of Expected Operations})}{(\text{Insurer's Prior Benefit Payment}) \times (\text{Number of Prior Operations})}$$

Calculation of the increase is as follows:

$220	New Average Surgeon's Charge
−100	Plan Deductible
$120	New Average Benefit Payment
×103%	Increase in Number of Operations
$123.60	New Claim Cost
−100.00	Prior Claim Cost ($200 charge − $100 deductible)
23.6%	Increase in Insurer's Claims Cost

der the particular plan being insured. While insurers' methods differ in estimating the degree to which future claims will be different from past claims experience, the objective is the same—to estimate future claims as accurately as possible.

MARGIN

It is usual for an insurer to add a margin to the premium to protect the insurer from higher than anticipated claim results. The margin for adverse claims fluctuations, commonly referred to as a margin for contingencies, typically will vary with the size of the group and type of coverage. As the size of the group increases, the probability of extreme fluctuations in the claims level decreases and, therefore, the required margin percentage decreases. Higher margins generally are needed in situations where the coverage insured is subject to complex forces that make it difficult to predict the ultimate effect, or where the base of past experience that has been available to estimate future claims results has been modest.

The amount of margin needed for a given coverage or group also may be related to the experience refund formula applied to the group. In situations where the refund depends on the experience of an individual group, higher margins may be needed to take into account the fact that monies refunded to groups with favorable experience are not available to offset losses on groups with unfavorable experience.

In such situations experience refunds are recognized as one of the insurer's costs of doing business, and sufficient margins are included in the premium to support the adopted refund scale. Also, the insurer may wish to increase its normal margin in situations where unfavorable past experience has led to a deficit balance in a policyholder's experience refund account in an effort to accelerate its recovery of such losses.

Instead of or in addition to the margin, the insurer may require the establishment of a Premium Stabilization Reserve. The reserve is typically built up from experience refunds for which the policyholder may be eligible. The insurer maintains these funds at interest and may use the reserve to cover any future experience losses or premium increases.

An insurer's needed margin for adverse claims experience, therefore, will depend on:

- the confidence the insurer has in its ability to predict future claims levels (The greater its confidence, the smaller will be its margin requirements.); or

- the degree to which its experience refund formula provides for refunds to its policyholders with favorable experience. (In general, the larger the amount the formula returns as a result of favorable experience, the larger will be the insurer's margin requirements.)

When refunds are based on the aggregate experience of the insurer's portfolio rather than on the experience of a particular group, the margin for adverse claim results added to the premium will be based on that required for the entire block of such business.

Although the results of individual groups might vary greatly, unfavorable experience on some groups will be offset by favorable experience on other groups, and the margin required will depend upon the coverages in question and the total size of the portfolio.

EXPECTED FUTURE EXPENSES

The insurer will provide for meeting its anticipated expense for the future period by arriving at the amounts believed to be adequate to cover claim costs for the period to which the rates will apply, and establishing an appropriate margin for contingencies.

If a significant variation is anticipated from one group to another in the area of services or other costs, the expense component of the premium rate should take such variations into account. For larger experience-rated groups it is common to relate expenses in the development of a group's premium to the actual charges that will be made against the group in the experience refund formula.

An insurer's expenses in the first year of a policy generally exceed those of the renewal years due to costs associated with prospecting, proposal preparation, underwriting, contract drafting and issuance. In some situations, higher first-year commissions are paid to the agent. Normally, it is competitively impractical to charge these higher expenses fully in the first year. They must be amortized over time and recovered from premiums received from the group or portfolio of groups in subsequent years.

CONTRIBUTION TO SURPLUS (OR PROFIT)

The premium charged a policyholder must also provide for the establishment and maintenance of the insurer's surplus funds. Surplus funds are designed to provide policyholders with the assurance that their claims will be honored even during periods when current costs exceed the insurer's current income. The surplus charge is usually established as a percentage of premium depending on the size of the group (the larger the group, the lower the percentage), and the type of coverage (the more uncertain or subject to fluctuation the probable experience, the higher the percentage). In establishing the percentage of premium surplus charge, the insurer will include investment income earned on cash flow and reserves, to the extent that the full amount of this income is not credited back to the policyholder in the experience-rating formula.

For groups on which a separate experience refund account is maintained, the surplus charge must take into consideration any losses to be absorbed by the insurer from groups that terminate with deficit balances in their accounts. Also, in the case of stock insurance companies, surplus earnings are required to provide a return on the investment of the insurance company's stockholders.

EXPERIENCE-RATED CALCULATION METHODS

Insurers use various methods in developing the total amount of premium required for any particular experience-rated group. Three general methods—desired loss ratio, incurred loss ratio, and split retention—are used. (Examples of these methods appear in the "For Enrichment" section that follows.) All three take into account each of the elements of the premium discussed in this chapter: expected future claims, margin for higher than anticipated claims, expected future expenses, and the insurer's surplus objective.

For purposes of simplicity, expenses and contribution to surplus are often combined in the premium rate formula and are referred to as "retention," a term that indicates amounts to be retained by the insurer for items other than claims charged to the group. Retention can be broken down into constant and variable charges. "Constant retention" consists of charges that are independent of the size of the group's premium, such as a flat charge to provide for the establishment of records needed to pay claims for each group or for the drafting of an employee booklet. "Variable retention" applies to retention items that are related to the premium charged for the group, such as taxes and commissions.

"Margin" refers to the margin for higher than anticipated claim results. "Loss ratio" is the relationship of claims to premiums.

(*Continued on page 173*)

FOR ENRICHMENT

Note: This section provides those students with a special interest in the mathematical aspects of rating with further information. Students will *NOT* be tested on material in this section.

DESIRED LOSS RATIO METHOD

This first general method develops the required dollar amount of premium for groups eligible for experience refunds. It is shown below:

$$\text{Required Premium} = \frac{\text{Expected Claims}}{1 - (\text{Margin }\%) - (\%\text{ of Required Premium for Total Retention})}$$

In this equation, the numerator reflects the dollar amount of expected claims. The denominator represents the "desired loss ratio"—that is, the claims loss ratio needed to produce premiums adequate to cover claims, margin, expenses, and the insurer's contribution to surplus or profit. The following example illustrates this method:

Assumptions:

Expected Claims	=	$200,000
Margin	=	7%
Total Retention	=	13%

Experience Rating Calculation:

$$\text{Required Premium} = \frac{\$200{,}000}{1-.07-.13} = \frac{\$200{,}000}{.80} = \$250{,}000$$

Each element of the premium may be determined separately as follows:

Expected Claims	=	\$200,000
Margin	= (.07) (\$250,000) =	17,500
Total Retention	= (.13) (\$250,000) =	32,500
Required Premium		\$250,000

INCURRED LOSS RATIO METHOD

This second general method derives the required percentage rate increase. The formula is demonstrated below.

$$\text{Required Percentage Premium Rate Increase} = \frac{(\text{Incurred Loss Ratio})(\text{Trend})(\text{Margin})}{1 - (\%\text{ of Required Premium for Total Retention})}$$

The Incurred Loss Ratio in the numerator reflects the ratio of total claims to total premiums during the previous rating period. By increasing this ratio by the expected trend, the insurer arrives at the loss ratio that can be expected to emerge in the coming rating period. A margin is added to the numerator to protect the insurer from higher than anticipated claims.

The denominator reflects the loss ratio needed for the group to break even—the loss ratio required to produce premiums adequate to cover claims and total expenses. (The insurer's contribution to surplus or profit is included in total expenses.)

Dividing the expected loss ratio (numerator) by the loss ratio required to break even results in the required premium rate increase. This second method produces a percentage rate increase, whereas the first method develops the dollar amount of premium needed.

SPLIT RETENTION METHOD

The third general method also used for developing the required premium for groups eligible for experience refunds is:

Required Premium =

Expected Claims + Margin + Constant Retention Items + % of Required Premium for Retention Items Based on Premiums

This may be written as:

$$\text{Required Premium} = \frac{(\text{Expected Claims})(1 + \text{Margin }\%) + \text{Constant Retention Items}}{1 - (\%\text{ of Required Premium for Retention Items Based on Premiums})}$$

In this method the retention is separated into constant and variable expenses. Constant expenses are reflected in the numerator and variable expenses are in the denominator. This formula produces the dollar amount of premium needed.

BENEFIT UNITS

In the examples above, the focus has been on the aggregate amount of group health insurance premium required from a group. In actual practice, however, rates are developed in terms of units of coverage. Although it is important to develop the value of the claims incurred during the experience period, knowledge of the exact amount of incurred claims is not particularly helpful, unless the number of benefit units (individuals insured) during the period is known. As might be imagined, it makes a significant difference in the rate that must be developed for a future period if a given level of claims experience stemmed from 2,000 benefit units or from 20,000.

A common unit of comparison for experience rated groups is the premium dollars earned by the insurer during the experience period. For example, assuming no changes in the benefit plan or in the characteristics of the insured group during the experience period, if the earned premium during the experience period was $300,000 and it was determined that, if all circumstances were to be unchanged during the future period, $360,000 of premium would be needed, the current unit rates could be increased by 20 percent to achieve the desired $360,000 premium ($360,000 divided by $300,000 = 1.20).

The most common benefit units, by type of coverage, for which premium rates are developed are:

Type of Group Insurance Coverage	*Benefit Unit*
Life	Each $1,000 of benefit
Accidental Death and Dismemberment	Each $1,000 of principal sum
Short-Term Disability	Each $10 of weekly benefit
Long-Term Disability	Each $100 of monthly benefit or covered payroll
Medical and Dental Care	Each employee and each category of dependents insured

After the premium rates have been determined, these rates are then applied to benefit units to develop the premium for each coverage. The total premium payable by the policyholder is the sum of the premium for each coverage provided by the policy.

SPECIAL RATE CONSIDERATIONS

Certain rating considerations apply in group insurance, depending on the premium rating class of the group.

MANUALLY RATED GROUPS

Usually, the rates for all participants in experience-rated groups are adjusted at the same time for any particular coverage, and the period for which the new rates will apply will be the same for all. Special consideration must be given to the establishment of manual rates, however.

Rates charged various manually rated policyholders will take effect at many different dates—whenever changes in the level of claims experience for a particular coverage are expected. For example, if a medical care rate schedule that will be applicable to all new manually rated plans issued during the next calendar year is being developed, it must be recognized that some groups will join on January 1, while coverage for others will not be effective until December 31. For coverage with increasing costs, such as medical care expense, the rate that would be sufficient to cover the first 12 months of expected claims of a January 1 group would not be sufficient to cover the first 12 months of expected claims of a group for which coverage begins on the following December 31.

The solution to this problem requires a choice between two general alternatives. When the expected difference in cost between the January 1 and December 31 groups is small, many insurers choose to establish a single scale of premium rates based on the average cost expected from all groups that will be insured in the coming year. For example, premium rates might be established for all groups at a level that would be appropriate for a group that joined in the middle of the year on July 1. However, in a situation where the difference in cost between groups joining at different times during the year is considered to be significant, the insurer might choose to establish a scale of premium rates containing a built-in adjustment factor that would result in premium rates that would vary according to the date the program went into effect. In such situations, adjustments typically would be made either monthly or quarterly.

EXPERIENCE-RATED GROUPS

LARGE INDIVIDUAL CLAIMS

Insurers commonly give special consideration to unusually large individual claims when evaluating the past claims experience of experience-rated groups. When insurers determine claims to be truly unusual and not likely to be repeated in the future, all or a portion of them are eliminated from the projection of the future claims experience. This action is fully consistent with the insurer's objective of predicting, as accurately as possible, future claims costs for the group in question. On a more formal basis, insurers typically pool individual medical claims above a certain level, such as $25,000, $50,000, or $100,000. By excluding the amount of any claim above these levels, insurers protect a group's experience against severe claim fluctuations resulting from unusually large individual claims. A separate premium charge is made for the pooling protection.

BENEFIT CHANGES

Adjustments are made in the evaluation of past claims experience when there has been a benefit change for a group during the experience period. In addition, the projection of future claims experience may have to be adjusted to take into account any benefit changes that may become effective between the experience period and the implementation of a new rate basis.

The key to such adjustments is an evaluation of the relative costs of the plan before and after the benefit change. When the change has occurred during the experience period, the objective is to modify the experience to what it would have been had the new benefit schedule been effective during the entire experience period. When the benefit change has taken place after the close of the experience period, the objective is to modify the expected claim experience for the former plan to what might be expected under the new program.

In most situations the best estimate of the difference in claims cost among varying benefit provisions probably can be found by developing a ratio between the claims component in the insurer's manual rate schedule for the new plan to that of the former plan. For example, if the insurer's manual rates indicated that 10 percent more claims could be expected under the new plan when compared with the former plan, a 10 percent increase in expected claims would be considered appropriate when the plan is being changed after the conclusion of the experience period.

If the benefit change had been made during the experience period, it would only be necessary to adjust the actual experience for that portion of the period during which the new benefits had not been available. This will provide a basis for projecting experience to a period for which the new benefits will be available for the entire period.

RATE CHANGES

It is necessary to make special provisions in the development of new premium rate levels for experience-rated groups in situations where rates have been changed during the experience period. The easiest way to illustrate this is with an example. Assume that premiums of $200,000 have been earned during a 12-month experience period, but premiums of $250,000 are required for the next 12 months. Based on this premise, a 25 percent increase ($250,000/$200,000) in the unit rates would be required. However, if there was a rate change midway through the 12-month period such that the $200,000 of earned premium represents $75,000 of earned premium for the first 6 months of experience and $125,000 for the last 6 months, no rate adjustment would be required since it can be assumed that earned premiums for the last 6 months will continue to be earned in the future. Over the next 12 months $250,000 ($125,000 for each of the next six-month periods)—the required premium—will be earned and no adjustment in the current rates is needed.

To arrive at a proper adjustment in the current rates where there has been a change in rates during the experience period, it is necessary to compare the required future premium level with that which would have been earned during the experience period if the current rates had been applied throughout the period (since this is the amount that will be earned in the future if no change were to be made), rather than with the premium level that was actually earned during the period.

APPLICATION TO OTHER RATE CATEGORIES

Problems posed by large individual claims, benefit changes, and rate changes also arise in evaluating past experience for an insurer's overall block of manually rated business as well as for partially experience-rated (blended manual-experience rated) groups. These problems generally are solved by the application of the principles previously described. It is often quite helpful in analyzing questions relating to manually rated groups to recognize that an insurer's portfolio of manually rated groups may be regarded as one very large experience-rated group, composed of many small subsidiaries. Similarly, while great variation exists among insurance companies in the specific formulas used to blend manual rates with the rates that would be produced by full experience rating for groups that fall between the insurer's manually rated and experience-rated categories, the same techniques are used to solve similar problems for such groups.

ADMINISTRATION OF PREMIUMS

Insurers determine premium rates charged by an insurer during the first year of a group policy as part of the initial underwriting process that also includes a review of the coverages to be insured, benefit levels, and administrative procedures. The rates established at the inception of the plan usually are guaranteed for the first 12 months if the plan is not changed during that period, although longer rate guarantee periods are sometimes granted. Premium rates for subsequent policy periods are determined as part of a rate review process, which may include the determination of any experience refunds for prior periods of coverage. At the end of the first policy year, new rates usually are established. Depending on the provisions of the contract, these rates also may be guaranteed for a stated time.

Since the major portion of an insurer's premium income comes from business that has been in force for a year or more, the overall profit or loss of a group operation depends a good deal on effective rerating.

TIMING OF RERATING ACTIONS

Most insurers give a policyholder at least 30 days' notice before implementing a rate increase. (In some instances, particularly for larger cases, 60 or even 90 days' notice may be given.) When 30 days' notice is given, an insurer commences its rerating procedures approximately 60 to 90 days prior to the premium change date. This presents no problem if the insurer bases its new premium rate levels on its schedule of manual rates.

Considering the lead time required to implement a rate increase, an insurer usually bases a rate increase on only the first nine months of paid claims so that the increase becomes effective on the first policy anniversary. In many cases insufficient claims experience then exists for the insurer to obtain a satisfactory estimate of first-year incurred claims experience. The insurer may choose, therefore, either on a case-by-case basis or as a matter of general practice, to defer commencing rerating procedures until completion of the first policy year. This procedure means that the new premium rates generally are not effective until three or four months after the first policy anniversary.

Making both the rerating and the experience refund calculations for a group at the same time enables an insurer both to realize some administrative savings and to have a better picture of the group's emerging claims experience. It also enables the group representative to deliver and discuss both actions with the policyholder at one time.

On the other hand, the insurer may conclude that nine months of the policyholder's first-year experience indicates sufficiently unfavorable experience to require a rate increase on the first policy anniversary. In subsequent years, too, the experience of the group may indicate hat premiums should be increased at the first opportunity, regardless of the date that the experience refund review is completed. In such instances the insurer will probably give up the convenience and modest administrative savings that result from combining rerating and experience refund actions, to avoid potentially large losses resulting from delaying necessary rate increases.

ANALYSIS OF EMERGING CLAIMS EXPERIENCE

All insurers base their rerating action for experience-rated groups on both mathematical formulas and informed judgment. Special analysis of the claims paid to the group, involving their timing, types, and causes, and any other factors that might affect claims projection for the next rate period, may be required. These studies may also indicate the need for claim control procedures or modifications in the benefits.

Insurers use information from this analysis to identify the reasons for past claims results and to estimate the probable future experience of the group. For example, if claims were high during an early part of the experience period but have decreased in recent months, the insurer will decide whether the earlier experience shows a chance upward fluctuation or the more recent experience a chance downward fluctuation. Similarly, a significant portion of the claims experienced could be for several group members who are not likely to have similar claims in the future. In this instance the insurer must decide whether to expect lower claims in the future or to anticipate similar claims from different individuals.

SPECIAL SITUATIONS AFFECTING RATES

In setting premium levels for a particular group, the insurer must take account of special situations that may exist. Although most insurers attempt to charge premiums in proportion to the risk covered, in some circumstances margins available from a particular coverage might be used to offset a premium increase needed for another coverage. For example, a life insurance margin in a program combined with medical care can be used to maintain a medical care premium rate below the level that would otherwise be required. Often a rate increase is not requested unless the expected claims for all coverages combined require such a step.

Also, rate adjustments for different lines of coverage that have virtually no effect on the total amount of premium payable for a group are often waived. This procedure avoids causing the policyholder the inconvenience associated with making the necessary changes in its accounting procedures.

Other situations also occur. If the group policyholder has several coverages combined for experience refund purposes, margins for adverse claim results on any particular coverage might be smaller than otherwise would be needed. If the insurer has established a claim fluctuation reserve in the group's experience refund account from favorable results of prior years, it may consider the availability of these funds to cover future plan costs in determining level of premium. When the experience account for a group is in a deficit position, some insurers will establish a higher contingency margin level in an effort to recover the deficit over a reasonable time. Naturally, such a decision must weigh the likelihood of increased terminations at the higher premium level against the level of the deficit recovery expected.

ALTERNATIVES TO RATE INCREASES

An insurer frequently will suggest to a policyholder alternatives to increased premium rates—ways that may lessen or eliminate the need for higher premiums or make higher premiums more acceptable. These alternatives are discussed below.

A REDUCTION IN BENEFITS

When the policyholder does not wish to accept an increase in premium rates, or when the size of the increase is quite large, the insurer may suggest a reduction in benefits in an effort to reduce or eliminate the proposed rate increase. Suggestions will vary, depending on the type of coverages provided and the existing benefits. For example:

- An increase in the elimination period or a reduction in the duration of benefits for disability income coverages;
- Under a comprehensive major medical plan, an increase in the deductible, a change in the coinsurance percentage, or a reduction or elimination of full coverage areas;
- If the benefits include basic medical care protection, application of a deductible to each hospital confinement; or
- The addition of managed care features to reduce the cost and/or utilization of services.

Often the insurer will provide the policyholder with several options for program changes, all of which would achieve the desired cost reduction.

CHANGES IN POLICY PROVISIONS

A claims review may indicate that revisions in certain policy provisions, such as a change in eligibility requirements, would be beneficial. For example, a claims study might reveal that a large number of claims were for persons employed by the policyholder for only a short period. An increase in the length of the waiting period for eligibility might improve the experience in this case.

ADDING NEW BENEFITS, UPDATING EXISTING BENEFITS

Health care costs continue to rise steadily. Group plans, therefore, require regular updating to maintain a reasonable relationship between the benefits provided and the expenses likely to be incurred. A needed rate increase may be more acceptable if it is combined with the addition of new benefits or updating of existing benefits.

Benefits added to the plan could

possibly reduce the overall cost of claims. For example, if the experience under hospital coverage is unfavorable because of a number of confinements for purely diagnostic services, a diagnostic x-ray and laboratory examination benefit might be added. The benefit would pay for diagnostic services in a doctor's office, a clinic, or on an outpatient basis at a hospital, in conjunction with a requirement that such testing, when medically feasible, be done in advance of admission to the hospital. This plan addition could reduce the size of the increase required in the hospital premium rates.

RETROSPECTIVE PREMIUM AGREEMENT

In some situations the insurer may offer to continue coverage at a rate level below that which it requires for the group, in exchange for a formal binding agreement from the policyholder. The policyholder agrees to pay the insurer for any deficits, up to a specified amount, that are incurred as a result of the lower rate level.

These agreements (Retrospective Premium Agreements) may be offered to larger (fully experience rated) groups in two instances: when there has been an unusual increase in recent claims experience or, more generally, where a difference of opinion exists as to the likely future claims level. Naturally, before offering this alternative, the insurer will consider the potential willingness and ability of the policyholder to meet such an obligation. Some insurers deny this arrangement to groups that have a cumulative plan deficit, since payment under the retrospective agreement would be a virtual certainty.

PREMIUM STABILIZATION RESERVE

In establishing a premium rate level, the insurer's primary motive is to secure adequate funds to cover future claims, expenses, contribution to surplus (profit), and margin. To the extent that an alternate source of funds is available to cover these items, the insurer generally is willing to reduce the risk and margin components of the premium rate. In the event that a policyholder has established a Premium Stabilization Reserve the insurer can reduce premium rates since, in the event of adverse experience, the insurer may use some or all of the funds in the Premium Stabilization Reserve to reduce the deficit.

CLAIMS EDUCATION AND CONTROL PROGRAM

An analysis of a group's claims may indicate abuse by the insured persons or providers of health care. In such situations a claims education and control program may be effective in reducing future claims, thus ultimately permitting smaller rate increases.

REDUCED RATE GUARANTEE PERIOD

The insurer and policyholder may disagree on the interpretation of past claims experience or projected claims or over some complex aspect of the rate-setting process. When such misunderstandings occur, the insurer may agree to a lower renewal rate adjustment in return for the opportunity to change rates, if necessary, before the end of the insurer's normal rate guarantee period.

ALTERNATIVES FOR BENEFIT PLAN FUNDING

During the 1960s, with rare exception the traditional insurance contract was the arrangement under which group benefit plans were funded. The insurance company was regarded by the buyer as the expert in its field and best qualified to manage all financial aspects of the group insurance program. However, large employers from time to time contemplated funding their insurance in some way other than conventional fully insured group plans.

Early in the 1970s many corporations experienced reduced profits and cash flow problems. At the same time, insurance plans became more liberal with accompanying increases in reserving requirements. Escalating inflation and greater utilization increased the cost of providing insurance benefits. Corporate money managers became concerned with making better use of corporation funds. Interest in the financial aspects of group insurance programs was heightened by an economic climate in which the cost of borrowing money for corporate purposes rose to an historic high.

All of this gave added impetus to consideration of alternate financing mechanisms. Employer involvement in plan administration through self-accounting methods and self-payment of claims replaced to some extent the traditional role of the insurer and created a need for developing the employer's own skilled insurance specialists.

Generally, the buyer interested in such alternatives has one or both of the following primary objectives in mind:

- the control and use of reserve funds normally available to an insurer for investment purposes under a conventional fully insured plan, and
- the reduction or elimination of state premium taxes and risk and contingency charges that normally are part of the cost under a conventional fully insured plan.

Accordingly, a number of techniques have been developed by insurers that modify conventional methods of funding group insurance and offer an adequate guarantee of comparable benefits. The techniques have two main subdivisions: funding arrangements with fully insured plans and alternatives that make the benefit plan either fully or partially self-funded. These techniques are discussed in detail in Part C of this course.

SUMMARY

Insurers take great care in pricing their products to achieve specific objectives and to ensure equitable treatment of policyholders. This function requires skill in mathematical and statistical analysis and the delicate balancing of insurer and policyholder goals.

KEY TERMS

Actuary
Adequacy
Alternate Funding
Blended Rate
Claim Frequency
Claim Severity
Competitive Rates
Constant Retention
Contribution to Surplus
Cost Shifting
Credibility
Equity
Expected Claims
Expected Expenses
Experience Period
Experience Rating
Intercompany Study
Intracompany Study
Loss Ratio
Manual Premium Rate
Margin
Medical Claim Trend
Net Premium
Pooling
Premium Rating Class
Premium Stabilization Reserve
Principle of Large Numbers
Rate Guarantee Period
Rate Manual
Rerating
Retention
Retrospective Premium
Retrospective Premium Agreement
Society of Actuaries
Trend
Utilization
Variable Retention

VIII

THE CONTRACT

INTRODUCTION

An insurance contract is simply a legal contract that binds both the insurance company and the policyholder to certain agreements. The contract and insurance policy can be thought of as synonymous. The insurance policy is the written evidence of specific insurance protection. It is the legal description of the type and scope of insurance protection provided and it also identifies the rights and responsibilities of insurer and insured toward that protection.

A policy usually sets forth the contractual agreement. However, a contract may exist even without issuance of an actual policy if the actions of the parties and the documents involved otherwise satisfy the legal requirements. On the other hand, even if an insurer issues a policy, the contract might not be legally enforceable against the insurer if fraud or material misrepresentation exists in the application or if either party fails to meet any of the essential elements for the formation of a contract.

BASIC COMPONENTS

Although a group insurance contract has certain unique features, it also contains the four basic elements of all contracts: *offer, acceptance, consideration, and a meeting of the minds.*

In the usual sales situation, the insurer presents a proposal that describes the insurance plan to the prospective policyholder. This proposal invites the prospective policyholder to make an offer, which the prospect does by completing an application and paying the required premium.

The insurer then either accepts or rejects the offer. The insurer accepts by approving the application and issuing the policy.

Following acceptance of an offer, each party to the contract—the insurer and the prospective policyholder—either gives or gives up something. The applicant's consideration is payment of the required premium; the insurer's consideration is its promise to provide the benefits described in the policy.

In addition, both parties to the contract must reach a meeting of minds—that is, understand and agree to their rights and obligations under the contract.

CHARACTERISTICS OF GROUP POLICIES

The group insurance contract, a master policy between the insurer and the policyholder, describes not only the benefits of the group insurance plan but also the terms and conditions under which they are provided. The contract represents mutual agreement to these terms and conditions by both parties—insurer and policyholder.

The group insurance contract is based on a good-faith business relationship. Drafting the precise benefit descriptions, reviewing them with the policyholder and, where necessary, filing them with the insurance department involved and receiving approval, requires a considerable amount of time. Several months beyond the policy effective date may elapse before the contract is issued; however, coverage is in effect. All administration, including the payment of claims, proceeds as though the contract had been issued on its effective date.

TERMS AND CONDITIONS

Certain terms and conditions characterize a group policy. Policies specify the:

- types and levels of benefits available to eligible persons in the group,
- requirements a group member must meet in order to become insured,
- provisions relating to claim, administrative, and legal aspects,
- circumstances under which coverage may terminate, and
- benefits that may be available to insureds after coverage has terminated.

The certificate may or may not be part of the contract. Usually it is not. Courts in some states, however, have enforced its description of the plan provisions. In those instances where the certificate is not part of the contract, if the certificate description differs from that of the contract, courts have held that the insured person who relied on the certificate was misled.

FORMAT FOR ISSUANCE

A policy may combine in one contract all the coverage of the plan—life, accidental death and dismemberment, hospital, surgical, and other medical care expense benefits. This method avoids duplication of policy provisions that are common to all coverages.

On the other hand, an insurer may issue a separate policy for each major line of coverage, adding supplemental coverages to these policies—for example, supplemental accident expense benefits added to a hospital expense policy. The definition of a "major line" differs somewhat among insurance companies, but it usually means group life insurance, accidental death and dismemberment insurance, short-term or long-term disability income insurance, medical—especially comprehensive major medical—and dental insurance. Supplemental major medical insurance is usually written as part of a hospital expense policy, except that it is written as a separate policy when the basic benefits are provided by an insurer other than the one that underwrites the major medical plan. Dental insurance may be written as a separate policy or offered as a supplemental benefit under a major medical plan.

Normally insurers use either the combined or separate type of policy form, but *not* both. Even when an insurer issues several separate policies, however, it may still consider them together in determining a premium refund to policyholder because of favorable claims experience (called experience refund), in calculating commissions, and for administrative functions.

CONTRACT REVISION

Policyholders often revise the type or levels of benefits in their plans and may change other provisions as well. To effect these changes, insurers use policy riders to describe the changes to the group insurance policy.

The policyholder signifies acceptance of the revision described in the rider by signing and returning it to the insurer. Some insurers issue contract amendments that do not require policyholder acceptance when the policyholder itself requests a change that involves a liberalization of the plan. A revision that reduces benefits, however, requires the policyholder's signature.

INSURANCE DEPARTMENT MATTERS

State insurance departments play a significant role in group insurance operations. Since policy forms require state approval before use, states exercise considerable control over the group insurance business.

Both the number and complexity of state laws and regulations are increasing at a rapid pace. Small group reform has come under intense state scrutiny and legislative activity.

STATE OF ISSUE (SITUS)

The state of issue or situs of a group insurance contract is the jurisdiction in which the contract is delivered or issued for delivery. It usually is the state where the policyholder has its headquarters but could also be the state where the majority of the policyholder's employees are located, provided a company officer authorized to make decisions pertaining to insurance matters also is located in that state. The laws and regulations of the state of issue usually control the interpretation and effect of the contract on all insured persons, even those located in other states. The exception to this is when the insured persons reside in a state that considers itself extraterritorial.

"Extraterritorial" means that all or certain portions of the laws of the state where the insured resides will govern the provisions of the group insurance contract, regardless of contract situs. For example, Texas considers itself extraterritorial with respect to all of its group insurance laws. Therefore, if a policy is issued in Tennessee but covers residents of Texas, the laws of Texas govern the provisions of the insurance contract that apply to Texas residents.

FILINGS

Most states require insurers to file group insurance policy and certificate forms with the state insurance department. If the filings meet with the department's approval, the insurer may then use the forms in that state. An insurance company that intends to do business in a number of states that require the filing of these forms will submit them to the insurance department of each of these states.

An insurer entering the group insurance field in a state where filing is required files all the forms it intends to use in that state. An insurer that has offered group coverage for a long time will already have a number of approved forms on file with the state insurance department; it will file new forms only when the approved forms do not meet new statutory requirements or when the insurer proposes new policy provisions or benefits that the approved forms cannot accommodate.

Over the years, insurance departments either have approved policy forms as submitted or have required the insurers to modify their forms in order to obtain approval. This procedure has produced a high degree of uniformity in both form and content among all group insurance contracts. Group insurance contracts also have been affected by court decisions, providers of medical care, competition, federal legislation (such as ADEA, TEFRA, DEFRA, COBRA, Medicare), state legislation, and published guidelines of several state insurance departments, notably New York, Pennsylvania, and California. The National Association of Insurance Commissioners' Model Group Life Insurance Act and Model Group Health Insurance Act are major influences affecting the standardization of important contract provisions.

METHODS OF FILING NEW FORMS

An insurer that has to file a new policy form decides among several methods: a general, limited, or one-case filing. A general filing involves submitting the proposed policy form to the insurance department of each state where the insurer does business. For a limited filing, the insurer submits the form only to the insurance department of the state where the form will be used. A "one-case" filing restricts the use of the policy form to the contract of the group policyholder named in the filing.

The determination of whether to undertake a general, limited, or "one-case" filing depends upon the circumstances. If the form involved is a new type of contract that will be issued to all group insurance policyholders, obviously a general filing is necessary. On the other hand, if the form provides for a special type of benefit developed to suit the needs of a particular policyholder, a more restricted filing will suffice; a "one-case" filing may be all that is necessary. To expand the scope of the approval, however, allowing for use of the benefit in other contracts issued in the same jurisdiction, the insurance company may decide to make a limited filing. Some insurance companies use a limited rather than "one-case" filing whenever possible because of its greater flexibility.

FLEXIBILITY OF CONTRACT FORMS

The basic policy and its provisions, filed with state insurance departments prior to issuance, usually contain a number of variations in the policy provisions. The insurer then may make all these variations available to policyholders so they can select the specific provisions that best suit their needs. The policy forms also may have blank spaces where the provisions of the plan purchased by the policyholder may be inserted, such as the dollar amount of daily room and board allowance in a hospital expense benefit plan.

These "variables" and "fill-in" areas in new policy forms, plus those in forms already approved, not only reduce the number of filings required of an insurer but also add to the flexibility insurers have in adapting their contracts to the needs of policyholders. The same basic contract form may be used to describe different benefit plans, conditions of eligibility, and termination provisions.

THE APPLICATION

The insurer receives from the application essential information regarding the group risk. The form itself may either be a long- or a short-form application. The long form shows the details of employee eligibility as well as the types and amounts of coverage. It gives the underwriter much of the information needed to evaluate the group and provide the benefit plan desired. When a short form is used, detailed information about the new plan is usually furnished to the underwriters on work sheets completed by group field personnel.

In either case the policyholder receives the final application with the policy. This application states that the policy has been approved by the insurer and its terms accepted by the policyholder. Signed by the policyholder and attached to the policy, it becomes a part of the contract.

Whatever the form of the application—short form or long form—the insurer must give its approval. An agent cannot pass on the acceptability of any insurance or modify or expand the issued contract. Insurance applied for becomes effective when an insurer's home office approves the application and all legal requirements regarding issuance have been met, including enrolling the minimum number of persons.

CONTRACT PROVISIONS

Group insurance contracts contain a number of specific definitions and provisions. Some provisions are general; others apply to either the policyholder or the persons insured under the contract. Details of these aspects of the contract follow.

DEFINITIONS

As in any contract, the terms used in a group policy should be easy to understand. To achieve this goal, policies define some of the key words and phrases used in the policy. Terms that relate to an individual's coverage and to premium payment are defined in the contract, as are such terms as "policy month" and "policy year." Without definitions there can be disagreement over what constitutes "treatment" or even "illness." Persons insured will attach their own meanings to these terms unless the definitions are established clearly in the contract.

Because of legislation, court decisions, and insurance industry efforts to provide more liberal coverage, the definitions of many of the terms used in the contract continually change. For example, the definition of a "physician" originally recognized only those licensed to practice medicine and surgery. It has been expanded by many insurance companies, especially under major medical plans, to include any legally qualified medical and non-medical practitioners as well as personnel such as social workers and nutritionists.

The definition of "dependents" varies little among insurance companies. They are usually defined as follows:

1. The spouse of an employee, provided:
   - the employee and spouse are not legally separated;
   - the spouse is not on active service in any branch of the armed forces or merchant marine of any country.

2. An unmarried child of an employee (including a stepchild) who is principally dependent on the employee for support and maintenance, and who is:
   - under age 19;
   - age 19 but under age 23 or 26 and a registered student in regular, full-time attendance at an accredited secondary school, college, or university with legal residence with the employee;
   - incapable of self-sustaining employment by reason of mental retardation or a physical handicap and who became incapable prior to attaining the age limit in the contract.

The above definition is a medical one. Dependent life defines a child as 15+ days of age, and only the first two items above apply.

When both a husband and a wife are insured under the same policy as employees, usually one or the other, but not both, may elect to cover their mutual dependents. Some states allow both spouses to cover mutual dependents.

In some contracts the medical definition of a dependent child also may include other members of the family, such as a foster child who permanently resides with the person insured and is dependent on that person for support and maintenance or a child in the process of adoption.

GENERAL PROVISIONS

In addition to definitions, a number of provisions generally appear in a group contract.

CLERICAL ERROR

If an error or omission occurs in the administration of a group policy, what the person's insurance should be is considered the correct basis or amount. For example, an employee promoted to a position that makes him/her eligible for a higher amount of life insurance would be entitled to that amount, even though the insurance records have not been revised to show the higher amount. Appropriate premium adjustments, of course, will be made. Failure of the policyholder to report a termination, however, will not continue insurance coverage on the individual.

INCONTESTABILITY

If a life insurance policy has been in force for a reasonable period (usually two years), the insurer cannot take the position that a valid contract does not exist unless the premiums are not paid. Similarly, no statement made by an insured individual relating to personal insurability may be used to dispute that person's insurance coverage after coverage has been in force for a certain period (usually two years).

ENTIRE CONTRACT

The policy and the application of the policyholder (and insured persons, if required) are the entire contract between the policyholder and the insurance company. Statements on the applications by the policyholder and by persons insured are considered representations, not warranties. In a "representation," the accuracy of the statements made by a person when applying for the contract or for individual coverage are not absolutely guaranteed. Since the statements are representations, the insurance company may not cancel insurance or reduce benefits on the basis of these statements unless they materially affect the underwriting of the coverage. If these representations were considered warranties, any misstatement, no matter how immaterial, would void the insurance.

In any event, no statement made by the policyholder or any insured person may be used by the insurer to void the policy or as a defense against a claim unless the statement is:

- in writing,
- signed by the person insured, and
- furnished to the insured or to that person's beneficiary.

Fraud, of course, voids the contract under any circumstances.

The courts have determined (*Cutler vs. Hartford Life Insurance Co.* and *Layman vs. Continental Assurance Co.*) that an insurer cannot claim material misrepresentation under group life insurance unless the insured or the insured's beneficiary received a copy of the application prior to the insured's death. Although these decisions relate to life insurance, the same principle, presumably, would apply to health insurance, since the language of the law is comparable.

MISSTATEMENT OF AGE

If the age of any individual insured under a group insurance policy has been misstated and, as a result, the person is insured for an amount different from that provided by the plan for a person at the correct age, the person's insurance is adjusted to the correct amount. The premiums are also adjusted.

RECORDS AND REPORTS

The insurance company or the policyholder, depending on the type of administration agreed upon, maintains records of all persons insured, including such information as their names, ages, amounts of insurance, insurance effective date, and, for group life or accidental death and dismemberment policies, their beneficiaries.

The policyholder agrees to furnish the insurer with information on individuals covered by the policy that the insurer needs to administer the coverage and determine premiums. The insurer has the right to inspect records of the policyholder for any purpose relating to the provisions of the insurance policy.

CERTIFICATE OF INSURANCE

Although not required in all states, a provision that requires that persons insured be issued a certificate describing the essential features of the group coverage commonly is included in all group contracts wherever issued. In addition to a schedule of amounts and description of benefits, these certificates contain information about age limits, notice and proof of loss requirements, the insurer's right to examine the claimant, and the conditions under which benefits are payable. The right to convert to individual coverage when group coverage ends also is described.

The certificate is not a contract between the certificate holder and the insuring company, nor between the certificate holder and the policyholder. Most often, one certificate is issued for all coverages in the group plan. When a plan is changed, certificate riders may be used to show the change or, if the change is substantial, new certificates may be issued showing the revised plan as of the date the change was made.

Certificates vary considerably among insurers in type and format. The trend is toward issuing certificates in booklet form and describing the conditions of coverage and other plan features in nontechnical, easy-to-understand language.

NOTICE, PROOF OF LOSS, AND PAYMENT OF CLAIMS

Specific provisions in health insurance contracts apply to:

- the time limit for submitting a notice of claim to the insurance company, usually 20 days from date of loss,
- the time limit for submitting proofs of loss, usually 90 days, and
- the time that the insurance company has to make payment, usually 60 days after proof of loss has been filed.

The health insurance statutes of some states require that insurers include many of these provisions in all health insurance policies.

Late submission of either notice or proof of loss does not affect the consideration of a claim, if there is good reason for it. When permitted by law, some insurers require the submission of proof within one year from the normal time limit, to avoid problems with claims that are unreasonably old. Insurers generally include provisions relating to claim payments in all their contracts, even if there is no governing statute in the state of issue.

FACILITY OF PAYMENT

The facility of payment provision permits the insurer to pay a portion of the proceeds of a life insurance policy directly to those who have incurred expenses in connection with the insured's fatal illness or burial. The maximum that may be paid is shown in the provision and usually is limited to a specific amount. The amount paid by the insurer is then deducted from the total death benefit and the balance is paid to the beneficiary.

ASSIGNMENT OF BENEFITS

Medical care expense policies usually state that no assignment is binding on the insurer unless it is in writing and has been filed at the home office. Although group medical benefits normally are payable directly to the insured person, most contracts permit the insured to assign benefits to the providers of medical care services. Even in the absence of a specific contract provision permitting an assignment of benefits, insurers commonly not only accept such assignments but promote their use by making provision for them on the claim forms that the insured person completes.

Group life and accidental death and dismemberment policies allow an employee to make an absolute assignment. Although insurers accept no responsibility as to whether or not the assignment made by any employee is legally binding on them, they will consider such an assignment valid if it is made without consideration to: (1) their estates, (2) a trustee of a trust under which any such person is one of the beneficiaries, or (3) one or more of the following persons:

- the employee's spouse,
- the employee's lineal descendants (including legally adopted children), or
- the employee's lineal ascendants (including legally adoptive parents).

The assignment must be in writing and accepted by both the policyholder and the insurance company. While the assignment is in effect, the assignee has the sole right to exercise any of the rights and privileges previously given to the employee, including naming a beneficiary and exercising the conversion privilege. If the assignee does not designate a beneficiary, claim payments will be made to the assignee. The assignee cannot, however, designate a beneficiary for payments under a rider providing survivor income benefits; payment under these plans will go only to those persons provided for under the rider.

OTHER PROVISIONS

Health insurance contracts contain provisions concerning the payment of benefits if the insured is a minor, is otherwise not competent to give a release, or if the insured person has died while some benefits remain unpaid. Unassigned benefits usually will be paid to the surviving spouse, to any surviving children, or to the executors or administrators of the insured's estate.

Contracts also may stipulate that an insured person may not start legal action earlier than 60 days after filing proof of loss, and that the legal action must be brought within two years of the time for filing proof of loss.

To permit the gathering of all the detailed information about a claim needed to judge its merits, the contract gives the insurer the right and opportunity to examine the insured whenever and as often as required, within reason. The insurance company usually pays for this examination. In addition, where not prohibited by law, the insurer has the right to order an autopsy.

PROVISIONS RELATING TO THE POLICYHOLDER

The following material deals with those provisions that specifically impact on a group policyholder.

EFFECTIVE DATE

The effective date of the group contract is established by agreement between the policyholder and the insurer. Usually, this date is shown on the face page of the policy and applies to all of its sections unless there is a special arrangement to have one or more of the coverages become effective at some later date. Group insurance transferred from one insurer to another places the effective date of the new contract immediately following the termination date of the old one to provide continuous coverage for persons insured when the transfer occurs.

INFORMATION REQUIRED OF THE POLICYHOLDER

The contract imposes certain duties on the policyholder. Among them is the requirement to furnish certain information to the insurer concerning persons becoming insured or changes in classification or status that have a bearing on the amount of insurance coverage. This information is essential when the insurance company is to administer all phases of the plan, including premium billing.

PREMIUMS

The frequency of premium payment is stated in the contract. Almost all group policyholders pay premiums monthly; a few pay annually, semi-annually, or quarterly.

Initial premium rates shown in the policy are the rates used to calculate the initial premium. At renewal insurers commonly omit premium rates from the policy; instead, they use a letter or some other form of notice to tell the policyholder of the renewal rates. Most policies guarantee initial premium rates for 12 months unless the terms of the policy are changed. Occasionally, however, rates are guaranteed for as little as three months or as long as two or three years, depending on the coverage.

After the initial guarantee period, rates may be changed only at certain times. Practices vary but, typically, rates may be changed:

- on any premium due date, provided the insurer notifies the policyholder at least 31 days before the premium due date, or
- when the terms of the policy are changed.

GRACE PERIOD

Group contracts provide for a grace period (commonly 31 days after the due date) during which the policyholder may pay overdue premiums without an interest penalty. During this time the coverage remains in force unless the policyholder has given the insurer written notice of contract termination. If by the end of the grace period the overdue premium has not been paid, the contract terminates. Because coverage is in force and the insurer is liable for claims incurred during the grace period, the policyholder is liable for the premium for this period.

EXPERIENCE REFUNDS

The contracts may have a specific provision for the return of premium to the policyholder in the form of an experience refund, determined as of the policy anniversary date if the contract is in force and premiums have been paid. Policyholders who have transferred their group plan to another insurer as of a date other than the policy anniversary also may be eligible for a refund from the former insurer. (This depends on the practice of the former insurer.) In this instance, the refund is based on the period ending as of the date of termination.

The experience refund may be in cash or, at the policyholder's option, either applied to subsequent premiums or left on deposit with the insurer. Further, the provision in the policy may state that, if the total employees' contributions exceed the cost of the insurance after the experience refund, the employer will use the excess for the benefit of the employees. Policyholders usually do this by waiving or reducing contributions or by providing increased benefits.

AUTHORITY TO MODIFY THE CONTRACT

The policy provisions are modified only by agreement between the policyholder and the insurance company. Brokers, agents, or other representatives of the insurer do not have the right to make changes in contract provisions. The contract specifically designates those who do have the authority to modify it. Usually, these authorized persons are the officers of the insurance company.

RIGHT TO TERMINATE

Generally, a policyholder may terminate its policy on any premium due date, giving 31 days' advance written notice to the insurer; the insurer, however, usually has only a limited right of termination. The insurer exercises this termination right most often when the policyholder has failed to maintain minimum enrollment requirements. In such cases, 31 days' advance notice generally is given to the policyholder. For the typical employer group, these participation requirements may be expressed in the contract as a percentage of all employees eligible to participate in the plan, such as 75 percent, or as a numerical minimum, such as ten employees—or both.

For an association or a union group plan, different participation requirements may apply. A minimum requirement of ten participants is not unusual. The insurance company usually may terminate the coverage as of a premium due date, though some contracts restrict the insurer's right to terminate to a policy anniversary.

PROVISIONS RELATING TO THE PERSONS INSURED

The following provisions affect the persons insured under a group plan.

ELIGIBILITY

The definition of eligible persons varies depending on whether an employer group or some other entity is the policyholder. The date on which a person becomes eligible for coverage normally is the later of the effective date of the plan or the first day after completion of a probationary waiting period.

EFFECTIVE DATE OF COVERAGE

The rules defining effective date of coverage vary, depending on whether or not the persons to be insured are contributing part of the premium. When the policyholder is paying the full cost of the group plan, a request for coverage is not necessary; nevertheless, the enrollees are asked to complete enrollment cards for record purposes and for beneficiary designations. Coverage automatically begins on an employee's eligibility date. When employees contribute, the eligible person applies for coverage by completing an enrollment card that includes authorization for payroll deductions—the usual method used by the policyholder to collect employee contributions.

If application is made on or before the date the person becomes eligible, coverage usually begins on the eligibility date. If application is made more than 31 days *after* the person becomes eligible, the contract normally requires the late entrant to submit evidence of insurability. This requirement also applies to persons seeking reinstatement of insurance coverage after they have voluntarily cancelled it. If the evidence submitted is satisfactory, coverage may begin on the date the home office underwriters approve the application or, in some contracts, on the date the evidence was submitted.

Rather than require evidence of insurability from late applicants, however, some insurers defer the effective date of coverage for three months or provide reduced benefits for a limited period of time. This is common in the case of late applicants for dependent coverage. Insurance coverage also may be deferred in any of the situations described above until the first day of a policy month or even until the policy anniversary.

Whether the group is contributory or noncontributory, insurers defer the usual effective date of coverage if, on that date, the employee is not actively at work because of illness or injury. The "actively-at-work" requirement is not an appropriate basis for establishing coverage for dependents; therefore, the contract may require that the dependent not be confined in a hospital, in a similar institution, or at home on the effective date. A disabled employee's coverage begins on return to full-time work; the dependent's coverage begins when the individual is no longer confined. (This requirement usually does not apply to newborn children of an employee if dependent coverage is in effect on the date of birth.) Dependent coverage cannot become effective until the employee's coverage is in effect.

In order to provide uninterrupted coverage, insurers often waive these provisions—particularly for coverage transferred from one insurer to another where individuals involved have been insured under a previous insurer's policy.

BENEFITS

Contracts include benefit provisions that fully describe the conditions and level of benefits as well as limitations of coverage. The number and type of these provisions depend on the plan the policyholder buys.

COORDINATION OF BENEFITS

In many families, both husband and wife are employed. An increasing number of people also are insured under more than one health benefits plan. Since both the employee and dependents may make claims to the employee's insurer, whether the employee or any dependent is insured under another insurance plan, total benefits received may exceed the expenses incurred. This situation permits an insured to make a "profit," leading to overutilization of the benefit plan and to increased health insurance premium rates. Inclusion of a Coordination of Benefits (COB) provision avoids such overpayment. This provision, common in group policies, takes into account total benefits paid to a person who has overlapping coverage under more than one plan. The total benefit payments will not exceed, and may be less than, the total expenses. Details about the COB provision appear in the Group B and C text under "Claims."

PREEXISTING CONDITIONS

Both short- and long-term disability plans and medical care expense plans may contain a preexisting conditions provision. This item excludes or limits the benefits for an injury or sickness that has existed during a specified period—such as three or six months—prior to a person's becoming insured. Insurer practice determines the size of the groups and the types of coverage to which this provision applies, except in such cases as New York, which does not allow for preexisting provisions in groups of 300 or more lives. Insurers also usually waive this provision for transferred cases of a certain minimum size, such as 25 employees, although they may restrict benefit amounts to the lesser of the two benefit plans—

the new or the replaced. In many states, 41 at last count, small group reform initiatives have restricted the applicability of preexisting contractual provisions.

Group plans may cover preexisting conditions on the same basis as any other condition once the individual has been insured for a certain period of time or meets other criteria. For example, the preexisting condition limitation in a medical care expense policy ceases to apply on the earliest of the following dates:

- the end of three consecutive months during which no charges were incurred for the preexisting condition or any related condition,
- the end of six consecutive months during which the employee was continuously insured and actively at work, or
- the end of 12 consecutive months during which the person was continuously insured.

INSURING CLAUSE

The insuring clause provides that the insurer agrees to pay the benefits described in the policy to each individual who is insured and who, according to the terms of the policy, is entitled to the benefits. The clause also specifies that proof of loss must be submitted to the insurer before claim payment will be made.

LIFE INSURANCE: MAXIMUM CONTRIBUTION

The New York State Insurance Department limits the contribution of insured individuals to the cost of term life insurance, for nonhazardous industries, to the greater of $.60 a month per $1,000, or 75 percent of the premium rate.

A contribution higher than 60 cents is permitted, however, for certain hazardous industries.

The maximum contributions established in the New York regulation have generally been accepted as the maximum amount an individual can contribute. Michigan has a similar regulation, except the maximum for a nonhazardous risk is the lesser of 60 cents and 75 percent of the rate.

BENEFICIARY DESIGNATION

Under both life insurance policies and the death benefit of accidental death and dismemberment insurance, the insured person has the right to name or change the beneficiary. (Statutes may prohibit naming the employer as the beneficiary.) Insureds may change a beneficiary on written request to the insurance company, or to the policyholder if the group is self-administered. The change will be effective on the date of the request or of its receipt in the insurer's home office, whichever is specified in the contract. For a self-administered group, receipt by the policyholder is equivalent to receipt by the insurer.

If the insured dies without naming a beneficiary or if the beneficiary dies before the insured, the insurer will try to establish a payee for the life insurance benefits. This payee will be identified through the "successive preference beneficiary" procedure, which often is included in the contract. Under this procedure, the first of the following classes in which there is a survivor will become the beneficiary:

- the employee's spouse,
- surviving children,
- surviving parents,
- surviving brothers or sisters, or
- executors or administrators.

TERMINATION OF AN INDIVIDUAL'S INSURANCE

The provisions for terminating an individual's insurance vary depending on the type of group and coverage. The most common termination provisions are those based on conditions pertaining to employment in plans that cover employees. These provisions terminate coverage at the earliest of:

- the date the group policy terminates,
- the date the policy is amended to terminate the eligibility of the class of employees to which the employee belongs,
- at the end of the period for which the last premium has been paid for the employee,
- the date employment terminates,
- or the date the employee transfers out of a class eligible for coverage.

In a union or an association group, coverage terminates when membership terminates. Under credit life, coverage terminates when the debt is repaid or there is failure to pay the premium. Survivor income coverage, dependent life insurance, and dependent health insurance terminate when the insured employee no longer has an eligible family member. Dependent coverage ends earlier if an employee's insurance terminates or for a particular dependent if that person no longer meets the definition of an eligible dependent in the policy.

EXTENDED BENEFITS

Group insurance contracts generally extend benefits if coverage ends for any reason. Some policies require a premium payment, and other policies waive such payment.

Life Insurance. Insurers are required to continue group term coverage for a person who has a conversion right for the period during which the person is eligible to convert to permanent insurance, whether or not disabled at the time of termination. Therefore, if an insured employee dies within 31 days after termination of employment, the beneficiary will receive the same death benefit that would have been payable if the termination had not occurred. If an insured dependent under a dependent life plan dies within 31 days following termination of the dependent life coverage, the dependent's death benefit also will be paid.

Life insurance policies also may provide special benefits for insureds who are totally and permanently disabled when their insurance coverage ends.

In the event an employee (1) has insurance cease due to termination or amendment of the policy, (2) has been continuously insured under the policy for five years immediately prior to termination, or (3) dies within 31 days following termination, the beneficiary will receive the lesser of:

- a specified amount, such as $2,000 to $10,000 (as required by state law), or
- the amount the employee was last insured for, less the amount of any group life insurance for which the employee became insured within 31 days following termination.

Medical and Disability Benefits. Insurers may provide extended medical care benefits to a disabled insured whose coverage terminates for any reason, if the person insured (1) is totally disabled when the insurance terminates and (2) has been continuously disabled until the date covered medical services are received. Only medical services received for the disabling condition qualify for benefits. Similar provisions apply to dependents' coverage. For extended dental or vision care benefits, however, an individual does not have to be disabled.

The extended benefit period generally is three months for basic medical care benefits and a year to 24 months for major medical benefits. The length of this period may depend, however, on whether an individual or the group itself terminates. For an individual termination the major medical extended benefit may run to the end of the calendar year following the year in which insurance terminated.

Many states have adopted the NAIC Discontinuance and Replacement regulation. This regulation requires all group health insurance policies to extend benefits 90 days for hospital and medical, 12 months for major medical, and a period of accrued liability in the case of disability coverage.

COVERAGE CONTINUATION

Except for disability income insurance, group contracts usually provide continuation of coverage on an employee who is disabled, temporarily laid off, or on leave of absence. Disability income insurance may not continue since the individual receives no income from the policyholder; therefore, there is no income to replace. However, some insurers will cover short-term disability premiums for the period benefits are being paid.

A majority of states require group medical policies to provide a right of continuation of varying periods depending on state law. Such rights are usually available to the employee upon termination of employment, and to the spouse and eligible dependents if coverage ends because of divorce or death of the employee.

Federal law (COBRA), applicable to employers of 20 or more employees, requires employers to include in their health benefit plans a right of continuation for employees upon termination of employment for any reason (other than gross misconduct) or upon reduction of hours worked. That right of continuation applies to spouses and dependents upon divorce (or legal separation) from the employee, death of the employee, or the employee becoming eligible for Medicare. Dependent children also may continue coverage when their eligibility as a dependent otherwise terminates. Continued coverage under these provisions terminates

- when the policy is terminated for failure to pay the premium required of each continuee,
- when other similar coverage is obtained (unless the similar coverage contains a pre-existing conditions exclusion or limitation), when the continuee is entitled to Medicare, or
- on the date for termination stated in the law.

CONVERSION PRIVILEGE

The conversion privilege permits employees and dependents to continue their insurance protection with an individual policy or group certificate if coverage under a group life insurance or medical care expense policy ceases when:

- the employee terminates employment in a class of employees insured under the group policy,
- the policy is amended to terminate coverage on the class to which the employee belongs,
- the group policy is terminated, or
- a dependent child, reaches the limiting age.

Although evidence of insurability is not required, the person usually must apply in writing and pay the first premium within 31 days of termination of the group coverage. Those who voluntarily discontinue their insurance coverage while still employed are not eligible to convert.

Under various state laws, conversion rights are required only upon expiration of any applicable continuation of coverage. Frequently, under such state laws, the spouse has a conversion right upon death of or divorce from the employee or group member.

Life Insurance Conversion. If an employee terminates employment or has coverage reduced, statutes in some states give the individual more than 31 days following termination or reduction of coverage in which to apply for conversion, especially if the person was not given proper notification of the right to convert. The individual conversion policy becomes effective at the expiration of the 31 days following termination or reduction of group coverage.

Insureds may choose to convert either the entire terminated amount that was in force under the group policy, or a lower amount, to any type of permanent individual life insurance the insurer usually offers. Some states, however, require insurers to offer one year, single premium, preliminary term insurance prior to permanent individual life insurance. Some insurers apply this practice in all states. Benefits for total and permanent disability and additional benefits for accidental death are not offered.

A spouse insured under a dependent life insurance plan may also convert to an individual policy if the employee's coverage ends. Conversion is on the same terms and conditions that apply to the employee's conversion right. Dependent children are not eligible to convert to individual life insurance policies except in those states that mandate this right.

If the employee has been continously insured for five years or more prior to termination, an individual life insurance conversion policy is available on termination of the policy or the class to which the employee belongs. The amount of insurance available is the lesser of a specified amount (such as $2,000 or $10,000) or the amount for which the employee was last insured, minus the amount of any group life insurance for which the employee became eligible after termination.

Medical Insurance Conversion. The conversion privilege is available to persons (1) who have been insured under a group medical care expense contract for at least three months, and (2) who terminate membership in the group and are not eligible for similar coverage under another group plan. Individuals have the right to convert both their own coverage and the coverage of all dependents who were insured under the group policy. A dependent child whose group coverage is terminating because of attaining the age limit also has the right to convert to individual insurance. A spouse whose coverage is terminating because of the death of the employee may convert both his or her own coverage and the coverage on dependent children. In some states, a spouse also has a conversion privilege when there is a divorce.

The group policy often states the benefits the converted coverage will provide. The individual may choose from the plan or plans required to be provided in the state where the group policy is issued. Such plans provide hospital, surgical, and/or major medical insurance, but the plan selected usually does not provide greater benefits than those that were available under the group policy.

New York was the first state to require that group medical care expense contracts contain a conversion privilege. It is now mandatory in many states. Some states require that the insured receive a written notice of the right to convert; otherwise, the time during which conversion is available is extended from 31 days to as long as 91 days.

COBRA

The Consolidated Omnibus Budget Reconciliation Act of 1985 (COBRA) sets forth certain regulations for continuation of medical care insurance for employees and their dependents. Basically, the Act provides as follows:

If an employee's insurance ends because of ceasing to be in an eligible class under this policy, which stays in effect, the employee may elect to continue medical care insurance, and dependents' medical care insurance. After the policy holder notifies the employee or eligible dependent of their right to continue coverage, the employee must then elect coverage within 60 days of the later of (1) the date of the qualifying event, or (2) the date the plan administrator gives notice of the right to elect this continuation. The employee will be required to pay all the premiums due.

Insurance for the employee may continue until the earliest of the following dates:

- end of the period for which the last premium has been paid by the employee,
- date a person is entitled to Medicare,
- end of a period of 18 months,
- date the person is insured under another group insurance plan not containing a pre-existing exclusion or limitation, or
- date the policy ends for all employees.

If medical care insurance ends for the listed dependents, they may elect to continue it. To do so, they usually must notify the policyholder within 60 days of the later of (1) the date of the qualifying event, or (2) the date the plan administrator gives them notice of their right to elect this continuation, whichever is later.

The dependent will be required to pay the premiums due. A spouse or dependent child may elect continuation if the insurance ends because the employee dies; the marriage ends by divorce, legal separation, or annulment; or the employee becomes entitled to Medicare.

A child who ceases to be defined as "dependent" in the policy may also elect continuation.

Insurance may continue until the earliest of:

- the end of the period for which the last premium has been paid by the dependent,
- the date the dependent is eligible for Medicare,
- the end of a period of 36 months,
- the date the dependent is insured under another group insurance plan, not containing a pre-existing exclusion or limitation, or
- the date the policy ends.

OPTIONAL MODES OF SETTLEMENT

The death benefit for which an individual is insured, under all employee group life insurance plans except survivor income benefits, is a specified amount of money payable in a lump sum. The Optional Modes of Settlement provision in group life policies, however, permits the insured to elect to have the death benefit paid in a number of different ways. The insured must give a written notice to the insurance company of the option selected but retains the right to change or revoke the election. Accidental death and dismemberment benefits also may be included in the election. If the insured did not select a mode of settlement before death, the beneficiary may do so by giving written notice to the insurance company. The options commonly available to both the insured and the beneficiary are:

1. *Deposit Option.* The proceeds are left on deposit with the insurance company and the interest is paid to the beneficiary. Full or partial withdrawal of the funds on deposit may be permitted.

2. *Installment Option—Fixed Period.* The proceeds are payable in equal installments for the number of years elected, usually not more than 30, based on a table of installments developed by the insurance company.

3. *Installment Option—Fixed Amount.* The proceeds are payable in equal installments until the proceeds plus interest on the unpaid balance are exhausted. The beneficiary may be permitted to make a complete or partial withdrawal of the funds.

4. *Life Income Option.* Several options are available:

- 10 or 20 years certain. The proceeds are payable in installments during the beneficiary's lifetime. If the beneficiary dies before the end of the 10- or 20-year "certain" period, installments will continue to be paid to a secondary beneficiary or to the beneficiary's executors or administrators for the balance of the "certain" period.

- "Refund certain." The proceeds are payable in installments during the beneficiary's lifetime. If the beneficiary dies before the total benefit is paid, the amount remaining goes to a secondary beneficiary or to the beneficiary's executors or administrators.

5. *Joint and Survivor Option—10 Years Certain.* The proceeds will be paid in equal installments during the lifetime of either of two named beneficiaries. The insured may also provide for the payment of the remaining "certain" (10 years) benefits to a secondary beneficiary, if both the beneficiaries should die before the end of the "certain" period.

6. *Annuity Option.* One additional option is available to the beneficiary when the beneficiary has the right to elect an optional mode of settlement. This option permits the beneficiary to purchase a single premium annuity on her/his own life. The beneficiary may choose any of the types of single premium annuities offered by the insurance company at the time of purchase.

SUMMARY

The group insurance policy/contract has certain characteristics in format and content unique to the group insurance business. State insurance departments oversee such contracts, which have not only general provisions but provisions that apply to either the master group policyholder (an employer, an association, etc.) or to the individuals insured under the group plan. The importance of the contract, representing the agreement between the involved parties, cannot be overemphasized.

KEY TERMS

Acceptance
Actively at Work
Amendment
Application
Assignment of Benefits
Beneficiary Designation
Certificate of Insurance
Clerical Error Provision
Consideration
Consolidated Omnibus Budget Reconciliation Act (COBRA)
Contract
Contract Filing
Contract Provision
Conversion Privilege
Coordination of Benefits (COB)
Dependents
Effective Date
Eligibility
Eligibility Date
Entire Contract
Experience Refund
Extended Benefits
Extraterritorial
Facility of Payment
General Filing
Grace Period
Incontestability
Insuring Clause
Late Application
Limited Filing
Major Line
Minimum Enrollment Requirement
Misstatement of Age
Mode of Settlement
National Association of Insurance Commissioners (NAIC)
Offer
One-Case Filing
Policy
Preexisting Conditions Provision
Proof of Loss
Representation
Rider
Settlement Option
Situs of Contract
State Insurance Department
Termination Provisions
Variable Policy Forms
Warranty

Appendix A

NAIC GROUP HEALTH INSURANCE DEFINITION AND GROUP HEALTH INSURANCE STANDARD PROVISIONS MODEL ACT

(WITH 1985 AMENDMENTS)

SECTION 1. GROUP HEALTH INSURANCE DEFINITION

Except as provided in Section 2, no policy of group health insurance shall be delivered in this state unless it conforms to one of the following descriptions:

A. A policy issued to an employer, or to the trustees of a fund established by an employer, which employer or trustees shall be deemed the policyholder, to insure employees of the employer for the benefit of persons other than the employer, subject to the following requirements:

(1) The employees eligible for insurance under the policy shall be all of the employees of the employer, or all of any class or classes thereof. The policy may provide that the term "employees" shall include the employees of one or more subsidiary corporations, and the employees, individual proprietors, and partners of one or more affiliated corporations, proprietorships or partnerships if the business of the employer and of such affiliated corporations, proprietorships or partnerships is under common control. The policy may provide that the term "employees" shall include retired employees, former employees and directors of a corporate employer. A policy issued to insure the employees of a public body may provide that the term "employees" shall include elected or appointed officials. (Last sentence of subsection (A)(1) may be deleted if its content is covered.)

(2) The premium for the policy shall be paid either from the employer's fund or from funds contributed by the insured employees, or from both. Except as provided in subsection (3), a policy on which no part of the premium is to be derived from funds contributed by the insured

employees must insure all eligible employees, except those who reject such coverage in writing.

(3) A insurer may exclude or limit the coverage on any person as to whom evidence of individual insurability is not satisfactory to the insurer.

B. A policy issued to a creditor or its parent holding company or to a trustee or trustees or agent designated by two or more creditors, which creditor, holding company, affiliate, trustee, trustees or agent shall be deemed the policyholder, to insure debtors of the creditor or creditors with respect to their indebtedness, subject to the following requirements:

(1) The debtors eligible for insurance under the policy shall be all of the debtors of the creditor or creditors, or all of any class or classes thereof. The policy may provide that the term "debtors" shall include (i) borrowers of money or purchasers or lessees of goods, services, or property for which payment is arranged through a credit transaction; (ii) the debtors of one or more subsidiary corporations; and (iii) the debtors of one or more affiliated corporations, proprietorships or partnerships if the business of the policyholder and of such affiliated corporations, proprietorships or partnerships is under common control.

(2) The premium for the policy shall be paid either from the creditor's funds, or from charges collected from the insured debtors, or from both. Except as provided in subsection (3), a policy on which no part of the premium is to be derived from funds contributed by insured debtors specifically for their insurance must insure all eligible debtors.

(3) An insurer may exclude any debtors as to whom evidence of individual insurability is not satisfactory to the insurer.

(4) The total amount of insurance payable with respect to an indebtedness shall not exceed the greater of the scheduled or actual amount of unpaid indebtedness to the creditor. The insurer may exclude any payments which are delinquent on the date the debtor becomes disabled as defined in the policy.

(5) The insurance may be payable to the creditor or any successor to the right, title, and interest of the creditor. Such payment or payments shall reduce or extinguish the unpaid indebtedness of the debtor to the extent of each such payment and any excess of the insurance shall be payable to the insured or the estate of the insured.

(6) Notwithstanding the preceding provisions of this section, insurance on agricultural credit transaction commitments may be written up to the amount of the loan commitment. Insurance on educational credit transaction commitments may be written up to the amount of the loan commitment less the amount of any repayments made on the loan.

C. A policy issued to a labor union, or similar employee organization, which shall be deemed to be the policyholder, to insure members of such union or organization for the benefit of persons other than the union or organization or any of its officials, representatives, or agents, subject to the following requirements:

(1) The members eligible for insurance under the policy shall be all of the members of the union or organization, or all of any class or classes thereof.

(2) The premium for the policy shall be paid either from funds of the union or organization, or from funds contributed by the insured members specifically for their insurance, or from both. Except as provided in subsection (3), a policy on which no part of the premium is to be derived from funds contributed by the insured members specifically for their insurance must insure all eligible members, except those who reject such coverage in writing.

(3) An insurer may exclude or limit the coverage on any person as to whom evidence of individual insurability is not satisfactory to the insurer.

D. A policy issued to a trust, or the trustee(s) of a fund, established or adopted by two or more employers, or by one or more labor unions of similar employee organizations, or by one or more employers and one or more labor unions or similar employee organizations, which trust or trustee(s) shall be deemed the policyholder, to insure employees of the employers or members of the unions or organizations for the benefit of persons other than the employers or the unions or organizations, subject to the following requirements:

(1) The persons eligible for insurance shall be all of the employees of the employers or all of the members of the unions or organizations, or all of any class or classes thereof. The policy may provide that the term "employees" shall include the employees of one or more subsidiary corporations, and the employees, individual proprietors, and partners of one or more affiliated corporations, proprietorships or partnerships if the business of the employer and of such affiliated corporations, proprietorships or partnerships is under common control. The policy may provide that the term "employees" shall include retired employees, former employees and directors of a corporate employer. The policy may provide that the term "employees" shall include the trustees or their employees, or both, if their duties are principally connected with such trusteeship.

(2) The premium for the policy shall be paid from funds contributed by the employer or employers of the insured persons, or by the unions or similar employee organizations, or by both, or from funds contributed by the insured persons or from both the insured persons and the employer(s) or union(s) or similar employee organization(s). Except as provided in subsection (3), a policy on which no part of the premium is to be derived from funds contributed by the insured persons specifi-

cally for their insurance must insure all eligible persons, except those who reject such coverage in writing.

(3) An insurer may exclude or limit the coverage on any person as to whom evidence of individual insurability is not satisfactory to the insurer.

E. A policy issued to an association or to a trust or to the trustee(s) of a fund established, created, or maintained for the benefit of members of one or more associations. The association or associations shall have at the outset a minimum of 100 persons and have been organized and maintained in good faith for purposes other than that of obtaining insurance; shall have been in active existence for at least one year; and shall have a constitution and by-laws which provide that (i) the association or associations hold regular meetings not less than annually to further purposes of the members, (ii) except for credit unions, the association or associations collect dues or solicit contributions from members, and (iii) the members have voting privileges and representation on the governing board and committees. The policy shall be subject to the following requirements:

(1) The policy may insure members of such association or associations, employees thereof or employees of members, or one or more of the preceding or all of any class or classes thereof for the benefit of persons other than the employee's employer.

(2) The premium for the policy shall be paid from funds contributed by the association or associations, or by employer members, or by both, or from funds contributed by the covered persons or from both the covered persons and the association, associations, or employer members.

(3) Except as provided in subsection (4), a policy on which no part of the premium is to be derived from funds contributed by the covered persons specifically for their insurance must insure all eligible persons, except those who reject such coverage in writing.

(4) An insurer may exclude or limit the coverage on any person as to whom evidence of individual insurability is not satisfactory to the insurer.

F. A policy issued to a credit union or to a trustee or trustees or agent designated by two or more credit unions, which credit union, trustee, trustees, or agent shall be deemed the policyholder, to insure members of such credit union or credit unions for the benefit of persons other than the credit union or credit unions, trustee or trustees, or agent or any of their officials, subject to the following requirements:

(1) The members eligible for insurance shall be all of the members of the credit union or credit unions, or all of any class or classes thereof.

(2) The premium for the policy shall be paid by the policyholder from the credit union's funds and, except as provided in subsection (3), must insure all eligible members.

(3) An insurer may exclude or limit the coverage on any member as to whom evidence of individual insurability is not satisfactory to the insurer.

G. A policy issued to cover persons in group where that group is specifically described by a law of this state as one which may be covered for group life insurance. The provisions of such law relating to eligibility and evidence of insurability shall apply.

SECTION 2. LIMITS OF GROUP HEALTH INSURANCE

Group health insurance offered to a resident of this state under a group health insurance policy issued to a group other than one described in Section 1 shall be subject to the following requirements:

A. No such group health insurance policy shall be delivered in this state unless the Commissioner (Substitute the appropriate title if "Commissioner" is not correct in the enacting state.) finds that:
   (1) the issuance of such group policy is not contrary to the best interest of the public;
   (2) the issuance of the group policy would result in economies of acquisition or administration; and
   (3) the benefits are reasonable in relation to the premiums charged.
B. No such group health insurance coverage may be offered in this state by an insurer under a policy issued in another state unless this state or another state having requirements substantially similar to those contained in subsections (A) (1), (2) and (3), has made a determination that such requirements have been met.
C. The premium for the policy shall be paid either from the policyholder's funds or from funds contributed by the covered persons, or from both.
D. An insurer may exclude or limit the coverage on any person as to whom evidence of individual insurability is not satisfactory to the insurer.

SECTION 3. NOTICE OF COMPENSATION

A. With respect to a program of insurance which is issued on a group basis would not qualify under Subsections (A), (B), (C), (D) and (F) of Section 1, of the Act, if compensation of any kind will or may be paid to;
   (1) a policyholder or sponsoring or endorsing entity in the case of group policy, or
   (2) a sponsoring or endorsing entity in the case of individual, blanket or franchise policies marketed by means of direct response solicitation,

   the insurer shall cause to be distributed to prospective insurers a written notice that compensation will or may be paid.
B. Such notice shall be distributed:
   (1) whether compensation is direct or indirect, and
   (2) whether such compensation is paid to or retained by the policyholder or sponsoring or endorsing entity, or paid to or retained by a third party

at the direction of the policyholder or sponsoring or endorsing entity, or an entity affiliated therewith by way of ownership, contract or employment.

C. The notice by this Section shall be placed on or accompany any application or enrollment form provided prospective insureds.

D. The following terms shall have the meanings indicated:

(1) "direct response solicitation" means a solicitation through a sponsoring or endorsing entity through the mails, telephone, or other mass communications media;

(2) "sponsoring or endorsing entity" means an organization which has arranged for the offering of a program of insurance in a manner which communicates that eligibility for participation in the program is dependent upon affiliation with such organization or that it encourages participation in the program.

SECTION 4. DEPENDENT GROUP HEALTH INSURANCE

Except for a policy issued under Section 1 (B), a group health insurance policy may be extended to insure the employees or members with respect to their family members or dependents, or any class or classes thereof, subject to the following:

A. The premium for the insurance shall be paid either from funds contributed by the employer, union, association or other person to whom the policy has been issued, or from funds contributed by the covered persons, or from both. Except as provided in Subsection (B), a policy on which no part of the premium for the family members or dependents coverage is to be derived from funds contributed by the covered persons must insure all eligible employees or members with respect to their family members or dependents, or any class or classes thereof.

B. An insurer may exclude or limit the coverage on any family member or dependent as to whom evidence of individual insurability is not satisfactory to the insurer.

SECTION 5. GROUP HEALTH INSURANCE STANDARD PROVISIONS

No policy of group health insurance shall be delivered in this state unless it contains in substance the following provisions, or provisions which in the opinion of the Commissioner are more favorable to the persons insured, or at least as favorable to the persons insured and more favorable to the policyholder, provided, however, (a) that provisions (E), (G) AND (L) shall not apply to policies insuring debtors; (b) that the standard provisions required for individual health insurance policies shall not apply to group health insurance policies; and (c) that if any provision of this section is in whole or in part inapplicable to or inconsistent with the coverage provided by a particular form of policy, the insurer, with the approval of the Commissioner (Substitute the appropriate title if "Commissioner" is not correct in the enacting state.) shall omit from such policy any inapplicable provision or part of provision, and shall modify any inconsistent provision or part of a provision in such manner as to make the provision as contained in the policy consistent with the coverage provided by the policy:

A. A provision that the policyholder is entitled to a grace period of thirty-one days for the payment of any premium due except the first, during which grace period the policy shall continue in force, unless the policyholder shall have given the insurer written notice of discontinuance in advance of the date of discontinuance and in accordance with the terms of the policy. The policy may provide that the policyholder shall be liable to the insurer for the payment of a pro data premium for the time the policy was in force during such grace period.

B. A provision that the validity of the policy shall not be contested except for nonpayment of premiums after it has been in force for two years from its date of issue; and that no statement made by any person covered under the policy relating to insurability shall be used in contesting the validity of the insurance with respect to which such statement was made after such insurance has been in force prior to the contest for a period of two years during such person's lifetime nor unless it is contained in a written instrument signed by the person making such statement; provided however, that no such provision shall preclude the assertion at any time of defenses based upon the person's ineligibility for coverage under the policy or upon other provisions in the policy.

C. A provision that a copy of the application, if any, of the policyholder shall be attached to the policy when issued, that all statements made by the policyholder or by the persons insured shall be deemed representations and not warranties, and that no statement made by any person insured shall be used in any contest unless a copy of the instrument containing the statement is or has been furnished to such person, or, in the event of the death or incapacity of the insured person, to the individual's beneficiary or personal representative.

D. A provision setting forth the conditions, if any, under which the insurer reserves the right to require a person eligible for insurance to furnish evidence of individual insurability satisfactory to the insurer as a condition to part or all of the individual's coverage.

E. A provision specifying the additional exclusions or limitations, if any, applicable under the policy with respect to a disease or physical condition of a person, not otherwise excluded from the person's coverage by name or specific description effective on the date of the person's loss, which existed prior to the effective date of the person's coverage under the policy. Any such exclusion or limitation may only apply to a disease or physical condition for which medical advice or treatment was received by the person during the 12 months prior to the effective date of the person's coverage. In no event shall such exclusion or limitation apply to loss incurred or disability commencing after the earlier of (a) the end of a continuous period of 12 months commencing on or after the effective date of the person's coverage during all of which the person has received no medical advice or treatment in connection with such disease or physical condition; and (b) the end of the two-year period commencing on the effective date of the person's coverage.

F. If the premiums or benefits vary by age, there shall be a provision specifying an equitable adjustment of premiums or of benefits, or both, to be made in the event the age of a covered person has been misstated, such provision to contain a clear statement of the method of adjustment to be used.

G. A provision that the insurer will issue to the policyholder for delivery to each person insured a certificate setting forth a statement as to the insurance protection to which that person is entitled, to whom the insurance benefits are payable, and a statement as to any family member's or dependent's coverage.

H. A provision that written notice of claim must be given to the insurer within 20 days after the occurrence or commencement of any loss covered by the policy. Failure to give notice within such time shall not invalidate nor reduce any claim if it can be shown not to have been reasonably possible to give such notice and that notice was given as soon as was reasonably possible.

I. A provision that the insurer will furnish to the person making claim, or to the policyholder for delivery to such person, such forms as are usually furnished by it for filing proof of loss. If such forms are not furnished before the expiration of 15 days after the insurer received notice of any claim under the policy, the person making such claim shall be deemed to have complied with the requirements of the policy as a proof of loss upon submitting within the time fixed in the policy for filing proof of loss, written proof covering the occurrence, character, and extent of the loss for which claim is made.

J. A provision that in the case of claim for loss of time for disability, written proof of such loss must be furnished to the insurer within 90 days after the commencement of the period for which the insurer is liable, and that subsequent written proofs of the continuance of such disability must be furnished to the insurer at such intervals as the insurer may reasonably require, and that in the case of claim for any other loss, written proof of such loss must be furnished to the insurer within 90 days after the date of such loss. Failure to furnish such proof within such time shall not invalidate nor reduce any claim if it was not reasonably possible to furnish such proof within such time, provided such proof is furnished as soon as reasonably possible and in no event, except in the absence of legal capacity of the claimant, later than one year from the time proof is otherwise required.

K. A provision that all benefits payable under the policy other than benefits for loss of time will be payable not more than 60 days after receipt of proof, and that, subject to due proof of loss, all accrued benefits payable under the policy for loss of time will be paid not less frequently than monthly during the continuance of the period for which the insurer is liable, and that any balance remaining unpaid at the termination of such period will be paid as soon as possible after receipt of such proof.

L. A provision that benefits for loss of life of the person insured shall be payable to the beneficiary designated by the person insured. However, if the policy contains conditions pertaining to family status the beneficiary may be the family member specified by the policy terms. In either case, payment of these benefits is subject to the provisions of the policy in the event no such designated or specified beneficiary is living at the death of the person insured. All other benefits of the policy shall be payable to the person insured. The policy may also provide that if any benefit is payable to the estate of a person, or to a person who is a minor or otherwise not competent to give a valid release, the insurer may pay such benefit, up to an amount not exceeding $(5,000), to any relative by blood or connection by marriage of such person who is deemed by the insurer to be equitably entitled thereto.

M. A provision that the insurer shall have the right and opportunity to examine the person of the individual for whom claim is made when and so often as it may reasonably require during the pendency of claim under the policy and also the right and opportunity to make an autopsy in case of death where it is not prohibited by law.

N. A provision that no action at law or in equity shall be brought to recover on the policy prior to the expiration of 60 days after proof of loss has been filed in accordance with the requirement of the policy and that no such action shall be brought at all unless brought within three years from the expiration of the time within which proof of loss is required by the policy.

O. In the case of a policy insuring debtors, a provision that the insurer will furnish the policyholder for delivery to each debtor insured under the policy a certificate of insurance describing the coverage and specifying that the benefits payable shall first be applied to reduce or extinguish the indebtedness.

Appendix B

NAIC GROUP LIFE INSURANCE DEFINITION AND GROUP LIFE INSURANCE STANDARD PROVISIONS MODEL ACT

(WITH 1984 AMENDMENTS)

SECTION 1. GROUP LIFE INSURANCE DEFINITION

Except as provided in Section 2. herein, no policy of group life insurance shall be delivered in this state unless it conforms to one of the following descriptions:

A. A policy issued to an employer, or to the trustees of a fund established by an employer, which employer or trustees shall be deemed the policyholder, to insure employees of the employer for the benefit of persons other than the employer, subject to the following requirements:

(1) The employees eligible for insurance under the policy shall be all of the employees of the employer, or all of any class or classes thereof. The policy may provide that the term "employees" shall include the employees of one or more subsidiary corporations, and the employees, individual proprietors, and partners of one or more affiliated corporations, proprietorships or partnerships if the business of employer and of such affiliated corporations, proprietorships or partnerships is under common control. The policy may provide that the term "employees" may include the individual proprietor or partners if the employer is an individual proprietorship or partnership. The policy may provide that the term "employees" may include retired employees, former employees and directors of a corporate employer. A policy issued to insure the employees of a public body may provide that the term "employees" shall include elected or appointed officials. (Last sentence of Subsection (1) may be deleted if its content is covered by other statutes.)

(2) The premium for the policy shall be paid either from the employer's funds or from funds contributed by the insured employees, or from

both. Except as provided in subsection (3), a policy on which no part of the premium is to be derived from funds contributed by the insured employees must insure all eligible employees, except those who reject such coverage in writing.

(3) An insurer may exclude or limit the coverage on any person as to whom evidence or individual insurability is not satisfactory to the insurer.

B. A policy issued to a creditor or its parent holding company or to a trustee or trustees or agent designated by two or more creditors, which creditor, holding a company, affiliate, trustee, trustees or agent shall be deemed the policyholder, to insure debtors of the creditor, or creditors, subject to the following requirements:

(1) The debtors eligible for insurance under the policy shall be all of the debtors of the creditor or creditors, or all of any class or classes thereof. The policy may provide that the term "debtors" shall include (i) borrowers of money or purchase or lessees of goods, services, or property for which payment is arranged through a credit transaction; (ii) the debtors of one or more subsidiary corporations; and (iii) the debtors of one or more affiliated corporations, proprietorships, or partnerships if the business of the policyholder and of such affiliated corporations, proprietorships, or partnerships is under common control.

(2) The premium for the policy shall be paid either from the creditor's funds, or from charges collected from the insured debtors, or from both. Except as provided in subsection (3), a policy on which no part of the premium is to be derived from the funds contributed by insured debtors specifically for their insurance must insure all eligible debtors.

(3) An insurer may exclude any debtors as to whom evidence of individual insurability is not satisfactory to the insurer.

(4) The amount of the insurance on the life of any debtor shall at no time exceed the greater of the scheduled or actual amount of unpaid indebtedness to the creditor.

(5) The insurance may be payable to the creditor or any successor to the right, title, and interest of the creditor. Such payment shall reduce or extinguish the unpaid indebtedness of the debtor to the extent of such payment and any excess of the insurance shall be payable to the estate of the insured.

(6) Notwithstanding the provisions of the above subsections, insurance on agricultural credit transaction commitments may be written up to the amount of the loan commitment on a non-decreasing or level term plan. Insurance on educational credit transaction commitments may be written up to the amount of the loan commitment less the amount of any repayments made on the loan.

C. A policy issued to a labor union, or similar employee organization, which shall be deemed to be the policyholder, to insure members of such union or organization for the benefit of persons other than the union or organization or any of its officials, representatives, or agents, subject to the following requirements:

(1) The members eligible for insurance under the policy shall be all of the members of the union or organization, or all of any class or classes thereof.

(2) The premium for the policy shall be paid either from funds of the union or organization, or from funds contributed by the insured members specifically for their insurance, or from both. Except as provided in subsection (3), a policy on which no part of the premium is to be derived from the funds contributed by insured debtors specifically for their insurance must insure all eligible debtors.

(3) An insurer may exclude any debtors as to whom evidence of individual insurability is not satisfactory to the insurer.

D. A policy issued to a trust or to the trustee(s) of a fund established or adopted by two or more employees, or by one or more labor unions or similar employee organizations, or by one or more employers and one or more labor unions or similar employee organizations, which trust or trustee(s) shall be deemed the policyholder, to insure employees of the employers or members of the unions or organizations for the benefit of persons other than the employees or the unions or organizations, subject to the following requirements:

(1) The persons eligible for insurance shall be all of the employees of the employers or all the members of the unions or organizations, or all of any class or classes thereof. The policy may provide that the term "employees" shall include the employees of one or more subsidiary corporations, and the employees, individual proprietors, and partners of one or more affiliated corporations, proprietorships or partnerships if the business of the employer and of such affiliated corporations, proprietorships or partnerships in under common control. The policy may provide that the term "employees" shall include the individual proprietor or partners if the employer is an individual proprietorship or partnership. The policy may provide that the term "employees" shall include retired employees, former employees and directors of the corporate employer. The policy may provide that the term "employees" shall include the trustees or their employees, or both, if their duties are principally connected with such trusteeship.

(2) The premium for the policy shall be paid from funds contributed by the employer or employers of the insured persons, or by the union or unions or similar employee organizations, or by both, or from funds contributed by the insured persons or from both the insured persons and the employer(s) or union(s) or similar employee organization(s). Except as provided in subsection (3), a policy on which no part of the premium is to be derived from funds contributed by the insured persons specifically for their insurance must insure all eligible persons, except those who reject such coverage in writing.

(3) An insurer may exclude or limit the coverage on any person as to whom evidence of individual insurability is not satisfactory to the insurer.

E. A policy issued to an association or to a trust or to the trustee(s) of a fund established, created, or maintained for the benefit of members of one or more associations. The association or associations shall have at the outset a minimum of 100 persons; shall have been organized and maintained in good faith for purposes other than that of obtaining insurance; shall have been in active existence for at least two years; and shall have a constitution and by-laws which provides that (i) the association or associations hold regular meetings not less than annually to further purposes of the members, (ii) members, and (iii) the members have voting privileges and representation on the governing board and committees. The policy shall be subject to the following requirements;

(1) The policy may insure members of such association or associations, employees thereof the employees of members, or one or more of the preceding or all of any class or classes thereof for the benefit of persons other than the employee's employer.

(2) The premium for the policy shall be paid from funds contributed by the association or associations, or by employer members, or by both the covered persons or the association, associations, or employer members.

(3) Except as provided in subsection (4), a policy on which no part of the premium is to be derived from funds contributed by the covered persons specifically for the insurance must insure all eligible persons, except those who reject such coverage in writing.

(4) An insurer may exclude or limit the coverage on any person as to whom evidence of individual insurability is not satisfactory to the insurer.

F. A policy issued to a credit union or to a trustee or trustees or agent designated by two or more credit unions, which credit union, trustee, trustees, or agent shall be deemed policyholder, to insure members of such credit union or credit unions for the benefit of persons other than the credit union or credit unions, trustee or trustees, or agent or any of their officials, subject to the following requirements:

(1) The members eligible for insurance shall be all of the members of the credit union or credit unions, or all of any class or classes thereof.

(2) The premium for the policy shall be paid by the policyholder from the credit union's funds and, except as provided in subsection (3), must insure all eligible members.

(3) An insurer may exclude or limit the coverage on any members as to whom evidence of individual insurability is not satisfactory to the insurer.

SECTION 2. LIMITS OF GROUP LIFE INSURANCE

Group life insurance offered to a resident of this state under a group life insurance policy issued to a group other than one described in Section 1 shall be subject to the following requirements:

A. No such group life insurance policy shall be delivered in this state unless the Commissioner finds that:
   (1) The insurance of such group policy is not contrary to the best interest of the public;
   (2) The issuance of the group policy would result in economies of acquisition or administration; and
   (3) The benefits are reasonable in relation to the premiums charged.

B. No such group life insurance coverage may be offered in this state by an insurer under a policy issued in another state unless this state or another state having requirements substantially similar to those contained in subsections (A)(1), (2) and (3) has made a determination that such requirements have been met.

C. The premium for the policy shall be paid either from the policyholder's funds or from funds contributed by the covered persons, or from both.

D. An insurer may exclude or limit the coverage on any person as to whom evidence of individual insurability is not satisfactory to the insurer.

SECTION 3. NOTICE OF COMPENSATION

A. With respect to a program of insurance which if issued on a group basis would not qualify under Subsections (A), (B), (C), (D) and (F) of Section 1 of this Act, if compensation of any kind will or may be paid to:
   (1) A policyholder or sponsoring or endorsing entity in the case of a group policy, or
   (2) a sponsoring or endorsing entity in the case of individual, blanket or franchise policies marketed by means of direct response solicitation, the insurer shall cause to be distributed to prospective insureds in a written notice that compensation will or may be paid.

B. Such notice shall be distributed
   (1) whether compensation is direct or indirect, and
   (2) whether such compensation is paid to or retained by the policyholder or sponsoring or endorsing entity, or paid to or retained by a third party at the direction of the policyholder or sponsoring or endorsing entity, or any entity affiliated therewith by a way of ownership, contract or employment.

C. The notice required by this Section shall be placed on or accompany any application or enrollment from provided prospective insureds.

D. The following terms shall have the meanings indicated:
   (1) "direct response solicitation" means a solicitation through a sponsoring or endorsing entity through the mails, telephone, or other mass communications media;
   (2) "sponsoring or endorsing entity" means an organization which has arranged for the offering of a program of insurance in a manner which communicates that eligibility for participation in the program is depen-

dent upon affiliation with such organization or that it encourages participation in the program.

SECTION 4. DEPENDENT GROUP LIFE INSURANCE

Except for a policy issued under Section 1(B), a group life insurance policy may be extended to insure the employees or members against loss due to the death of their spouses and dependent children, or any class or classes thereof, subject to the following:

A. The premium for the insurance shall be paid either from funds contributed by the employer, union, association or other persons to whom the policy has been issued, or from funds contributed by the covered persons, or from both. Except as provided in subsection (B), a policy on which no part of the premium for the spouse's and dependent child's coverage is to be derived from funds contributed by the covered persons must insure all eligible employees or members with respect to their spouses and dependent children, or any class or classes thereof.
B. An insurer may exclude or limit the coverage on any spouse or dependent child as to whom evidence of individual insurability is not satisfactory to the insurer.
C. The amounts of insurance for any covered spouse or dependent child under the policy may not exceed 50% of the amount of insurance for which the employee or member is insured.

SECTION 5. GROUP LIFE INSURANCE STANDARD PROVISION

No policy of group life insurance shall be delivered in this state unless it contains in substance the following provisions, or provisions which in the opinion of the Commissioner are more favorable to the persons insured, or at least as favorable to the persons insured and more favorable to the policyholder, provided, however, (a) that provisions (F) to (K) inclusive shall not apply to policies insuring the lives of debtors; (b) that the standard provisions required for individual life insurance policies shall not apply to group life insurance policies; and (c) that if the group life insurance policy is on a plan of insurance other than the term plan, it shall contain a nonforfeiture provision or provisions which in the opinion of the Commissioner is or are equitable to the insured persons and to the policyholder, but nothing herein shall be construed to require that group life insurance policies contain the same nonforfeiture provisions as are required for individual life insurance policies:

A. A provision that the policyholder is entitled to a grace period of thirty-one days for the payment of any premium due except the first, during which grace period of death benefit coverage shall continue in force, unless the policyholder shall have given the insurer written notice of discontinuance in advance of the date of discontinuance and in accordance with the terms of the policy. The policy may provide that the policyholder shall be liable to the insurer for the payment of a pro rata premium for the time the policy was in force during such a grace period.

B. A provision that the validity of the policy shall not be contested except for nonpayment of premiums, after it has been in force for two years from its date of issue; and that no statement made by any person insured under the policy relating to his insurability shall be used in contesting the validity of the insurance with respect to which such statement was made after such insurance has been in force prior to the contest for a period of two years during such person's lifetime nor unless it is contained in a written instrument signed by him; providing, however, that no such provision shall preclude the assertion at any time of defenses based upon provisions in the policy which relate to eligibility for coverage.

C. A provision that a copy of the application, if any, of the policyholder shall be attached to the policy when issued, that all statements made by the policyholder or by the persons insured shall be deemed representations and not warranties, and that no statement made by any person insured shall be used in any contest unless a copy of the instrument containing the statement is or has been furnished to such person or, in the event of death or incapacity of the insured person, to his beneficiary or personal representative.

D. A provision setting forth the conditions, of any, under which the insurer reserves the right to require a person eligible for insurance to furnish evidence of individual insurability satisfactory to the insurer as a condition to part or all of his coverage.

E. A provision specifying an equitable adjustment of premiums or of benefits or of both to be made in the event the age of a person insured has been misstated, such provision to contain a clear statement of the method of adjustment to be made.

F. A provision that any sum becoming due by reason of the death of the person insured shall be payable to the beneficiary designated by the person insured, except that where the policy contains conditions pertaining to family status the beneficiary may be the family member specified by the policy terms, subject to the provision of the policy in the event there is no designated beneficiary, as to all or any part of such sum, living at the death of the person insured, and subject to any right reserved by the insurer in the policy and set forth in the certificate to pay at its option a part of such sum not exceeding $2,000 to any person appearing to the insurer to be equitably entitled thereto by reason of having incurred funeral or other expenses incident to the last illness or death of the person insured.

G. A provision that the insurer will issue to the policyholder for delivery to each person insured a certificate setting forth a statement as to the insurance protection to which he is entitled, to whom the insurance benefits are payable, a statement as to any dependent's coverage included in such certificate, and the rights and conditions set forth in (H), (I), (J) and (K) following.

H. A provision that if the insurance, or any portion of it, on a person covered under the policy or on the dependent of a person covered, ceases because of termination of employment or of membership in the class or classes eligible for coverage under the policy, such person shall be entitled to have issued to him by the insurer, without evidence of insurability, an individual policy of life insurance without disability or other supplementary benefits, provided application for the individual policy shall be made, and the first premium paid to the insurer, within thirty-one days after such termination and provided further that:
   (1) The individual policy shall, at the option of such person, be on any one of the forms then customarily issued by the insurer at the age and for the amount applied for, except that the group policy may exclude the option to elect term insurance.
   (2) The individual policy shall be in an amount not in excess of the amount of life insurance which ceases because of such termination, less the amount of any life insurance for which such person becomes eligible under the same or any other group policy within thirty-one days after such termination, provided that any amount of insurance which shall have matured on or before the date of such termination as an endowment payable to the person insured, whether in one sum or in installments or in the form of an annuity, shall not, for the purposes of this provision, be included in the amount which is considered to cease because of such termination; and
   (3) The premium on the individual policy shall be at the insurer's then customary rate applicable to the form and amount of the individual policy to the class of risk to which such person then belongs, and to the individual age attained on the effective date of the individual policy. Subject to the same conditions set forth above, the conversion privilege shall be available (i) to surviving dependent, if any, at the death of the employee or member, with respect to the coverage under the group policy which terminates by reason of such death and (ii) to the dependent of the employee or member upon termination of coverage of the dependent, while the employee or member remains insured under the group policy, by reason of the dependent ceasing to be a qualified family member under the group policy.

I. A provision that if the group policy terminates or is amended so as to terminate the insurance of any class of insured persons, every person insured thereunder at the date of such termination whose insurance terminates, including the insured dependent of a covered person, and who has been so insured for at least five years prior to such termination date shall be entitled to have issued by the insurer an individual policy of life insurance, subject to the same conditions and limitations as are provided by (H) above, except that the group policy may provide that the amount of such individual policy shall not exceed the smaller of (a) the amount of the person's life insurance protection ceasing because of the termination or amendment of the group policy, less the amount of life insurance for which he is or becomes eligible; under the group policy issued or reinstated by the same or another insurer within thirty-one days after such termination, and (b) $10,000.

J. A provision that if a person insured under the group policy, or the insured dependent of a covered person, dies during the period within which the individual would have been entitled to have an individual policy issued in accordance with (H) or (I) above and before such an individual policy shall have become effective, the amount of life insurance which he would have been entitled to have issued under such individual policy shall be payable as a claim under the group policy, whether or not application for the individual policy or the payment of the first premium therefore has been made.

K. Where active employment is a condition of insurance, a provision that an insured may continue coverage during the insured's total disability by timely payment to the policyholder of that portion, of any, of the premium that would have been required from the insured had total disability not occurred. The continuation shall be on a premium paying basis for a period of six months from the date on which the total disability started, but not beyond the earlier of (a) approval by the insurer of continuation of the coverage under any disability provision which the group insurance policy may contain or (b) the discontinuance of the group insurance policy.

L. In the case of a policy insuring the lives of debtors, a provision that the insurer will furnish to the policyholder for delivery to each debtor insured under the policy a certificate of insurance describing the coverage and specifying that the death benefit shall first be applied to reduce or extinguish the indebtedness.

SECTION 6. SUPPLEMENTARY BILL RELATING TO CONVERSION PRIVILEGES

If any individual insured under a group life insurance policy hereafter delivered in this state becomes entitled under the terms of such policy to have an individual policy of life insurance issued without evidence of insurability, subject to making of application and payment of the first premium within the period specified in such policy, and if such individual is not given notice of the existence of such right at least 15 days prior to the expiration date of such period, then in such event the individual shall have an additional period within which to exercise such right, but nothing herein contained shall be construed to continue any insurance beyond the period provided in such policy. This additional period shall expire 15 days next after the individual is given such notice but in no event shall such additional period extend beyond 60 days next after the expiration date of the period provided in such policy. Written notice presented to the individual or mailed by the policyholder to the last known address of the individual or mailed by the insurer to the last known address of the individual as furnished by the policyholder shall constitute notice for the purpose of this paragraph.

Appendix C

NAIC GROUP COORDINATION OF BENEFITS MODEL REGULATION

(WITH 1989 REVISIONS)

SECTION 1. AUTHORITY

This regulation is adopted and promulgated by [title of supervisory authority] pursuant to Section . . . of the Insurance Code. It replaces the regulation of similar purpose which took effect on ____________.

SECTION 2. PURPOSE AND APPLICABILITY

The purpose of this regulation is to:

A. Permit, but not require, plans to include a coordination of benefits (COB) provision;
B. Establish an order in which plans pay their claims;
C. Provide the authority for the orderly transfer of information needed to pay claims promptly;
D. Reduce duplication of benefits by permitting a reduction of the benefits paid by a plan when the plan, pursuant to rules established by this regulation, does not have to pay its benefits first;
E. Reduce claims payment delays; and
F. Make all contracts that contain a COB provision consistent with this regulation.

SECTION 3. DEFINITIONS

The following words and terms, when used in this regulation, shall have the following meanings unless the context clearly indicates otherwise:

A. Allowable Expenses
   (1) "Allowable Expense" means the necessary, reasonable and customary item of expense for health care when the item of expense is covered at

least in part under any of the plans involved, except where a statute requires a different definition.

(2) Notwithstanding the above definition, items of expense under coverages such as dental care, vision care, prescription drug or hearing aid programs may be excluded from the definition of Allowable Expense. A plan which provides benefits only for any such items of expense may limit its definition of Allowable Expenses to like items of expense.

(3) When a plan provides benefits in the form of service, the reasonable cash value of each service will be considered as both an Allowable Expense and a benefit paid.

(4) The difference between the cost of a private hospital room and the cost of a semi-private hospital room is not considered an Allowable Expense under the above definition unless the patient's stay in a private hospital room is medically necessary in terms of generally accepted medical practice.

(5) When COB is restricted in its use to specific coverage in a contract (for example, major medical or dental), the definition of "Allowable Expense" must include the corresponding expenses or services to which COB applies.

(6) When benefits are reduced under a Primary Plan because a covered person does not comply with the plan provisions, the amount of such reduction will not be considered an Allowable Expense. Examples of such provisions are those related to second surgical opinions, precertification of admissions or services, and preferred provider arrangements.

   (a) Only benefit reductions based upon provisions similar in purpose to those described above and which are contained in the Primary Plan may be excluded from Allowable Expenses.

   (b) This provision shall not be used by a Secondary Plan to refuse to pay benefits because an HMO member has elected to have health care services provided by a non-HMO provider and the HMO, pursuant to its contract, is not obligated to pay for providing those services.

NOTE: This Paragraph (6) is not intended to allow a Secondary Plan to exclude expenses that are applied towards the satisfaction of the deductible, copayments or coinsurance amounts required by the Primary Plan, except for the benefit reductions expressly described in this paragraph.

B. Claim

A request that benefits of a plan be provided or paid is a claim. The benefits claimed may be in the form of:

(1) Services (including supplies);

(2) Payment for all or a portion of the expenses incurred;

(3) A combination of (1) and (2) above; or

(4) An indemnification.

C. Claim Determination Period

This is the period of time, which must not be less than twelve consecutive months, over which Allowable Expenses are compared with total benefits payable in the absence of COB, to determine whether overinsurance exists and how much each plan will pay or provide.

(1) The Claim Determination Period is usually a calendar year, but a plan may use some other period of time that fits the coverage of the group contract. A person may be covered by a plan during a portion of a Claim Determination Period if that person's coverage starts or ends during the Claim Determination Period.

(2) As each claim is submitted, each plan is to determine its liability and pay or provide benefits based upon Allowable Expenses incurred to that point in the Claim Determination Period. That determination is subject to adjustment as later Allowable Expenses are incurred in the same Claim Determination Period.

D. Coordination of Benefits

This is a provision establishing an order in which plans pay their claims.

E. Hospital Indemnity Benefits

These are benefits not related to expenses incurred. The term does not include reimbursement-type benefits even if they are designed or administered to give the insured the right to elect indemnity-type benefits at the time of claim.

F. Plan

Plan means a form of coverage with which coordination is allowed. The definition of Plan in the group contract must state the types of coverage which will be considered in applying the COB provision of that contract. The right to include a type of coverage is limited by the rest of this definition.

(1) The definition shown in the Model COB Provision, attached to this rule as Appendix A, is an example of what may be used. Any definition that satisfies this subsection may be used.

(2) This subchapter uses the term "plan." However, a group contract may, instead, use "program" or some other term.

(3) Plan may include:

(a) Group insurance and group subscriber contracts;

(b) Uninsured arrangements of group or group-type coverage;

(c) Group or group-type coverage through HMOs and other prepayment, group practice and individual practice plans;

(d) Group-type contracts. Group-type contracts which are not available to the general public and can be obtained and maintained only because of membership in or connection with a particular organization or group. Group-type contracts answering this description may be included in the definition of plan, at the option of the insurer or the service provider and the contract client, whether or not uninsured arrangements or individual contract forms are used and regardless of how the group-type coverage is designated (for example, "franchise" or "blanket"). Individually underwritten and issued guaranteed renewable policies would not be considered "group-type" even though purchased through payroll deduction at a premium savings to the insured since the insured would have the right to maintain or renew the policy independently of continued employment with the employer.

NOTE: The purpose and intent of this provision is to identify certain plans of coverage which may utilize other than a group contract but are administered on a basis more characteristic of group insurance. These "group-type" contracts are distinguished by two factors: (1) they are not available to the general public, but may be obtained only through membership in, or connection with, the particular organization or group through which they are marketed (for example: through an employer payroll withholding system), and (2) they can be obtained only through such affiliation (for example: the contracts might provide they cannot be renewed if the insured leaves the particular employer or organization in which case they would meet the "group-type" definition). On the other hand, if such contracts are guaranteed renewable, thereby allowing the insured the right to renewal regardless of continued employment or affiliation with the organization, they would not be considered "group-type."

(e) The amount by which group or group-type hospital indemnity benefits exceed $100 per day;

(f) The medical benefits coverage in group, group-type and individual automobile "no fault" and traditional automobile "fault" type contracts; and

(g) Medicare or other governmental benefits, except as provided in (4)(g) below. That part of the definition of plan may be limited to the hospital, medical and surgical benefits of the governmental program.

(4) Plan shall not include:

(a) Individual or family insurance contracts;

(b) Individual or family subscriber contracts;

(c) Individual or family coverage through Health Maintenance Organizations (HMOs);

(d) Individual or family coverage under other prepayment, group practice and individual practice plans;

(e) Group or group-type hospital indemnity benefits of $100 per day or less;

(f) School accident-type coverages. These contracts cover grammar, high school and college students for accidents only, including athletic injuries, either on a twenty-four-hour basis or on a "to and from school" basis; and

(g) A State plan under Medicaid, and shall not include a law or plan when, by law, its benefits are in excess of those of any private insurance plan or other non-governmental plan.

G. Primary Plan

A Primary Plan is a plan whose benefits for a person's health care coverage must be determined without taking the existence of any other plan into consideration. A plan is a Primary Plan if either of the following conditions is true:

(1) The plan either has no order of benefit determination rules, or it has rules which differ from those permitted by this subchapter. There may be more than one Primary Plan; or

(2) All plans which cover the person use the order of benefit determination rules required by this regulation, and under those rules the plan determines its benefits first.

H. Secondary Plan

A Secondary Plan is a plan which is not a Primary Plan. If a person is covered by more than one Secondary Plan, the order of benefit determination rules of this regulation decide the order in which their benefits are determined in relation to each other. The benefits of each Secondary Plan may take into consideration the benefits of the Primary Plan or plans and the benefits of any other plan which, under the rules of this regulation, has its benefits determined before those of that Secondary Plan.

I. This Plan

In a COB provision, this term refers to the part of the group contract providing the health care benefits to which the COB provision applies and which may be reduced because of the benefits of other plans. Any other part of the group contract providing health care benefits is separate from This Plan. A group contract may apply one COB provision to certain of its benefits (such as dental benefits), coordinating only with like benefits, and may apply other separate COB provisions to coordinate other benefits.

SECTION 4. MODEL COB CONTRACT PROVISION

A. General

Appendix A contains a model COB provision for use in group contracts. That use is subject to the provisions of B and C below and to the provisions of Section 5.

B. Flexibility

A group contract's COB provision does not have to use the words and format shown at Appendix A. Changes may be made to fit the language and style of the rest of the group contract or to reflect the difference among plans which provide services, which pay benefits for expenses incurred, and which indemnity. No other substantive changes are allowed.

C. Prohibited Coordination and Benefit Design

(1) A group contract may not reduce benefits on the basis that:

(a) Another plan exists;

(b) A person is or could have been covered under another plan, except with respect to Part B of Medicare; or

(c) A person has elected an option under another plan providing a lower level of benefits than another option which could have been elected.

(2) No contract may contain a provision that its benefits are "excess" or "always secondary" to any plan as defined in this regulation, except in accord with the rules permitted by this regulation.

SECTION 5. RULES FOR COORDINATION OF BENEFITS

Order of Benefits

A. General

The general order of benefits is as follows:

(1) The Primary Plan must pay or provide its benefits as if the Secondary Plan or Plans did not exist. A Plan that does not include a coordination of benefits provision may not take the benefits of another Plan as defined in Section 3 into account when it determines its benefits. There is one exception: a contract holder's coverage that is designed to supplement a part of a basic package of benefits may provide that the supplementary coverage shall be excess to any other parts of the plan provided by the contract holder.

(2) A Secondary Plan may take the benefits of another plan into account only when, under these rules, it is Secondary to that other plan.

(3) The benefits of the plan which covers the person as an employee, member or subscriber (that is, other than as a dependent) are determined before those of the plan which covers the person as a dependent.

B. Dependent Child/Parents Not Separated or Divorced

The rules for the order of benefits for a dependent child when the parents are not separated or divorced are as follows:

(1) The benefits of the plan of the parent whose birthday falls earlier in a year are determined before those of the plan of the parent whose birthday falls later in that year;

(2) If both parents have the same birthday, the benefits of the plan which covered the parent longer are determined before those of the plan which covered the other parent for a shorter period of time;

(3) The word "birthday" refers only to month and day in a calendar year, not the year in which the person was born;

(4) A group contract which includes COB and which is issued or renewed, or which has an anniversary date on or after sixty days after the effective date of this subchapter shall include the substance of the provision in B (1), (2) and (3) above. Until that provision becomes effective, the group contract may instead contain wording such as:

"Except as stated in C below, the benefits of a plan which covers a person as a dependent of a male are determined before those of a plan which covers the person as a dependent of a female."

(5) If the other plan does not have the rule described in B (1), (2) and (3) above, but instead has a rule based upon the gender of the parent; and if, as a result, the plans do not agree on the order of benefits, the rule based upon the gender of the parent will determine the order of benefits.

C. Dependent Child/Separated or Divorced Parents

If two or more plans cover a person as a dependent child of divorced or separated parents, benefits for the child are determined in this order:

(1) First, the plan of the parent with custody of the child;

(2) Then, the plan of the spouse of the parent with the custody of the child; and

(3) Finally, the plan of the parent not having custody of the child.

(4) If the specific terms of a court decree state that one of the parents is responsible for the health care expenses of the child, and the entity obligated to pay or provide the benefits of the plan of that parent has actual knowledge of those terms, the benefits of that plan are determined first. The plan of the other parent shall be the Secondary Plan. This paragraph does not apply with respect to any Claim Determination Period or Plan Year during which any benefits are actually paid or provided before the entity has that actual knowledge.

(5) If the specific terms of the court decree state that the parents shall share joint custody, without stating that one of the parents is responsible for the health care expenses of the child, the plans covering the child shall follow the order of benefit determination rules outlined in Section 5B, Dependent Child/Parents Not Separated or Divorced.

D. Active/Inactive Employee

The benefits of a plan which covers a person as an employee who is neither laid off nor retired (or as that employee's dependent) are determined before those of a plan which covers that person as a laid off or retired employee (or as that employee's dependent). If the other plan does not have this rule; and if, as a result, the plans do not agree on the order of benefits, this rule is ignored.

E. Longer/Shorter Length of Coverage

If none of the above rules determines the order of benefits, the benefits of the plan which covered an employee, member or subscriber longer are determined before those of the plan which covered that person for the shorter term.

(1) To determine the length of time a person has been covered under a plan, two plans shall be treated as one if the claimant was eligible under the second within twenty-four hours after the first ended.

(2) The start of a new plan does not include:

   (a) A change in the amount of scope of a plan's benefits;

   (b) A change in the entity which pays, provides or administers the plan's benefits; or

   (c) A change from one type of plan to another (such as, from a single employer plan to that of a multiple employer plan).

(3) The claimant's length of time covered under a plan is measured from the claimant's first date of coverage under that plan. If that date is not readily available, the date the claimant first became a member of the

group shall be used as the date from which to determine the length of time the claimant's coverage under the present plan has been in force.

SECTION 6. PROCEDURE TO BE FOLLOWED BY SECONDARY PLAN

Total Allowable Expenses

A. When it is determined, pursuant to Section 5, that this Plan is a Secondary Plan, it may reduce its benefits so that the total benefits paid or provided by all plans during a Claim Determination Period are not more than total Allowable Expenses. The amount by which the Secondary Plan's benefits have been reduced shall be used by the Secondary Plan to pay Allowable Expenses, not otherwise paid, which were incurred during the Claim Determination Period by the person for whom the claim is made. As each claim is submitted, the Secondary Plan determines its obligation to pay for Allowable Expenses based on all Claims which were submitted up to that point in time during the Claim Determination Period.

B. The benefits of the Secondary Plan will be reduced when the sum of the benefits that would be payable for the Allowable Expenses under the Secondary Plan in the absence of this COB provision and the benefits that would be payable for the Allowable Expenses under the other Plans, in the absence of provisions with a purpose like that of this COB provision, whether or not claim is made, exceeds those Allowable Expenses in a Claim Determination Period. In that case, the benefits of the Secondary Plan will be reduced so that they and the benefits payable under the other plans do not total more than those Allowable Expenses.
   (1) When the benefits of this Plan are reduced as described above, each benefit is reduced in proportion. It is then charged against any applicable benefit limit of this Plan.
   (2) Paragraph B (1) above may be omitted if the plan provides only one benefit, or may be altered to suit the coverage provided.

SECTION 7. MISCELLANEOUS PROVISIONS

A. Reasonable Cash Values of Services
   A Secondary Plan which provides benefits in the form of services may recover the reasonable cash value of providing the services from the Primary Plan, to the extent that benefits for the services are covered by the Primary Plan and have not already been paid or provided by the Primary Plan. Nothing in this provision shall be interpreted to require a plan to reimburse a covered person in cash for the value of services provided by a plan which provides benefits in the form of services.

B. Excess and Other Nonconforming Provisions
   (1) Some plans have order of benefit determination rules not consistent with this regulation which declare that the plan's coverage is "excess"

to all others, or "always secondary." This occurs because certain plans may not be subject to insurance regulation, or because some group contracts have not yet been conformed with this regulation pursuant to Section 2.

(2) A plan with order of benefit determination rules which comply with this regulation (Complying Plan) may coordinate its benefits with a plan which is "excess" or "always secondary" or which uses order of benefit determination rules which are inconsistent with those contained in this regulation (Noncomplying Plan) on the following basis:

(a) If the Complying Plan is the Primary Plan, it shall pay or provide its benefits on a primary basis;

(b) If the Complying Plan is the Secondary Plan, it shall, nevertheless, pay or provide its benefits first, but the amount of the benefits payable shall be determined as if the Complying Plan were the Secondary Plan. In such a situation, such payment shall be the limit of the Complying Plan's liability; and

(c) If the Noncomplying Plan does not provide the information needed by the Complying Plan to determine its benefits within a reasonable time after it is requested to do so, the Complying Plan shall assume that the benefits of the Noncomplying Plan are identical to its own, and shall pay its benefits accordingly. However, the Complying Plan must adjust any payments it makes based on such assumption whenever information becomes available as to the actual benefits of the Noncomplying Plan.

(3) If the Noncomplying Plan reduces its benefits so that the employee, subscriber, or member receives less in benefits than he or she would have received had the Complying Plan paid or provided its benefits as the Secondary Plan and the Noncomplying Plan paid or provided its benefits as the Primary Plan, and governing State laws allow the right of subrogation set forth below, then the Complying Plan shall advance to or on behalf of the employee, subscriber or member an amount equal to such difference.

However, in no event shall the Complying Plan advance more than the Complying Plan would have paid had it been the Primary Plan less any amount it previously paid. In consideration of such advance, the Complying Plan shall be subrogated to all rights of the employee, subscriber or member against the Noncomplying Plan. Such advance by the Complying Plan shall also be without prejudice to any claim it may have against the Noncomplying Plan in the absence of such subrogation.

C. Allowable Expense

A term such as "usual and customary," "usual and prevailing," or "reasonable and customary," may be substituted for the term "necessary, reasonable and customary." Terms such as "medical care" or "dental care" may be substituted for "health care" to describe the coverages to which the COB provisions apply.

D. Subrogation

The COB concept clearly differs from that of subrogation. Provisions for one may be included in health care benefits contracts without compelling the inclusion or exclusion of the other.

SECTION 8. EFFECTIVE DATE; EXISTING CONTRACTS

A. This subchapter is applicable to every group contract which provides health care benefits and which is issued on or after the effective date of this regulation, which is ____________.

B. A group contract which provides health care benefits and was issued before the effective date of this regulation shall be brought into compliance with this regulation by the later of:

(1) The next anniversary date or renewal date of the group contract; or

(2) The expiration of any applicable collectively bargained contract pursuant to which it was written.

APPENDIX A. MODEL COB PROVISIONS

Coordination of the Group Contract's Benefits with Other Benefits

I. APPLICABILITY

A. This Coordination of Benefits ("COB") provision applies to This Plan when an employee or the employee's covered dependent has health care coverage under more than one Plan. "Plan" and "This Plan" are defined below.

B. If this COB provision applies, the order of benefit determination rules should be looked at first. Those rules determine whether the benefits of This Plan are determined before or after those of another plan. The benefits of this Plan:

(1) Shall not be reduced when, under the order of benefit determination rules, This Plan determines its benefits before another plan; but

(2) May be reduced when, under the order of benefits determination rules, another plan determines its benefits first. The above reduction is described in Section IV "Effect on the Benefits of This Plan."

II. DEFINITIONS

A. "Plan" is any of these which provides benefits or services for, or because of, medical or dental care or treatment:

(1) Group insurance or group-type coverage, whether insured or uninsured. This includes prepayment, group practice or individual practice coverage. It also includes coverage other than school accident-type coverage.

(2) Coverage under a governmental plan, or coverage required or provided by law. This does not include a state plan under Medicaid (Title XIX, Grants to States for Medical Assistance Programs, of the United States Social Security Act, as amended from time to time).

Each contract or other arrangement for coverage under (1) or (2) is a separate plan. Also, if an arrangement has two parts and COB rules apply only to one of the two, each of the parts is a separate plan.

B. "This Plan" is the part of the group contract that provides benefits for health care expenses.

C. "Primary Plan/Secondary Plan:" The order of benefit determination rules state whether This Plan is a Primary Plan or Secondary Plan as to another plan covering the person.

When This Plan is a Primary Plan, its benefits are determined before those of the other plan and without considering the other plan's benefits.

When This Plan is a Secondary Plan, its benefits are determined after those of the other plan and may be reduced because of the other plan's benefits.

When there are more than two plans covering the person, This Plan may be a Primary Plan as to one or more other plans, and may be a Secondary Plan as to a different plan or plans.

D. "Allowable Expense" means a necessary, reasonable and customary item of expense for health care; when the item of expense is covered at least in part by one or more plans covering the person for whom the claim is made.

The difference between the cost of a private hospital room and cost of a semi-private hospital room is not considered an Allowable Expense under the above definition unless the patient's stay in a private hospital room is medically necessary either in terms of generally accepted medical practice, or as specifically defined in the plan.

When a plan provides benefits in the form of services, the reasonable cash value of each service rendered will be considered both an Allowable Expense and a benefit paid.

When benefits are reduced under a Primary Plan because a covered person does not comply with the plan provisions, the amount of such reduction will not be considered an Allowable Expense. Examples of such provisions are those related to second surgical opinions, precertification of admissions or services, and preferred provider arrangements.

E. "Claim Determination Period" means a calendar year. However, it does not include any part of a year during which a person has no coverage under This Plan, or any part of a year before the date this COB provision or a similar provision takes effect.

III. ORDER OF BENEFIT DETERMINATION RULES

A. General. When there is a basis for a claim under This Plan and another plan, This Plan is a Secondary Plan which has its benefits determined after those of the other plan, unless;

(1) The other plan has rules coordinating its benefits with those of This Plan; and

(2) Both those rules and This Plan's rules in Subsection B below, require that This Plan's benefits be determined before those of the other plan.

B. Rules. This Plan determines its order of benefits using the first of the following rules which applies:

(1) Non-Dependent/Dependent. The benefits of the plan which covers the person as an employee, member or subscriber (that is, other than as a dependent) are determined before those of the plan which covers the person as a dependent.

(2) Dependent Child/Parents not Separated or Divorced. Except as stated in Paragraph B (3) below, when This Plan and another plan cover the same child as a dependent of different persons, called "parents:"

(a) The benefits of the plan of the parent whose birthday falls earlier in a year are determined before those of the parent whose birthday falls later in that year; but

(b) If both parents have the same birthday, the benefits of the plan which covered one parent longer are determined before those of the plan which covered the other parent for a shorter period of time.

However, if the other plan does not have the rule described in (a) immediately above, but instead has a rule based upon the gender of the parent, and if, as a result, the plans do not agree on the order of benefits, the rule in the other plan will determine the order of benefits.

(3) Dependent Child/Separated or Divorced. If two or more plans cover a person as a dependent child of divorced or separated parents, benefits for the child are determined in this order:

(a) First, the plan of the parent with custody of the child;

(b) Then, the plan of the spouse of the parent with the custody of the child; and

(c) Finally, the plan of the parent not having custody of the child.

However, if the specific terms of a court decree state that one of the parents is responsible for the health care expense of the child, and the entity obligated to pay or provide the benefits of the plan of that parent has actual knowledge of those terms, the benefits of that plan are determined first. The plan of the other parent shall be the Secondary Plan. This paragraph does not apply with respect to any Claim Determination Period or Plan Year during which any benefits are actually paid or provided before the entity has that actual knowledge.

(4) Joint Custody. If the specific terms of a court decree state that the parents shall share joint custody, without stating that one of the parents is responsible for the health care expenses of the child, the plans covering the child shall follow the order of benefit determination rules outlined in Paragraph III B(2).

(5) Active/Inactive Employee. The benefits of a plan which covers a person as an employee who is neither laid off nor retired (or as that employee's dependent) are determined before those of a plan which covers that person as a laid off or retired employee (or as that employee's dependent). If the other plan does not have this rule, and if, as a result, the plans do not agree on the order of benefits, this Rule (5) is ignored.

(6) Longer/Shorter Length of Coverage. If none of the above rules determines the order of benefits, the benefits of the plan which covered an employee, member or subscriber longer are determined before those of the Plan which covered that person for the shorter term.

IV. EFFECT ON THE BENEFITS OF THIS PLAN

A. When This Section Applies. This Section IV applies when, in accordance with Section III "Order of Benefit Determination Rules," This Plan is a Secondary Plan as to one or more other plans. In that event the benefits of This Plan may be reduced under this section. Such other plan or plans are referred to as "the other plans" in B immediately below.

B. Reduction in this Plan's Benefits. The benefits of This Plan will be reduced when the sum of:

(1) The benefits that would be payable for the Allowable Expense under This Plan in the absence of this COB provision; and

(2) The benefits that would be payable for the Allowable Expenses under the other plans, in the absence of provisions with a purpose like that of this COB provision, whether or not claim is made; exceeds those Allowable Expenses in a Claim Determination Period. In that case, the benefits of This Plan will be reduced so that they and the benefits payable under the other plans do not total more than those Allowable Expenses.

When the benefits of This Plan are reduced as described above, each benefit is reduced in proportion. It is then charged against any applicable benefit limit of This Plan.

V. RIGHT TO RECEIVE AND RELEASE NEEDED INFORMATION

Certain facts are needed to apply these COB rules. [Insurer] has the right to decide which facts it needs. It may get needed facts from or give them to any other organization or person. [Insurer] need not tell, or get the consent of, any person to do this. Each person claiming benefits under This Plan must give [insurer] any facts it needs to pay the claim.

VI. FACILITY OF PAYMENT

A payment made under another plan may include an amount which should have been paid under This Plan. If it does, [insurer] may pay that amount to the organization which made that payment. That amount will then be treated as though it were a benefit paid under This Plan. [Insurer] will not have to pay that amount again. The term "payment made" includes providing benefits in the form of services, in which case "payment made" means reasonable cash value of the benefits provided in the form of services.

VII. RIGHT OF RECOVERY

If the amount of the payments made by [insurer] is more than it should have paid under this COB provision, it may recover the excess from one or more of:

A. The persons it has paid or for whom it has paid;

B. Insurance companies; or

C. Other organizations.

The "amount of the payments made" includes the reasonable cash value of any benefits provided in the form of services.

Appendix D

NAIC MODEL REGULATION GROUP COVERAGE DISCONTINUANCE AND REPLACEMENT

SECTION 1. AUTHORITY

These rules and regulations are adopted and promulgated by [title of supervisory authority] pursuant to sections [s_______] of [the _______ Insurance Code].

SECTION 2. SCOPE

They are applicable to all insurance policies and subscriber contracts issued or provided by an insurance company or a non-profit service corporation on a group or group-type basis covering persons as employees of employers or as members of unions [or associations].

SECTION 3. DEFINITION

The term "group-type basis" means a benefit plan, other than "salary budget" plans utilizing individual insurance policies or subscriber contracts, which meets the following conditions:

(a) Coverage is provided through insurance policies or subscriber contracts to classes of employees or members defined in terms of conditions pertaining to employment or membership.
(b) The coverage is not available to the general public and can be obtained and maintained only because of the covered person's membership in or connection with the particular organization or group.
(c) There are arrangements for bulk payment of premiums or subscription charges to the insurer or non-profit service corporation.
(d) There is sponsorship of the plan by the employer, union, [or association].

SECTION 4. EFFECTIVE DATE OF DISCONTINUANCE FOR NONPAYMENT OF PREMIUM OR SUBSCRIPTION CHARGES

(a) If a policy or contract subject to these rules and regulations provides for automatic discontinuance of the policy or contract after a premium or subscription charge has remained unpaid through the grace period allowed for such payment, the carrier shall be liable for valid claims for covered losses incurred prior to the end of the grace period.

(b) If the actions of the carrier after the end of the grace period indicate that it considers the policy or contract as continuing in force beyond the end of the grace period (such as, by continuing to recognize claims subsequently incurred), the carrier shall be liable for valid claims for losses beginning prior to the effective date of written notice of discontinuance to the policyholder or other entity responsible for making payments or submitting subscription charges to the carrier. The effective date of discontinuance shall not be prior to midnight at the end of the third scheduled work day after the date upon which the notice is delivered.

SECTION 5. REQUIREMENTS FOR NOTICE OF DISCONTINUANCE

(a) Any notice of discontinuance so given by the carrier shall include a request to the group policyholder or other entity involved to notify employees covered under the policy or subscriber contract of the date as of which the group policy or contract will discontinue and to advise that, unless otherwise provided in the policy or contract, the carrier shall not be liable for claims for losses incurred after such date. Such notice of discontinuance shall also advise, in any instance in which the plan involves employee contributions, that if the policyholder or other entity continues to collect contributions for the coverage beyond the date of discontinuance, the policyholder or other entity may be held solely liable for the benefits with respect to which the contributions have been collected.

The carrier will prepare and furnish to the policyholder or other entity at the same time a supply of a notice form to be distributed to the employees or members concerned indicating such discontinuance and the effective date thereof, and urging the employees or members to refer to their certificates or contracts in order to determine what rights, if any, are available to them upon such discontinuance.

SECTION 6. EXTENSION OF BENEFITS

(a) Every group policy or other contract subject to these rules and regulations hereafter issued, or under which the level of benefits is hereafter altered, modified, or amended, must provide a reasonable provision for extension of benefits in the event of total disability at the date of discontinuance of the group policy or contract, as required by the following paragraphs of this section.

(b) In the case of a group life plan which contains a disability benefit extension of any type (e.g., premium waiver extension, extended death benefit in event of total disability, or payment of income for a specified period during total disability), the discontinuance of the group policy shall not operate to terminate such extension.

(c) In the case of a group plan providing benefits for loss of time from work or specific indemnity during hospital confinement, discontinuance of the policy during a disability shall have no effect on benefits payable for that disability or confinement.

(d) In the case of hospital or medical expense coverages other than dental and maternity expense, a reasonable extension of benefits or accrued liability provision is required. Such a provision will be considered "reasonable" if it provides an extension of at least twelve months under "major medical" and "comprehensive medical" type coverages, and under other types of hospital or medical expense coverages provides either an extension of at least ninety days or an accrued liability for expenses incurred during a period of disability or during a period of at least ninety days starting with a specific event which occurred while coverage was in force (e.g., an accident).

(e) Any applicable extension of benefits or accrued liability shall be described in any policy or contract involved as well as in group insurance certificates. The benefits payable during any period of extension or accrued liability may be subject to the policy's or contract's regular benefit limits (e.g., benefits ceasing at exhaustion of a benefit period or of maximum benefits).

SECTION 7. CONTINUANCE OF COVERAGE IN SITUATIONS INVOLVING REPLACEMENT OF ONE CARRIER BY ANOTHER

(a) This section shall indicate the carrier responsible for liability in those instances in which one carrier's contract replaces a plan of similar benefits of another.

(b) Liability of prior carrier. The prior carrier remains liable only to the extent of its accrued liabilities and extensions of benefits. The position of the prior carrier shall be the same whether the group policyholder or other entity secures replacement coverage from a new carrier, self-insures, or foregoes the provision of coverage.

(c) Liability of Succeeding Carrier.

1. Each person who is eligible for coverage in accordance with the succeeding carrier's plan of benefits (in respect of classes eligible and activity at work and non-confinement rules) shall be covered by that carrier's plan of benefits.

2. Each person not covered under the succeeding carrier's plan of benefits in accordance with paragraph 1 above must nevertheless be covered by the succeeding carrier in accordance with the following rules if such individual was validly covered (including benefit extension) under the prior plan on the date of discontinuance and if such individual is a member of the class or classes of individuals eligible for coverage under the succeeding carrier's plan. Any reference in the following rules to an individual who was or was not totally disabled is a reference to the individual's status immediately prior to the date the succeeding carrier's coverage becomes effective.
   a. The minium level of benefits to be provided by the succeeding carrier shall be the applicable level of benefits of the prior carrier's plan reduced by any benefits payable by the prior plan.
   b. Coverage must be provided by the succeeding carrier until at least the earliest of the following dates:
      i) the date the individual becomes eligible under the succeeding carrier's plan as described in paragraph 1, above.
      ii) for each type of coverage, the date the individual's coverage would terminate in accordance with the succeeding carrier's plan provisions applicable to individual termination of coverage (e.g., at termination of employment or ceasing to be eligible dependent, as the case may be).
      iii) in the case of an individual who was totally disabled, and in the case of a type of coverage for which Section (6) requires an extension of accrued liability, the end of any period of extension or accrued liability which is required of the prior carrier by Section (6) or, if the prior carrier's policy or contract is not subject to that Section, would have been required of that carrier had its policy or contract been subject to Section (6) at the time the prior plan was discontinued and replaced by the succeeding carrier's plan.
3. In the case of a pre-existing conditions limitation included in the succeeding carrier's plan, the level of benefits applicable to pre-existing conditions of persons becoming covered by the succeeding carrier's plan in accordance with this subsection during the period of time this limitation applies under the new plan shall be the lessor of:
   a. the benefits of the new plan determined without application of the pre-existing conditions limitation; and
   b. the benefits of the prior plan.
4. The succeeding carrier, in applying any deductibles or waiting periods in its plan, shall give credit for the satisfaction or partial satisfaction of the same or similar provisions under a prior plan providing similar benefits. In the case of deductible provisions, the credit shall apply for the same or overlapping benefit periods and shall be given for expenses

actually incurred and applied against the deductible provisions of the prior carrier's plan during the 90 days preceding the effective date of the succeeding carrier's plan but only to the extent these expenses are recognized under the terms of the succeeding carrier's plan and are subject to a similar deductible provision.

5. In any situation where a determination of the prior carrier's benefit is required by the succeeding carrier, at the succeeding carrier's request the prior carrier shall furnish a statement of the benefits available or pertinent information, sufficient to permit verification of the benefit determination or the determination itself by the succeeding carrier. For the purposes of this section, benefits of the prior plan will be determined in accordance with all of the definitions, conditions, and covered expense provisions of the prior plan rather than those of the succeeding plan. The benefit determination will be made as if coverage had not been replaced by the succeeding carrier.

SECTION 8. EFFECTIVE DATE

The rules and regulations shall take effect on [at least 120 days after promulgation].

Group A and B Glossary

ACCELERATED DEATH BENEFIT
An advance payment of a portion of the face amount of Life insurance due to a terminal illness

ACCIDENT
An unforeseen and unintended event.

ACCIDENT INSURANCE
A form of health insurance against loss by accidental bodily injury.

ACCIDENTAL BODILY INJURY
An injury sustained as the result of an accident.

ACCIDENTAL DEATH AND DISMEMBERMENT INSURANCE (AD&D)
A form of health and accident insurance that provides payment to an insured's beneficiary or the insured in the event of death or specific bodily losses resulting from an accident.

ACCIDENTAL DEATH BENEFIT
A lump sum payment upon the loss of life of an insured person due to the direct cause of an accident. (See Principal Sum.)

ACCIDENTAL MEANS
The unexpected and unforeseen cause of an accident. The "means" that caused the mishap must be accidental in order to claim benefits under the policy.

ACCOUNTING
The process of recording, summarizing, and allocating all items of income and expense of the company and analyzing, verifying, and reporting the results.

ACCUMULATION PERIOD
The maximum time during which an individual must incur covered expenses to satisfy a required deductible. (38) The credited hours of work during a previous period used to determine eligibility. (12)

ACQUISITION COST
The cost to the insurer of placing new business in force (includes the cost of clerical work, agent's commission, sales promotion expense, etc.).

ACTIVELY AT WORK
A requirement (a form of individual evidence of insurability) that an insured be at his or her usual place of employment on the date insurance takes effect. Since this definition is impractical for dependents, plans usually require that, if a dependent is hospital-

confined on the date the insurance would become effective, the effective date of insurance will be deferred until release from the hospital.

ACTIVITIES OF DAILY LIVING (ADL)
Usual activities of an insured in the nonoccupational environment, such as mobility, personal hygiene, dressing, sleeping, and eating. Skills required for community or social living also are included.

ACTUARY
An accredited, professionally trained-in-insurance-mathematics person, who calculates rates, reserves, dividends and other valuations and produces statistical studies and reports.

ADDITION
A person who becomes insured subsequent to the effective date of the group policy.

ADMINISTRATION
The handling of all functions related to the operation of the group insurance plan once it becomes effective. The claim function may or may not be included.

ADMINISTRATION MANUAL
A book of instructions provided the policyholder by the insurer that outlines and explains the duties of the plan administrator.

ADMINISTRATIVE ALLOWANCE
A fee or commission paid to an agent, consultant or administrator for performing case administrative functions normally handled by the insurer.

ADMINISTRATIVE SERVICES ONLY (ASO) AGREEMENT
A contract for the provision of certain services to a group employer, eligible group, trustee, etc., by an insurer or its subsidiary. Such services often include actuarial activities, benefit plan design, claim processing, data recovery and analysis, employee benefits communication, financial advice, medical care conversions, preparation of data for reports to governmental units, and stop-loss coverage.

ADMINISTRATOR
The individual or third-party firm responsible for the administration of a group insurance program. Accounting, certificate issuance, and claims settlement may be included activities.

ADVERSE SELECTION
The tendency of persons with poorer-than-average health expectations to apply for or continue insurance to a greater extent than persons with average or better health expectations.

AFFILIATE
A corporation of which a majority of the capital stock is owned or controlled by any or all the stockholders, directors, or officers of another corporation, who also own or control a majority of the stock of the other corporation.

AGE DISTRIBUTION
A distribution of either eligible or insured employees under a group life plan by either their insurance year of birth, their attained age, or year of birth, for the purpose of determining rates.

AGE RESTRICTION
The limitation on benefits when the insured person attains a specified age.

AGENT
Anyone, except a duly-licensed broker, who solicits insurance or aids in

the placing of risks, delivery of policies, or collection of premiums on behalf of an insurance company.

AGGREGATE AMOUNT (LIMIT)
The maximum sum for which an insurer is liable for any single loss, a series of losses, or for the entire duration of a contract.

ALLOCATED BENEFITS
Benefits for which the maximum amount payable for specific services is itemized in the group contract.

ALLOWABLE EXPENSE
A term used in a Coordination of Benefits provision to define any necessary, reasonable, or customary item of expense that is covered, at least in part, by one or more of the plans under which an individual is insured.

AMENDMENT
A formal document changing the provisions of the group contract and signed jointly by authorized representatives of the insurer and the policyholder.

ANNOUNCEMENT MATERIAL
Written communications used to solicit, enroll, and explain a group insurance program.

ANNUAL STATEMENT
The end-of-year report, as of December 31, of an insurer to a state insurance department showing assets and liabilities, receipts and disbursements, and other financial data.

APPLICATION
A signed request by a prospective policyholder for group insurance coverage. The application is made part of the group policy after it has been signed by the policyholder upon receipt of the policy formally establishing the risk.

APPROPRIATENESS OF CARE
Term used to describe the proper setting—an acute care hospital, an extended care facility, etc., for delivery of medical care that best responds to a patient's diagnosis.

ASSIGN
To transfer one's interest (policy benefits) to another (a third party). (The action is called an assignment.)

ASSIGNMENT OF BENEFITS
A provision in a health benefits claim form by which the insured directs the insurance company to pay any benefits directly to the provider of care on whose charge the claim is based.

ASSOCIATION GROUP INSURANCE
Group insurance provided to a professional or trade association by which eligible members are covered under one master policy.

ASSURANCE
Term synonymous with "insurance," more commonly used in Canada and Great Britain.

ATTAINED AGE
The age attained at one's last birthday, which does not change until the next birthday.

AUTOMATIC REINSURANCE
A type of reinsurance in which the insurer must cede and the reinsuring company must accept all risks within certain contractually defined areas. The reinsuring company undertakes in advance to grant reinsurance to the extent specified in the agreement in every case where the ceding company

accepts the application and retains its own limit.

BACK CHARGE
A charge made to a policyholder on a current billing statement for premium due for an insured whose insurance became effective earlier.

BACK DATE
To issue insurance for a person or group effective on a date earlier than the date of the issuance.

BASE PLAN
Any basic medical care plan that provides limited first-dollar hospital, surgical, or medical benefits, as contrasted with major medical benefit plans that provide comprehensive hospital, surgical, and medical benefits.

BASIC COMPENSATION
The basic salary or wages paid to an employee excluding overtime, bonuses, and other forms of additional compensation. It may or may not include commission income. Basic compensation is a means of establishing an employee's benefits and contributions.

BASIC COVERAGE
Refers to base plan benefits over which major medical benefits may be superimposed.

BENEFICIARY DESIGNATION
The person(s) designated to receive group life and/or accidental death benefits upon the death of an insured.

BENEFIT
The amount payable by an insurer to a claimant, assignee, or beneficiary under each coverage in the group contract.

BENEFIT FORMULA
A formula or rule for determining the amount of benefit payable under each contingency covered by a group insurance contract. The formula frequently takes into account salary and position or years of employment at the time the benefit is paid.

BENEFIT WAITING PERIOD
The period of time that must elapse before benefits are payable under a group insurance contract.

BLANKET POLICY
A contract between an insurer and a policyholder that provides for combining all major and minor coverages in a single master group policy. This type of coverage contrasts to issuing an individual master group policy for each major coverage with riders for the minor coverages attached to the applicable major policy.

BLUE CROSS
A nonprofit membership corporation providing protection against the costs of hospital care in a limited geographic area.

BLUE SHIELD
A nonprofit membership corporation providing protection against the costs of surgery and other items of medical care in a limited geographic area.

BROKER
A state-licensed person who places business with several insurers and who represents the insurance buyer rather than the insurance company, even though paid commissions by the insurer.

BROKER OF RECORD
A broker who has been designated or appointed in writing by a client to

provide certain insurance and service.

CAPITATION
A method of payment for health services in which a physician or hospital is paid a fixed amount for each person served regardless of the actual number or nature of services provided to each person.

CARRIER
A term sometimes used to identify the party (insurer) to the group contract that agrees to underwrite (carry the risk) and provide certain types of coverage and service.

CARVE-OUT
The term often used when referring to the integrated plan method of providing health benefits coverage to Medicare-eligible employees.

CASE
The term used to refer to the entire group plan of a policyholder.

CASE SUMMARY CARD
A form distributed by an insurer's home office summarizing vital information concerning a new case or a change in an existing case. (The card is sometimes referred to as an abstract.)

CASH CLAIMS
Cash disbursed, drafts redeemed, or drafts drawn for the settlement of group insurance claims.

CASH PREMIUM
Premium received by the insurer as distinguished from premium earned.

CASH SURRENDER VALUE
The amount available to a policyholder upon surrender of the policy (usually whole life).

CASUALTY INSURANCE
Type of insurance concerned with losses caused by injury to persons or damage to the property of others. It includes automobile, liability, aviation, bonding, and theft insurance.

CEDE
Activity of an insurer under a reinsurance treaty.

CENSUS DATA
Any statistical information (such as age, sex, income, insurance classification, or dependent status) on persons eligible for or insured under a group policy that is used to determine premium rates or benefits.

CERTIFICATE HOLDER
The insured person under a group plan who has been issued a certificate of insurance.

CERTIFICATE OF INSURANCE
A document delivered to the insured that summarizes the benefits and principal provisions of the group plan (may be distributed in booklet form).

CERTIFICATE RIDER
A document that amends and/or supplements the certificate of insurance.

CHARITY
The charges for services provided to needy patients without expectation of payment (sometimes called free care).

CLAIM
A demand to the insurer by, or on behalf of, the insured person for the payment of benefits under a policy.

CLAIM COST CONTROL
Efforts made by an insurer both inside and outside its own organization to contain and direct claim payments

so that health insurance premium dollars are used as efficiently as possible.

CLAIM LAG
The time between incurred date of a claim and its submission to the insurer for payment; also used to mean the time between claim incurred and payment (check or draft issue or redemption).

CLAIM LIST
A list of claims paid under a plan or coverage for a specified time which may include such information as identification of the covered person, cause of the claim, and kind and amount of charges paid.

CLAIM MANUAL
An instruction manual supplied to the administrator of the group plan by the insurer that describes the procedures to follow in processing a claim. It is usually a part of the administration manual.

CLAIM RESERVES
Funds retained by an insurer to settle incurred but unpaid claims that may also include reserves for potential claim fluctuation.

CLAIMANT
Insured or beneficiary exercising the right to receive benefits.

CLASS
The category into which insureds are placed in order to determine the amount of coverage for which they are eligible under the policy.

CLERICAL ERROR PROVISION
A policy provision that an eligible person, who submits a proper written request for coverage, shall not be denied coverage if the policyholder fails to give proper notice to the insurer, because of a clerical error.

CLOSED CLAIM
A claim under which all apparent benefits have been paid.

COINSURANCE
The arrangement by which the insurer and the insured share a percentage of covered losses after the deductible is met.

COLLATERAL DEPENDENTS
Persons made eligible for dependent coverage under a group contract by expansion of the definition of dependent (parents, grandparents, brothers, sisters, or others who depend upon the insured for a major portion of their support).

COLLECTIVE BARGAINING
A negotiation between organized labor and employer(s) on matters such as wages, hours, working conditions, and health and welfare programs.

COMMISSION
The percent of premium paid by an insurer to a duly-licensed agent or broker who sells the insurance to a policyholder and is designated by the insurer to receive the commissions.

CONSERVATION
The attempt by an insurer to prevent the lapse of a policy or its transfer to another insurer.

CONTESTABILITY
The insurer's ability to investigate possible misrepresentation in an insurance application and challenge the policy's validity.

CONTINGENCY RESERVE
A reserve established to share among all policyholders the cost to the insurer of unpredictable, catastrophic losses.

CONTINGENT BENEFICIARY
The person(s) or party legally entitled to the proceeds of an insurance policy upon death of the insured if the primary beneficiary does not survive the insured.

CONTRACT
A binding agreement between two or more parties for doing or not doing certain things. A contract of insurance is embodied in a written document usually called the policy.

CONTRACT RATE
The premium rate for a group insurance coverage that is specified in a master policy.

CONTRIBUTION
That part of the insurance premium paid by either the policyholder or the insured or both.

CONTRIBUTORY PLAN
A term used to describe a group insurance plan under which the insured shares in the cost of the plan with the policyholder.

CONVERSION CHARGE
A charge made by an insurer's group department for credit to its individual insurance department whenever group life or medical insurance is converted.

CONVERSION PRIVILEGE
The right given to the insured to change group life and/or medical care coverages to a form of individual insurance without medical examination. The conditions under which conversion can be made are defined in the master policy.

COORDINATION OF BENEFITS (COB)
A method of integrating benefits payable under more than one group health insurance plan so that the insured's benefits from all sources do not exceed 100% of allowable medical expenses.

CORRIDOR DEDUCTIBLE
A fixed out-of-pocket amount (e.g., $100) that the insured must pay above covered benefits of a basic plan before supplemental major medical plan benefits are payable.

COST CONTAINMENT
The control of the overall cost of health care services within the health care delivery system.

COST PLUS
An insurance arrangement whereby a policyholder is charged the amount of claims paid plus the insurer's retention.

COUNTERSIGNATURE
The signature of an authorized representative of an insurer validating an insurance contract.

COVERAGE
A major classification of benefits provided by a group policy (i.e., term life, short-term disability, major medical), or the amount of insurance or benefit stated in the group policy for which an insured is eligible.

COVERED CHARGES
Charges for medical care or supplies, which, if incurred by an insured or other covered person, create a liabil-

ity for the insurer under the terms of a group policy.

COVERED PERSON
Any person entitled to benefits under a group policy (insured or covered dependent).

CREDIBILITY
The weight assigned to a group's past claim experience in order to determine future expected claims for premium-setting purposes, or to determine claim charges for experience refund purposes for that group. Usually expressed as a percentage between 0% and 100%.

CREDIBILITY FACTORS
Numerical values expressing the degree of credibility assigned to actual claims experience for experience rating or analysis.

CREDITOR GROUP HEALTH INSURANCE
That form of coverage under which a borrower of money or purchaser of goods is indemnified in connection with a specific loan or credit transaction against loss of income resulting from an accident or illness.

CREDITOR GROUP LIFE INSURANCE
That form of coverage insuring lives of a group of persons who are in debt to a creditor under agreements to repay their indebtedness according to a fixed plan. The main purpose of the insurance is to liquidate the indebtedness in the event of the debtor's death prior to its repayment.

CUTBACK
A reduction in the amount or type of insurance on an individual who attains a specified age or condition (e.g., age 65 or 70, retirement, disability).

DAILY BENEFIT
A specified daily maximum amount payable for room and board charges under a hospital or major medical benefits policy.

DEATH BENEFIT
The payment made to a beneficiary at the time of death of an insured.

DECLINATION
The rejection of an application for insurance by the insurer.

DEDUCTIBLE
The amount of covered expenses that must be incurred by the insured before benefits become payable by the insurer.

DEFERRED PREMIUM
An arrangement that extends the grace period during which premiums may be paid beyond the usual 30 days.

DELINQUENT PREMIUM
Premium due the insurer that has not been paid by the end of the grace period.

DENTAL SERVICE CORPORATION
A professional group incorporated and organized on a nonprofit basis to provide dental care to consumer groups.

DEPENDENT
An insured's spouse (wife or husband), not legally separated from the insured, and unmarried child(ren) who meet certain eligibility requirements and who are not otherwise insured under the same group policy. The precise definition of a dependent varies by insurer.

DEPOSIT ADMINISTRATION FUNDS
Funds intended for the payment of benefits to plan participants that are held on an unallocated basis.

DEPOSIT PREMIUM
The amount paid by a prospective policyholder when an application is made for a group insurance policy. It is usually equal, at least, to the first month's estimated premium and is applied toward the actual premium when billed.

DESIGNATED BENEFICIARY
The person(s) or party designated by the insured to receive the proceeds of an insurance policy upon death of the insured.

DIAGNOSIS
The determination of the nature and circumstances of a disease condition.

DIAGNOSIS RELATED GROUP (DRG)
A system of categorizing inpatient medical services and assigning specific reimbursement fees to each category.

DIRECT CLAIM PAYMENT
A method of paying claims whereby the insured individuals deal directly with the insurance company rather than submitting claims through the group policyholder.

DIRECT COST
Acquisition and administrative costs directly attributable to particular group cases, which exclude any share of overhead expenses.

DIRECT WRITER
An insurer that deals directly with prospective policyholders without the participation of agents or brokers.

DISABILITY
A physical or mental condition that makes an insured incapable of performing one or more duties of his or her own occupation or, for total disability, of any occupation.

DISABILITY BENEFIT
A payment that arises because of the total and/or permanent disability of an insured; a provision added to a policy that provides for a waiver of premium in case of total and permanent disability.

DISABILITY INCOME BENEFITS
Loss-of-income benefits payable under group life (permanent and total disability income feature), short-term disability income, and long-term disability income insurance contracts. Sometimes called loss-of-time benefits.

DISABILITY INCOME INSURANCE
A form of health insurance that provides periodic payments when the insured is unable to work as a result of illness, disease, or injury.

DISABLED LIFE RESERVE
Funds reserved for payment of known and/or potential claims on lives of currently disabled insureds.

DISMEMBERMENT
The accidental loss of limb or sight.

DISTRIBUTION
The separation of all insureds (prospective or in force) under a group insurance plan by age, sex, location, income, dependency status, and benefit class for the purpose of computing gross premium rates.

DIVIDEND
The portion of the premiums collected that the insurer issuing group policies on a participating basis returns to a policyholder after taking into account the claims incurred, ex-

pense charges, risk charges, and changes in contingency reserves.

DOMESTIC COMPANY
An insurer doing business in the state in which it is incorporated.

DOUBLE INDEMNITY
An additional payment offered for injury or death occurring in a prescribed manner (e.g., accidental death on a common carrier such as a bus, plane, or train).

DOWNSCALE
The computation of the commissions due by applying the proper commission scale to the premiums received.

DRAFT BOOK CLAIM PAYMENT
A method of claim settlement whereby the insurer authorizes the policyholder to settle claims and to issue payment on behalf of the insurer.

DUE AND UNCOLLECTED PREMIUM
Premium due an insurer that has not been received as of some specified date.

DUE AND UNPAID CLAIMS
Incurred claims that are due but unpaid by the insurer as of some specified date.

DUPLICATE COVERAGE
Coverage of an insured under two or more policies for the same potential loss.

EACH PER CAUSE
Refers to a policy that determines the benefits payable separately, based on the covered expenses resulting from a given accident or illness.

EARNED PREMIUM
The part of the premium for coverage (protection) that has already been provided and that the insurer has, therefore, "earned."

EFFECTIVE DATE
The date that insurance coverage goes into effect (may refer to a case, a group contract, a coverage, a benefit, or an insured).

ELIGIBILITY
The provisions of the group policy that state the requirements members of the group and/or their dependents must satisfy to become insured.

ELIGIBILITY DATE
The date on which a member of an insured group may apply for insurance.

ELIGIBILITY PERIOD
The time following the eligibility date (usually 31 days) during which a member of an insured group may apply for insurance without evidence of insurability.

ELIGIBLE EMPLOYEES
Those employees who have met the eligibility requirements for insurance set forth in the group policy.

ELIGIBLE GROUP
A group of persons permitted, under state insurance laws and insurer underwriting practices, to be insured under a group policy; usually includes individual employer groups, multiple-employer groups, labor union groups, creditor-debtor groups, and certain association groups.

EMPLOYEE BENEFITS CONSULTANT
A person or firm specializing in the design, sale, and service of employee benefit plans, usually representing the policyholder in placing insurance coverage with an insurer or assisting

the employer in changing or enhancing a benefit program. Compensation is provided either by commissions from the insurer or by the policyholder on a fee-for-service basis.

EMPLOYEE CENSUS
Data, such as age, sex, occupation, earnings, and dependency status, relating to the insured persons under a group policy.

EMPLOYEE LIFE INSURANCE
Term coverage issued to the employees of a common employer by the use of a group policy.

EMPLOYEE-PAY-ALL PLAN
Group plan in which the insureds (employees) pay the entire premium.

EMPLOYER-PAY-ALL PLAN
Plan in which the employer (policyholder) pays the entire premium (which is referred to as a noncontributory plan).

ENDORSEMENT
The changing of provisions in a policy or certificate of insurance by means of an official entry over the signature of an officer of an insurer either on the policy or the certificate.

ENROLLMENT (SOLICITATION)
The process of explaining the proposed group insurance plan to eligible persons and assisting them in the proper completion of their enrollment cards.

ENROLLMENT CARD
A document signed by an eligible person as notice of desire to participate in the group insurance plan. For a contributory plan, this card also provides an employer with authorization to deduct contributions from an employee's pay. If group life and accidental death and dismemberment coverage are involved, the card usually includes the beneficiary's name and relationship.

EVIDENCE OF INSURABILITY
Proof, presented through written statements on an application form and/or through a medical examination, that an individual is eligible for a certain type of insurance coverage. In group insurance this form is required for eligibles who do not enroll during the open enrollment period (i.e., generally a 31-day period); who apply for reinstatement after having previously withdrawn from the plan; who apply for reinstatement after having received an overall maximum benefit; or who apply for excess amounts of group life or disability insurance.

EXCESS AMOUNTS
An amount of life or disability insurance offered a certain class of insureds that is more than the amount normally allowed, based on the total volume developed for the case. This excess amount of insurance usually is medically underwritten.

EXCLUSIONS (EXCEPTIONS)
Specified coverages, hazards, services, conditions, and the like that are not provided for (covered) under a particular contract.

EXEMPT EMPLOYEES
A classification designating those employees who are not subject to overtime compensation and working time limits under the federal Labor Standards Act.

EXPECTED MORTALITY
The number of deaths expected to occur in a given group within a specified time, usually expressed as a ratio of expected death claim payments to premium.

EXPENSE LOADING
That portion of a group insurance premium required to cover acquisition and administration costs.

EXPENSE RATIO
A percentage showing the relationship of expenses to earned premiums.

EXPERIENCE
The term used to describe the relationship between the premiums paid to an insurer and the benefits paid out over a fixed period (e.g., a policy year, the three most recent complete policy years).

EXPERIENCE ANALYSIS
Any statistical analysis of experience for all or any segment of the group business, such as a line or a territory; any group of cases, coverages, or benefits; or any single case, coverage, or benefit. It may include single or multiple experience periods, analysis of past and projection of future trends, plus various descriptive or inferential statistics.

EXPERIENCE RATING
The process of determining the premium rate for a group risk based wholly or partially on that risk's experience.

EXPERIENCE REFUND
The amount of premium returned by an insurer to a group policyholder when the financial experience of the particular group (or the experience refund class to which the group belongs) has been more favorable than anticipated in the premiums collected from the group.

EXPERIENCE-RELATED PREMIUM RATES
Premium rates for a group coverage that are based, wholly or partially, on the knowledge of past claims of the group.

EXPOSURE
The level of risk to a specific loss as measured by participation in a group, ratio of female lives to total lives, amounts at risk, or the like.

EXTENDED BENEFITS
The extension of certain benefits under specific conditions, beyond the termination of an insured's participation in a plan or the termination of the master policy.

EXTENDED DEATH BENEFIT
A provision in a group life contract stating that if the insured is totally and continuously disabled from the date the policyholder stops paying the premium for the insured's insurance until the date of the insured's death, the insurer will pay the amount of insurance in force on the insured's life at the date of cessation of premium payments provided that death occurs (a) within one year of the date of cessation of premium payments and (b) prior to the insured's 65th birthday.

EXTENDED INSURANCE
The extension of benefits under certain conditions beyond the termination date of insurance.

FACILITY OF PAYMENT
A contractual provision that the insurer may, under stated conditions, pay insurance benefits to persons

other than the insured, the designated beneficiary, or the estate of the insured.

FEE-FOR-SERVICE
Method of charging whereby a physician or other practitioner bills for each visit or service rendered.

FEE SCHEDULE
Maximum dollar or unit allowances for health services that apply under a specific contract.

FILING
The submission of a proposed policy form for approval to the insurance department of the jurisdiction where it will be issued.

501(c)(9) TRUST
This trust takes its name from the section of the Internal Revenue Code that permits more favorable tax treatment to qualifying trusts.

FOREIGN COMPANY
A term identifying an insurer doing business in any state other than the one in which it is incorporated.

FRANCHISE INSURANCE
A form of insurance in which individual policies are issued to the employees of a common employer or the members of an association under an arrangement by which the employer or the members of an association agree to collect premiums and remit them to the insurer.

FRATERNAL INSURANCE
A cooperative type of insurance provided by social organizations for their members. The social group may pay premiums into a fund and withdraw monies to pay claims upon the death of one of its members.

FRAUD
Deceit or trickery used to gain unfair or dishonest advantage.

GAIN-OR-LOSS REPORT
A financial statement that shows underwriting and investment gain or loss and related elements for a particular case, a group of cases, or an entire line of group business.

GENERALLY ACCEPTED ACCOUNTING PRINCIPLES (GAAP)
Rules of accounting and reporting business results developed by the American Institute of Certified Public Accountants.

GRACE PERIOD
A specified time (usually 31 days) following the premium due date during which the insurance remains in force and a policyholder may pay the premium without penalty.

GRACE PERIOD LIABILITY
An insurer's liability for claims incurred during the grace period.

GRADED LEVEL COMMISSIONS
A commission schedule (agreement) that provides the same commission percentages for premium increments of first and renewal years.

GROSS COST
The cost of an insurance program, over a specified time (e.g., a policy year), before taking dividends, rate credits, and such into consideration.

GROSS PREMIUM
The contracted premium (manual plus any loadings) before applying any discounts.

GROUP CASE
Expression used to refer collectively to the entire group plan of a policyholder.

GROUP CONTRACT (POLICY)
A contract of life or health insurance made with an employer or other entity (policyholder) that covers a group of persons identified as individuals by reference to their relationship to the contracting policyholder.

GROUP LIFE INSURANCE IN FORCE
The sum of the face amounts of group life insurance certificates outstanding at a given time; includes all employee and dependent insurance life exposed whether or not a specific premium is charged.

GROUP MONTHLY PREMIUM IN FORCE
The sum of monthly premiums billed at any given time to cover all outstanding group insurance.

GROUP NUMBER
The master policy number, assigned by the insurer's home office, that is used to identify a case and information pertaining to it. Various synonymous terms used are employer number, G-number, case number, file number, account number, company code number, or master policy number.

GROUP ORDINARY LIFE INSURANCE
Group permanent life insurance. Unlike group term, it has level premiums based on issue age and accumulates reserves and cash surrender values.

GROUP PAID-UP LIFE INSURANCE
Group permanent life insurance with employees' contributions used to purchase paid-up insurance, and with cash surrender values.

GROUP POLICYHOLDER
The legal entity to which the master policy is issued.

GROUP REPRESENTATIVE
A salaried employee of the insurer whose principal tasks are to assist agents and brokers in developing and soliciting prospects for group insurance and to install and service group contracts.

HAZARD
The measure of risk assumed by an insurer. It can involve physical, moral, or financial elements.

HEALTH INSURANCE
Types of coverage providing for the payment of benefits as a result of sickness or injury including insurance for losses from accident, disability, medical expense, or accidental death and dismemberment.

HEALTH MAINTENANCE ORGANIZATION (HMO)
An organization that provides for a wide range of comprehensive health care services for a specified group at a fixed periodic prepayment.

HIGH-LOW COMMISSION SCALE
A commission scale providing for the payment of a high first-year commission and lower renewal commissions.

HOME HEALTH CARE
A comprehensive, medically necessary range of health services provided by a recognized provider organization to a patient at home.

HOME OFFICE ADMINISTRATION
The method of insurance plan administration in which the insurer maintains the basic records for the persons covered.

HOSPITAL ADMISSION PLAN (HAP)
A plan used to facilitate admission of persons covered by group medical care insurance to hospitals and to as-

sure the prompt payment of applicable insurance benefits to hospitals.

HOSPITAL "EXTRAS" ALLOWANCE
The amount provided for in group policies to cover necessary hospital services and supplies other than room and board.

IDENTIFICATION (ID) CARD
A form provided to insureds that identifies them as members of a particular insurance plan and may provide basic information about their coverage. Although such cards do not guarantee eligibility for medical care benefits at any given time, they provide procedures for providers to follow to verify that a patient has health coverage.

IMMEDIATE MATERNITY
Coverage provided for pregnancies that commence prior to the date the individual becomes insured.

INCONTESTABILITY
Result of incontestable clause defined below.

INCONTESTABLE CLAUSE
The provision in a group life and/or health insurance policy that prevents the insurance company from disputing the validity of certain coverage under specific insurance conditions after the policy has been in effect for a certain time (usually two years).

INCREASE IN COVERAGE
An addition in benefits that becomes effective for an insured or a group of insureds as a result of a specific change in class, due to a wage or salary increase, occupational promotion, or negotiated enhancements to the benefits program.

INCURRED BUT UNPAID CLAIMS
Claims that have not been paid as of some specified date (may include both reported and unreported claims).

INCURRED BUT UNREPORTED CLAIMS
Claims that have not been reported to the insurer as of some specified date.

INCURRED CLAIM RESERVES
An estimation of claims actually incurred in the policy year but not paid as of the end of the policy year.

INCURRED CLAIMS
An amount equal to the claims paid during the policy year plus the change of the claim reserves as of the end of the policy year. The change in reserves represents the difference between the end of the year and beginning of the year claim reserves.

INDEMNIFY
To compensate for a loss.

INDEMNITY
A benefit paid by an insurance policy for an insured loss.

INDEPENDENT CONTRACTOR
One who agrees to perform services under a contract and who is not under the control of, nor an employee of, the party with which the contract is made.

IN FORCE
The total volume of insurance on the lives of covered employees at any given time (measured in terms of cases, lives, amount [volume] of insurance, or premium).

INITIAL RATE
A premium rate that is charged on the effective date of a new group policy.

INSIDE LIMITS
Specifications of benefits in an insurance plan that establish maximum service duration or amounts payable for a procedure, service, confinement, disability, or calendar year.

INSPECTION
A report describing and evaluating a risk usually provided to the insurer by a commercial company specializing in such services.

INSTALLATION
The process of assisting a group policyholder to set up the administrative practices essential to the proper handling of all initial and ongoing administrative activities of the plan.

INSTALLMENT DISABILITY INCOME BENEFITS
A provision in certain older group term life insurance policies that in the case of the total and permanent disability of an insured the insurer will pay the policy face amount in specified equal installments over a predetermined duration (e.g., five years).

INSURABILITY
Refers to the physical, moral, occupational, and financial status of a risk and its acceptability to the insurer.

INSURABLE INTEREST
The need of an insured or beneficiary to suffer a genuine loss should the event insured against occur.

INSURANCE
A plan of risk management that, for a price, offers the insured an opportunity to share the costs of possible economic loss through an entity called an insurer.

INSURANCE EXAMINER
The representative of a state insurance department assigned to participate in the official audit and examination of the affairs of an insurer.

INSURANCE MONTH
A period commencing on a given date (e.g., lst, l0th) of any calendar month and ending on a day (lst, 9th) of the next succeeding calendar month.

INSURANCE YEAR OF BIRTH
The year of birth for an individual insured under a group insurance plan that reflects the designated or insurance age of the individual on any policy anniversary.

INSURED
The person (employee, dependent, or group member) who is covered for insurance under the group policy and to whom, or on behalf of whom, the insurer agrees to pay benefits.

INSURER
The party to the insurance contract that promises to pay losses or benefits. Also, any corporation primarily engaged in the business of furnishing insurance protection to the public.

INSURING CLAUSE
The clause in a policy that names the parties to a contract and states what is covered by the policy.

INTEGRATED DEDUCTIBLE
A high fixed amount (e.g., $1,000) or the sum of the benefits paid under a base medical care plan, whichever is greater, that must be exceeded before supplemental major medical benefits are payable.

INTEGRATION
The combining of two or more benefit plans to prevent duplication of benefit payments.

INTERNATIONAL CLAIM ASSOCIATION (ICA)
An organization concerned with information and education in the area of life and health claims administration.

IRREVOCABLE ASSIGNMENT
The permanent legal transfer of one person's interest in an insurance policy to another person.

IRREVOCABLE BENEFICIARY
A beneficiary whose designation as such by the insured may not be changed without his or her consent.

JOB DESCRIPTION
A detailed listing of the requirements of the insured's predisability job, including specific physical and mental qualifications for performance, that is used to evaluate work potential in a rehabilitation case.

JOINT BENEFICIARY
Person or party legally entitled to share in the proceeds of an insurance policy.

KEY PERSON INSURANCE
A group plan designed to protect a business against the loss of income resulting from the disability of a central employee.

LAPSE
The termination of coverage provided in an insurance contract because of the nonpayment of premium(s) within the time due.

LAPSED POLICY
A group master contract that has automatically expired, as provided by its terms, because of nonpayment of premium.

LATE APPLICANT
An eligible person who applies for insurance after the normal 31-day open enrollment period.

LENGTH-OF-SERVICE SCHEDULE
A schedule of insurance under which employees are insured for an amount based on the length of time the employee has worked for the employer.

LENGTH OF STAY
The time a patient remains in a hospital or other health care facility. Measures use of health care facilities and reported as the average number of days spent in a facility per admission or discharge.

LEVEL COMMISSION SCALE
A method of assigning commission payments that applies the same commission rates to the premium each year, regardless of the policy year.

LEVEL PREMIUM BILLING
A method of premium billing that allows the policyholder to pay a certain set amount of premium on each due date during the policy year, based on an estimated annual premium, with an adjustment at the end of the policy year for coverage changes that have occurred during the policy year.

LEVEL SCHEDULE
A group plan in which everyone is insured for the same amount of benefits regardless of salary, position, or other circumstances.

LIABILITY
The probable cost of meeting an obligation.

LICENSE
Certification, issued by a state department of insurance, that an individual is qualified to solicit insurance applications for the period covered.

LIFE EXPECTANCY
The average number of years of life remaining for persons of a given age according to a particular mortality table.

LIMITS
The maximum amount of benefits payable for a given situation or occurrence; or age groups above and below which an insurer will not issue a policy or will offer restricted coverage.

LOADING FACTOR
The amount added to the net premium rate determined for a group insurance plan to cover the possibility that losses will be greater than statistically expected because of older average age, hazardous industry, large percentage of unskilled employees, or adverse experience.

LONG-TERM DISABILITY (LTD) INCOME INSURANCE
Benefits plan that helps replace earned income lost through inability to work because of disability caused by accident or illness.

LOSS
The amount of insurance or benefit for which the insurer becomes liable when the event insured against occurs.

LOSS RATIO (INCURRED BASIS)
The ratio of paid claims plus change in claim reserves to earned premiums.

LOSS RATIO (PAID BASIS)
The ratio of paid claims to earned premiums.

MALINGERING
The practice of feigning illness or inability to work in order to collect insurance benefits.

MALPRACTICE
Improper care or treatment by a physician.

MANAGED HEALTH CARE
Health care delivery arrangements that are designed to control health care costs and improve utilization of services.

MANUAL PREMIUM
The premium developed for a group's coverage from the insurer's standard rate tables.

MANUAL RATE
The premium rate developed for a group's coverage from the insurer's standard rate tables, usually contained in its rate manual or underwriting manual.

MASTER POLICY (MASTER CONTRACT)
The single or combined policy issued to a policyholder setting forth the provisions of a group insurance plan.

MAXIMUM BENEFIT
The highest amount any one individual may receive under an insurance contract.

MEDICAID
State programs with federal matching funds provided by Social Security under stipulated conditions of public as-

sistance to persons regardless of age whose income and resources are insufficient to pay for health care.

MEDICAL CASE MANAGEMENT

A system of patient or client assessment, planning, treatment, referral and follow-up to ensure provision of coordinated medical services. Also includes coordination of payment and reimbursement.

MEDICARE

A federally sponsored program that provides hospital benefits, supplementary medical care, and catastrophic coverages to elderly persons.

MINIMUM PREMIUM PLAN

A combination approach to funding an insurance plan aimed primarily at premium tax savings. The employer self-funds a fixed percent (e.g., 90%) of the estimated monthly claims and the insurance company insures the excess.

MINIMUM PREMIUM RATE

The lowest premium rate that an insurer may charge a policyholder during the first year the group insurance is in effect, based on its field manual premium rates.

MISREPRESENTATION

A false or misleading statement of fact on an insurance application, that influences an insurer to issue a policy it may not otherwise have issued.

MISSTATEMENT OF AGE

The declaration by an employee of an age that is lesser or greater than her or his actual age.

MONTHLY ADJUSTMENT BILLING

A method of premium billing by which the policyholder is billed on each premium due date for the insurance coverage on the actual number of persons covered by the group insurance plan.

MORBIDITY

The incidence and severity of sicknesses and accidents in a well-defined class or classes of persons.

MORBIDITY TABLE

A statistical table showing the average number of illnesses (and sometimes accidents) befalling a large group of persons.

MORTALITY

The death rate in a group of people as determined from prior experience.

MORTALITY TABLE

A mortality table shows the incidence of death in each age group.

MULTIPLE EMPLOYER GROUP

Employees of two or more employers, such as trade associations of employers in the same industry or union members who work for more than one employer, covered under one master contract.

MULTIPLE EMPLOYER TRUST (MET)

A legal trust established by a plan sponsor that brings together a number of small, unrelated employers for the purpose of providing group medical care coverage on an insured or a self-funded basis.

MULTIPLE INDEMNITY

A provision under which the principal sum of a policy will be multiplied by 100, 200, 300, or more percent in case of death from certain types of accidents.

MUTUAL COMPANY
An insurance company whose management is directed by a board of directors elected by the policyholders.

NATIONAL ASSOCIATION OF INSURANCE COMMISSIONERS (NAIC)
A national organization of state officials charged with regulating insurance, which has no official power but wields tremendous influence. The association was formed to promote national uniformity in insurance regulation.

NEGOTIATED TRUSTEESHIPS
A policy issued to the trustees of a fund established by a formal agreement concerning employees subject to collective bargaining, or employees of two employers who have signed the trust agreement.

NET COST
In group insurance it equals claims plus reserves plus expenses.

NET PREMIUM
Amount paid or earned premium after discounts.

NET PREMIUM RATE
That portion of the premium rate of a group that represents expected claims.

NET REVENUE
The amount of money actually received by a hospital resulting from charges for provided services, less deductions from bad debts, charity, and contractual adjustments.

NEW BUSINESS
For new cases, the increase of inforce business resulting from the sale of insurance coverage to a new policyholder; for additional business on existing cases, the increase resulting from the extension of coverage, addition of coverages, or the increase in coverages purchased by an existing policyholder.

NONCONTRIBUTORY PLAN
A term used to describe a group insurance plan under which the employer does not require employees to share in its cost.

NONDUPLICATION CLAUSE
A policy provision that results in a stricter application of coordination of benefits principles. When an individual is covered by two or more policies, this provision excludes expenses incurred that are covered by another policy.

NONEXEMPT EMPLOYEES
A classification of employees designating those who are subject to overtime compensation and working time limits under the federal Labor Standards Act.

NONOCCUPATIONAL INSURANCE
Insurance that does not provide benefits for an accident or sickness arising out of a person's employment.

NONPROFIT INSURERS
Corporations organized under special state laws to provide medical benefits on a not-for-profit basis (e.g., Blue Cross, Blue Shield, Dental Service Corporations).

NONVESTED RESERVES
Group case reserves (e.g., contingency) not owned by the policyholder, which are voluntary allocations of earnings rather than actual liabilities of the insurer. They may be

used for the policyholder's benefit (e.g., to pay claims) but are not returnable in the event of contract termination.

OCCUPANCY RATE
A measure of inpatient health facility use, determined by dividing available bed days by patient days.

OCCUPATIONAL SCHEDULE
A schedule of insurance under which persons are insured for an amount based on their job classifications.

OCCUPATIONAL THERAPY
A program of prescribed activities, emphasizing coordination and mastery, designed to assist the insured to regain independence, particularly in the activities of daily living (ADL).

OPEN ENROLLMENT
A time during which uninsured employees and/or their dependents may obtain coverage under an existing group plan without presenting evidence of insurability. Differs from a resolicitation in that a minimum number of applications are not required.

OPTIONAL MODES OF SETTLEMENT
The right of the insured or, under certain circumstances, the beneficiary, to elect to receive the proceeds of a life insurance policy other than as a lump sum.

ORTHOTICS
A specialized field relating to appliances, braces, and other devices used to support weight, align, prevent, or correct deformities, or improve the function of movable parts of the body.

OTHER INSURANCE CLAUSE
A provision in an insurance contract stating the effect on the policy of other coverages or insurance plans.

OUT-OF-POCKET EXPENSE
Those medical expenses that an insured must pay that are not covered under the group contract.

OVERINSURANCE
Coverage exceeding the probable loss to which it applies.

OVERRIDING COMMISSION
A commission paid to general agents or agency managers in addition to the commission paid the soliciting agent or broker.

PACKAGE PLAN (PACKAGING)
A plan consisting of several coverages each of which must be elected by eligible participants who must either accept or reject the entire package.

PACKAGE POLICY
A single contract that provides all the coverages in the group insurance plan.

PARENT COMPANY
A company that controls other companies (subsidiaries). When employees of a parent company and its subsidiaries have group insurance with a common insurer, the parent company is usually the group policyholder with which the insurer does business.

PARTIAL DISABILITY
Inability to perform one or more functions of one's regular job.

PARTIAL PAYMENT
A payment to a claimant where it is expected other payments will be made before the claim can be considered closed.

PARTICIPATION
The number of insureds covered under the group plan in relation to the

total number eligible to be covered, usually expressed as a percentage.

PAST SERVICE COST
The actuarial value (single sum) of the past service benefit as of the effective date of the establishment of the plan, or the date of the latest liberalization.

PAY-AS-YOU-GO
Deferring the cost of the coverages for retired employees until after their actual retirement.

PAYROLL DEDUCTION
The amount an employee consents to have taken from earnings as a contribution toward the cost of the group insurance plan.

PENDING CLAIM
A claim that has been reported but on which final action has not been taken.

PER DIEM COST
Literally, cost per day. Refers in general to hospital or other inpatient institutional costs per day or for a day of care. Per diem costs are averages and do not reflect true costs for each patient.

PERIOD OF DISABILITY
The period during which an employee is prevented from performing usual occupational duties, or during which a dependent cannot perform the normal activities of a healthy person of the same age or sex.

PERMANENT AND TOTAL DISABILITY
A disability that will presumably last for the insured's lifetime and prevent the insured from engaging in any occupation.

PERSISTENCY
The degree to which policies stay in force through the continued payment of renewal premiums.

PERSISTENCY FEES
Fees paid over and above the regular commissions as long as the case stays in force.

PERSONAL HEALTH STATEMENT
A general health questionnaire completed by an applicant for coverage under a group insurance plan, which is used as evidence of insurability.

POLICY
The document that sets forth the contract of insurance.

POLICY ANNIVERSARY
The manual date that separates the experience under a group policy for dividend and retroactive rate purposes. The period is normally 12 consecutive months.

POLICY CONSTANT
The factor that is added to the total premium in a group life rate calculation in recognition of the minimum expense loading associated with any case regardless of the size of the risk.

POLICY FEE
An amount sometimes charged in addition to the first premium as a fee for issuance of the policy; for example, group health conversion policies.

POLICYHOLDER
The legal entity (employer, union, trustees, creditor) to whom an insurer issues a contract.

POLICYHOLDER ADMINISTRATION (SELF-ADMINISTRATION)
Situation whereby the policyholder maintains all records and assumes re-

sponsibility regarding insureds covered under its insurance plan, including preparing the premium statement for each payment date and submitting it with a check to the insurer. Under this method the insurance company, in most instances, has the contractual prerogative to audit the policyholder's records.

POLICY NUMBER
That number assigned to a group contract that contains both the account number of the policy and the policy code number.

POLICY YEAR
The time that elapses between policy anniversaries, as specified in the policy.

POOLED CLAIMS
Claims applicable to pooled risks that are excluded from individual case experience rating.

POOLED PREMIUM
Premium applicable to pooled risks that is excluded from individual case experience rating.

POOLING
The combining of all premium, claims, expenses, and such for certain cases (usually small), types of coverage (e.g., all AD&D business), or excess classes (e.g., in group life insurance that are medically examined or are in excess of normal limits) in order to spread the risk.

POOLING CHARGE
A charge applicable to pooled risks provided in an individual case experience-rating refund formula that is included in the premium.

POOLING CREDIT
Credit for pooled claims provided in an individual case experience-rating refund formula.

PREADMISSION CERTIFICATION
A process under which an insurance company or precertification administrator reviews in advance admission to a health care institution to determine need and appropriateness and length of authorized stay.

PREEXISTING CONDITION
Any physical and/or mental condition or conditions that exist prior to the effective date of coverage under a contract.

PREEXISTING CONDITIONS PROVISION
A restriction on payments for those charges directly resulting from an accident or illness for which the insured received care or treatment within a specified period of time (e.g., three months) prior to the date of insurance.

PREFERRED PROVIDER ORGANIZATION (PPO)
An arrangement whereby a third-party payor contracts with a group of medical care providers to furnish services at lower-than-usual fees in return for prompt payment and a certain volume of patients.

PREFUNDED
Providing for the cost of coverage for retired employees during the time of their employment.

PREMIUM
The periodic payment required to keep a policy in force.

PREMIUM NOTICE (BILLING)
The statement requesting the policyholder to pay a premium on a particu-

lar due date. The insurer may enclose a premium remittance card that should be returned with the policyholder's check.

PREMIUM PAYMENT MODE (FREQUENCY)
The number of times premiums are payable in a policy year. For example, a policy on which premiums are paid monthly is said to have a monthly premium frequency.

PREMIUM RATE
The price of a unit of coverage or benefit.

PREMIUM REFUND
Monies returned to a policyholder, usually because of favorable experience (i.e., an experience-rating refund).

PREMIUM STATEMENT
The bill prepared by the insurer and sent to the policyholder for each premium due on a group plan administered by the insurer, or the bill submitted to the insurer as of each premium due date by a policyholder whose group plan is self-administered.

PREMIUM TAX
An assessment levied by a federal or state government usually on the net premium income collected in a particular jurisdiction by an insurer.

PRIMARY BENEFICIARY
The first person(s) designated to receive the proceeds of an insurance policy upon death of the insured.

PRIMARY CARE
First contact and continuing health care, including basic or initial diagnosis and treatment, health supervision, management of chronic conditions, preventive health services, and appropriate referral.

PRINCIPAL SUM
The amount payable in one sum in event of accidental death and, in some cases, accidental dismemberment.

PRODUCTION CREDIT
The new business volume and/or premium written on new and existing cases that is credited to an agent, broker, or group representative.

PROFESSIONAL ASSOCIATION PLANS
Plans designed for persons belonging to professional organizations (lawyers, doctors, educators, and the like) and written on a group or franchise basis as permitted by state law.

PROOF OF LOSS
Documentary evidence required by an insurer to prove a valid claim exists, such as a claim form or proof of death.

PROPOSAL
A quotation, submitted to a prospective group insurance policyholder by an insurance company primarily through an agent, broker, or group representative, which outlines the benefits available under a suggested plan and the costs to both employer and employees.

PRORATION
The modification of policy benefits because of a change in the insured's occupation or the existence of other insurance.

PROSPECTIVE RATING
A method of renewal rating that adjusts the rates for the coming policy year in accordance with such factors as known credible past experience,

insurance industry and insurance company trends, general business trends (e.g., inflation, deflation), current manual rates, and so forth.

PROSPECTIVE REIMBURSEMENT
Any method of payment in which rates of payment are established in advance for a defined period. These systems are designed to introduce constraints on cost increases and provide incentives for improved efficiency, in contrast with a system that reimburses for actual expenses incurred.

PROSTHETICS
A specialized field relating to the design and use of an artificial substitute for a missing body part such as an arm, leg, or eye.

PROVISION
A part of a group insurance contract that describes or explains a feature, benefit, condition, or requirement of the insurance protection afforded by the contract.

PROVISIONAL PREMIUM
An estimated premium paid prior to the exact determination of the total amount due.

QUOTATION
The offer to a prospective policyholder to underwrite specified insurance benefits at stated premium rates.

RATE REVIEW
A system for advance review of proposed costs and charges developed for health care institutions to determine their appropriateness.

REASONABLE AND CUSTOMARY (USUAL AND REASONABLE) CHARGE
A charge for health care consistent with the going rate or charge in a certain geographic area for identical or similar services.

REBATING
The illegal act of giving any valuable consideration, usually a part or all of the commissions, to a prospect as an inducement to buy insurance.

RECORD CARD (REGISTER)
A card used by the insurer and/or the administrator of the plan to indicate a person insured, coverages and amounts of insurance, beneficiary, and any other information necessary to successfully administer the group plan.

REDUCTION FORMULA
A contractual provision that periodically reduces the level of life insurance to some ultimate amount of coverage. The reduction formula is triggered by the attainment of a certain age or by change in employment status (e.g., retirement).

REHABILITATION
The physical or mental restoration of disabled insureds to maximum independence and productivity commensurate with their limitations.

REIMBURSEMENT
The payment of the actual charges incurred as a result of an accident or illness but not to exceed any maximums specified in the plan of insurance.

REINSTATE (REINSTATEMENT)
To place in force again, without the usual probationary or service period, a group contract or an individual's group insurance that for some reason has terminated.

REINSURANCE
Acceptance by one insurer (the reinsurer) of all or part of the risk of loss underwritten by another insurer (the ceding insurer).

REINSURANCE TREATY
An agreement between a reinsurer and a ceding company.

RELATIVE VALUE STUDY (RVS)
A guide (not a fee schedule) that attempts to show in a general way by a unit or point designation the relationship between the time, competency, experience, severity, and other factors required to perform services under usual conditions. Such a study becomes a schedule when dollar conversion factors are applied.

RENEWAL
An offer and acceptance of a premium for a new policy term.

RENEWAL DATE
The annual date on which the experience of an existing policy is scheduled to be reviewed.

RENEWAL RATING
The insurer's review of the premium rates and claims experience for a group plan from which the necessity of rate changes is determined.

RENEWAL SERVICE CALL
A periodic visit made by a representative of the insurance company to the policyholder. The purpose of the call is to discuss the group plan and render any service that appears necessary.

RENEWAL UNDERWRITING
The review of the financial experience of a group case and the establishment of the renewal premium rates and terms under which the insurance may be continued.

REPRESENTATION
A statement on an application that need only be substantially true. As a general rule, representations are considered fraudulent only when they relate to a matter material to the risk and were made with fraudulent intent.

RESERVE
A measure of an insurer's liability, present and future, for a particular obligation or a class of obligations.

RESOLICITATION (RECANVASS)
A campaign conducted to enroll persons in an existing group insurance plan who are eligible to participate in, but are not covered by, the insurance. Evidence of insurability may or may not be required for inclusion in the group.

RETALIATORY TAX (STATE)
Premium tax rate a state levies against a foreign insurer doing business in that state, which, in accordance with state laws, is the greater of the tax rate levied against domestic insurers, or the tax rate levied against domestic companies by the home state of the foreign insurer.

RETENTION
That portion of the premium kept by the insurer for expenses, contingencies, and contributions to surplus (profit).

RETENTION ESTIMATE
A projection of estimated expenses on a particular group insurance case.

RETROACTIVE RATE CREDIT
The portion of the premiums that the insurer, issuing group policies on a nonparticipating basis, returns to a policyholder after taking into account the claims incurred, expense charges, risk charges, changes in reserves, and profit.

RETROSPECTIVE PREMIUM AGREEMENT
A formal, binding agreement from the policyholder to pay the insurer for deficits incurred as a result of the insurer's agreement to continue coverage at a premium level that eliminates any margin for claim fluctuation.

RETROSPECTIVE RATING
A method of experience rating that adjusts the final premium of a risk in accordance with the experience of that risk during the term of the policy for which the premium is paid.

RIDER
An amendment that modifies the terms of the group contract or certificates of insurance. It may increase benefits, waive a condition or coverage, or alter in any other way the original contract.

RISK
The probable amount of loss foreseen by an insurer in issuing a contract.

RISK CHARGE
That portion of a group insurer's retention intended to be used (1) to spread the cost of catastrophic or epidemic losses over all groups, (2) to pay certain claims that may be pooled and not charged against the experience of a particular group, (3) to cover the experience deficits arising on the poorer risks in a given class, or (4) to contribute to the insurer's general surplus as protection against major losses affecting its entire group business.

RISK MARGIN
That portion of the insurer's retention other than for expenses, i.e., risk and other contingency charges and profits.

RULING
A judicial decision, or a decision of the commissioner of Internal Revenue relative to a specific tax question.

SCHEDULE
A listing of amounts payable for specified occurrences (e.g., surgical operations, laboratory tests, x-ray services, and such).

SCHEDULE OF INSURANCE
A list of the amounts of insurance per person for each coverage according to predetermined classifications, decided on by the policyholder and insurer.

SECOND SURGICAL OPINION
An attempt to verify the need for surgery by encouraging insureds to seek the advice of another physician or surgeon who will not perform the operation.

SELF-FUNDING
A medical benefit plan established by an employer or employee group (or a combination of the two) that directly assumes the functions, responsibilities, and liabilities of an insurer.

SELF-PAY PATIENTS
That group of persons, not covered by health insurance or public assistance for medical services received, who personally pay their hospital bills.

SERVICE FEES
Special compensation usually granted to consultants and/or brokers who directly perform many of the functions of group representatives and/or home offices, or commissions paid to the servicing agent after the vested commissions have ceased.

SERVICE-TYPE PLANS
Plans that provide benefits in the form of services rendered rather than in cash benefits (e.g., Blue Cross, Blue Shield, Dental Service Corporations).

SEX DISTRIBUTION
A male or female percentage analysis of insureds within a group.

SHORTFALL
The difference between the price of the service charged by the hospital and the actual portion of such charges accepted by hospitals as payment by a payor.

SIZE DISCOUNT
A discount or rate reduction allowed to groups that have a self-administered plan. The size of the reduction is based on the size of the initial gross monthly premium.

SOCIAL INSURANCE
A type of insurance coverage that pools risks by their transfer to an organization, usually governmental, that is required by law to provide certain benefits.

SOCIETY OF ACTUARIES
A professional organization of life, health insurance, and pension insurance mathematicians.

SPECIFICATIONS
A detailed listing of the qualifying factors of a certain group of individuals (type of risk, complete census data, contributions, past experience if a transferred case), the coverages (types, amounts, schedules), and services (self-administration, draft book claims, level commissions) that an insurance company gathers in order to obtain the right to administer the program.

STATE (COMPULSORY) DISABILITY PLAN
A plan of short-term income replacement insurance required by some states to cover eligible persons employed within that state.

STATE FUND
An insurer operated by a state government.

STATE OF ISSUE (SITUS)
The jurisdiction in which the group insurance contract is delivered or issued for delivery.

STATISTICAL FLUCTUATION
A result deviating from that expected or probable, based on collected data.

STEP-RATE PREMIUM
Premium rates for a single unit of group insurance (e.g., $1,000 life) scheduled according to age, occupation, or other classification of individual insureds. Most often used in employee-pay-all group life policies.

STOCK COMPANY
An insurance company owned by stockholders who elect a board of directors to manage the company.

SUBROGATION
The substitution of the insurer in place of an insured who claims medical expenses from a third party.

SURGICAL SCHEDULE
A list of cash or unit allowances up to a maximum amount an insurer will reimburse, based on the severity of the operation.

SURPLUS
The amount by which the value of an insurer's assets exceeds its liabilities.

TAX DISTRIBUTION
The distribution of premium by state to compute the premium tax due.

THIRD-PARTY ADMINISTRATION
That method by which an outside person or firm, not a party to a contract, maintains all records regarding the persons covered under the group insurance plan and may also pay claims using the draft book system.

THIRD-PARTY PAYOR
Any organization, public or private, that pays or insures health or medical expenses on behalf of beneficiaries or recipients.

TIME LIMIT
The set number of days in which a notice of claim or proof of a loss must be filed.

TRANSFERABLE SKILLS
Those abilities an insured has acquired through occupational or vocational endeavors that may be applied with minimal training in another occupation.

TRANSFERRED BUSINESS
A term used to describe a group insurance plan that is switched from one insurer to another.

TRAVEL ACCIDENT POLICIES
Limited contracts covering only accidents that occur while an insured person is traveling on business for an employer, away from the usual place of business and only on named conveyances.

TRUST
The care and management of property or funds by a person or third party for the benefit of another.

TRUST AGREEMENT
A legal document that establishes a trust fund, makes provisions as to how these funds shall be allocated, and appoints and defines the duties, responsibilities, and liabilities of the trustees.

TRUSTEE
A person appointed by a trust agreement to administer a trust fund. In group insurance, an individual (usually one of several) designated to administer a fund for purposes that include the purchase of group insurance.

TURNOVER
The rate of change in the number of new employees over the course of a year.

TWENTY-FOUR-HOUR COVERAGE
Insurance providing benefits at any time for an accident or sickness incurred either on or off the job.

TWISTING
An agent or broker inducing a policyholder to drop an existing policy in order to take a similar policy from him or her.

UNALLOCATED BENEFITS
Benefits in which reimbursement is provided up to a maximum amount but without setting specific limits on the extent of benefit for each service rendered.

UNDERWRITING
The process by which an insurer determines whether or not and on what basis it will accept an application for insurance.

UNDERWRITING PROFIT
An insurer's profit from its insurance operations as distinguished from its investment earnings.

UNEARNED PREMIUM
That portion of a premium for which the protection of the policy has not as yet been given.

UTILIZATION
A numerical measure of usage of a single service or type of service (e.g., hospital care, prescription drugs, physician visits).

UTILIZATION REVIEW
Evaluation of the necessity, appropriateness, and efficiency of the use of medical services, procedures, and facilities on a prospective, concurrent, or retrospective basis.

VESTED RESERVES
Reserves whose ownership is vested in the policyholder and which cannot be used by the insurer except to pay refunds or claims. In the event of case cancellation, any portion of the reserve not required to pay claims is returned to the policyholder.

VESTING
The commission practice or custom under which an insurer guarantees to an agent or broker the commissions paid in connection with an insurance contract for a predetermined time and subject to specified conditions (e.g., licensed with insurer, death, disability, retirement).

VOLUME DISCOUNT
A premium rate reduction application to new case coverages that is based on total case premium (for specific coverages) or total premium and premium per certificate (employee).

VOLUME LOADING
A premium rate increase applicable to new case coverages that is based on the total case premium (for specified coverages) or total premium and premium per certificate (employee).

WAITING PERIOD
The time a person must wait from the date of entry into an eligible class or application for coverage to the date the insurance is effective.

WAIVER
The voluntary surrender of a right or privilege known to exist.

WAIVER CARD
A form signed when an eligible person in a group wishes to surrender the right to enroll in a group insurance program.

WAIVER OF PREMIUM
A provision that, under certain conditions, a person's insurance will be kept in full force by the insurer without further payment of premiums. It is used most often in the event of permanent and total disability.

WARRANTY
A statement that guarantees the truth, when if breached is sufficient to render a policy void whether the matter warranted is material or not and whether or not it contributed to the loss.

WELL-BABY CARE
Those medical services, physician visits, and immunizations that are rec-

ommended by the American Pediatric Association as appropriate and routine care for a normal child from birth to one year of age.

WHOLESALE PLAN

A term life insurance plan under which a number of individual life insurance policies, based on individual applications, are issued at special rates to a selected group (also known as a franchise, blanket, or employee life plan).

WORKERS' COMPENSATION LAW

A statute imposing liability on employers to pay benefits and furnish care to employees injured and to pay benefits to dependents of employees killed in the course of and because of their employment.

Index

A

B

C

D

H

I

K

L

M

N

O

P

R

S